D1109952

a BOOK OF LEGAL LISTS

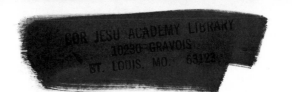

a BOOK OF LEGAL LISTS

The Best and Worst in American Law

With 100 Court and Judge Trivia Questions

BERNARD SCHWARTZ

New York   Oxford

Oxford University Press

1997

Oxford University Press

Oxford   New York
Athens   Auckland   Bangkok   Bogotá   Bombay
Buenos Aires   Calcutta   Cape Town   Dar es Salaam
Delhi   Florence   Hong Kong   Istanbul   Karachi
Kuala Lumpur   Madras   Madrid   Melbourne
Mexico City   Nairobi   Paris   Singapore
Taipei   Tokyo   Toronto

and associated companies in
Berlin   Ibadan

Copyright © 1997 by Bernard Schwartz

Published by Oxford University Press, Inc.
198 Madison Avenue, New York, NY 10016

Oxford is a registered trademark of Oxford University Press

Library of Congress Cataloging-in-Publication Data
Schwartz, Bernard, 1923–.
A book of legal lists: the best and worst in American law.
with 150 court and judge trivia questions / Bernard Scwartz.
p. cm.   Includes Index.
ISBN 0-19-510961-9
1. Law—United States—Miscellanea. 2. Law—United States—
Popular works. I. Title
KF387.S39 1997
349.73 — dc20
[347.3]   96-21979

Book design by Nicola Ferguson
Illustrations by Vicky Rabinowicz

1 3 5 7 9 8 6 4 2

Printed in the United States of America
on acid-free paper

Semper Uxori Suae

Preface

Irving Wallace, the novelist, begins his *Book of Lists* with a quote by H. Allen Smith: "The human animal differs from the lesser primates in his passion for lists of Ten Bests." Almost a hundred books of lists have been published—about motion pictures, the Bible, sports (both sports in general and individual sports: baseball, golf, tennis, soccer, rugby, and cricket), food, money, chess, women, music, and four books of general lists by Irving Wallace himself. As far as I have been able to determine, however, there has been no book of legal lists. I have tried to fill the gap with this book. It contains my lists of the best and worst in American law—from the greatest and worst Supreme Court Justices to the greatest legal motion pictures.

These lists are personal; experts in all the areas covered will disagree with many of my choices. They are, however, based on over half a century's experience in the law—as a student, professor, writer, and part-time counsel (in both government and private practice). I have tried to explain my choices in brief essays that follow each entry. At the least, they show that the lists are not my own ipse dixits, but are reasoned selections derived from a lifetime's work in law and legal history.

In addition, I have included 150 Trivia Questions on the Supreme Court and the ten greatest non-Supreme Court judges. Most of these have been published in the *Supreme Court Historical Society Quarterly*. I trust they will be of interest to a wider audience than the Court aficionados who normally read that publication.

Tulsa, Oklahoma   B. S.
October 1996

Contents

a
BOOK OF
LEGAL
LISTS

1

TEN

GREATEST

SUPREME COURT

JUSTICES

Who are the top ten Supreme Court Justices, and why does each deserve his place at the judicial apex?

To be sure, any such ranking is a personal matter, bound to be based on the lister's own subjective evaluation. After all, as Justice Felix Frankfurter pointed out, "Greatness in the law is not a standardized quality, nor are the elements that combine to attain it." There are no "objective" standards of comparison between Justices—no batting averages like those that distinguish the Ty Cobbses or Ted Williamses from their lesser counterparts.

Perhaps the most that can be done here is to apply Justice Potter Stewart's celebrated aphorism on pornography to Supreme Court greatness: "I could never succeed in [defining it]. But I know it when I see it." It may be impossible to say exactly what makes a great Justice. But we know greatness when we see it, and we *know* that the Justices on this list were great—in my opinion, the ten greatest in Supreme Court history.

What follows is a discussion of the selected Justices, with emphasis on the reasons for their apotheosis. Then, I will discuss some Justices included in other lists and why they are not on mine. I will conclude with an attempt to generalize from my list and determine what raises a Justice to the select pantheon.

— ★ — ★ — ★ —

Ten Greatest Supreme Court Justices

1. John Marshall (1755–1835), Chief Justice of the United States, 1801–1835

2. Oliver Wendell Holmes (1841–1935), Justice, United States Supreme Court, 1902–1932

3. Earl Warren (1891–1974), Chief Justice of the United States, 1953–1969

4. Joseph Story (1779–1845), Justice, United States Supreme Court, 1811–1845

5. William J. Brennan, Jr. (b. 1906), Justice, United States Supreme Court, 1956–1990

6. Louis D. Brandeis (1856–1941), Justice, United States Supreme Court, 1916–1939

7. Charles Evans Hughes (1862–1948), Justice, United States Supreme Court, 1910–1916; Chief Justice of the United States, 1930–1941

8. Hugo Lafayette Black (1886–1971), Justice, United States Supreme Court, 1937–1971

9. Stephen J. Field (1816–1899), Justice, United States Supreme Court, 1863–1897

10. Roger Brooke Taney (1777–1864), Chief Justice of the United States, 1836–1864

1. John Marshall

John Marshall (1755–1835) is at the top of every list of Supreme Court greats. "If American law," Oliver Wendell Holmes once said, "were to be represented by a single figure, skeptic and worshipper alike would agree that the figure could be one alone, and that one, John Marshall." Certainly, more has been written about the great Chief Justice than about any other judge. He was not merely the expounder of our constitutional law, but was also its author, its creator. "Marshall found the Constitution paper; and he made it power," said James A. Garfield. "He found a skeleton, and he clothed it with flesh and blood."

For Marshall, the Constitution was not to be applied formalistically; it must be applied in light of the overriding purpose of the Framers—to establish a nation endowed with necessary governmental powers. His three most important decisions ensured that the federal government would possess those powers: *Marbury v. Madison* (1803), establishing the supremacy of the Constitution and judicial power to review the constitutionality of laws; *McCulloch v. Maryland* (1819), holding that federal authority was not limited to the powers enumerated in the Constitution; and *Gibbons v. Ogden* (1824), giving a broad interpretation to the federal power to regulate commerce.

The key to the Marshall jurisprudence is his seminal dictum: "[W]e must never forget that it is a *constitution* that we are expounding." Justice Frankfurter termed this the "most important, single sentence in American Constitutional Law." It set the theme for constitutional construction— that the Constitution, in Frankfurter's words, is not to be read as "an insurance clause in small type, but a scheme of government . . . intended for the undefined and unlimited future."

Marshall read the Constitution to lay the legal foundation of an effective national government. More than any other jurist, he employed the law as a means to attain the political and economic ends that he favored. In this sense, he was the very paradigm, during our law's formative era, of the result-oriented judge.

Marshall was undoubtedly one of the greatest of legal reasoners. His opinions were based on supposedly timeless first principles that, once accepted, were led, by unassailable logic, to the conclusions that he favored. As Benjamin N. Cardozo put it, "The movement from premise to conclusion is put before the observer as something more impersonal than the working of the individual mind. It is the inevitable progress of an inexorable force."

Even Marshall's strongest critics were affected by the illusion. "All wrong, all wrong," we are told was the despairing comment of one critic, "but no man in the United States can tell why or wherein."

Marshall was described by a contemporary as "disposed to govern the world according to rules of logic." Marshall the logician is, of course, best seen in his magisterial opinions, which, to an age still under the sway of the syllogism, built up in broad strokes a body so logical that it baffled criticism from contemporaries. To Marshall, however, logic, like law, was only a tool. Indeed, the great Chief Justice's opinions may be taken as a prime judicial example of the famous Holmes aphorism: "The life of the law has not been logic: it has been experience." Marshall, more than any judge, molded his decisions to accord with what Holmes called "the felt necessities of the time." For Marshall, the Constitution was a tool; and the same was true of law in general. Both public law and private law were to be employed to lay down the doctrinal foundations of the polity and economy that served his nationalistic vision of the new nation.

Compared with Thomas Jefferson's, Marshall's vision may have been a conservative one. But the men had different conceptions of the American polity. Marshall himself saw all too acutely that the Jeffersonian theme was sweeping all before it. "In democracies," he noted in an 1815 letter, "which all the world confirms to be the most perfect work of political wisdom, equality is the pivot on which the grand machine turns." As he grew older, Marshall fought the spread of the equality principle, notably in the Virginia Convention of 1829/1830. For, as he wrote in the same letter, "equality demands that he who has a surplus of anything in general demand should parcel it out among his needy fellow citizens."

Yet, if Marshall's last effort—against the triumph of Jeffersonian and Jacksonian democracy—was doomed to failure, his broader battle for his conception of law was triumphantly vindicated. Even the least conversant with American law knows that it is the Marshall conception of the Constitution that has dominated Supreme Court jurisprudence. In addition, the Marshall Court decisions adapting the common law to the needs of the expanding market economy led the way to the remaking of private law in the entrepreneurial image. Free individual action and decision became the ultimate end of law, as it became that of the society itself. The law became a prime instrument for the conquest of the continent and the opening of the economy to people of all social strata. Paradoxically perhaps, it was Marshall, opponent of Jefferson–Jackson democracy though he may have been, whose conception of law laid the constitutional cornerstone for a legal system that furthered opportunity and equality in the marketplace to an extent never before seen.

2. Oliver Wendell Holmes

Oliver Wendell Holmes (1841–1935) was the most influential Associate Justice ever to sit on the Supreme Court. I have already quoted Holmes's statement that if American law were to be represented by a single figure, that figure would be John Marshall. If our law were to be represented by a second figure, most would say that it should be Holmes himself. It was Holmes, more than any other legal thinker, who set the agenda for modern jurisprudence. In doing so, he became as much a part of legend as law: the Yankee from Olympus—the patrician from Boston who made his mark on his own age and on ages still unborn as few men have done. Indeed, a major part of twentieth-century Supreme Court doctrine is a product of the Holmes handiwork.

In constitutional law, the two great Holmes contributions were the theory of judicial self-restraint and the expansive view of free speech.

Judicial self-restraint was a constant theme in Holmes's opinions. Holmes reiterated that, as a judge, he was not concerned with the wisdom of a challenged legislative act. The responsibility for determining what measures were necessary to deal with economic and other problems lay with the people and their elected representatives, not with judges.

But the theme of judicial restraint was overridden by another Holmes theme in cases involving freedom of expression. The governing criterion here was the "clear and present danger" test, which Holmes developed just after World War I. Under this test, speech may be restricted only if there is a real threat—a danger, both clear and present—that the speech will lead to an evil that the legislature has the power to prevent.

Holmes's contribution was, however, greater than these constitutional doctrines. It was Holmes, more than any other Justice, who, as stated, pointed the way to a whole new era of jurisprudence. For Holmes, the law should be consciously made to give effect to the policies that would best serve the society. Instead of a system based on logical deduction from a priori principles, the Holmes concept was one of law fashioned to meet the needs of the community. In the Holmes jurisprudence, the law was a utilitarian instrument for the satisfaction of social needs.

Thus it was Holmes who set legal thought on its coming course. As early as his book *The Common Law* (1881), in which he asserted, "The life of the law has not been logic," he was sounding the clarion of twentieth-century jurisprudence. If the law reflected the "felt necessities of the time," then those needs rather than any theory should determine what the law should be. These were not, to be sure, the views followed by American judges and lawyers at the beginning of this century—or even by the majority during Holmes's Supreme Court tenure. But the good that men do also lives after them. If the nineteenth century was dominated by the formalist jurisprudence of the day, the twentieth was, ultimately, to be that of Mr. Justice Holmes.

3. Earl Warren

The period during which Earl Warren (1891–1974) served as Chief Justice was the second formative era in our legal history, in which the law underwent changes as profound as those occurring in the country. The Warren Court led the movement to remake the law in the image of the evolving society. In terms of creative impact on the law, the Warren tenure can be compared only with that of John Marshall.

Warren's leadership abilities and skill as a statesman enabled him to rank as second only to Marshall among our Chief Justices. Those Justices who served with him stressed Warren's leadership abilities, particularly his skill in leading the conferences at which cases were discussed. As the *Washington Post* noted, "Warren helped steer cases from the moment they were first discussed simply by the way he framed the issues."

In his first conference on *Brown v. Board of Education* (1954), Warren presented the question before the Court in terms of racial inferiority. He told the Justices that segregation could be justified only by belief in the inherent inferiority of blacks, and if segregation was upheld, it had to be on that basis. A scholar such as Justice Frankfurter would certainly not have presented the case that way. But Warren went straight to the ultimate human values involved. In the face of such an approach, arguments based on legal scholarship would have seemed inappropriate, almost pettifoggery.

There is an antinomy inherent in every system of law: the law must be stable, yet it cannot stand still. It is the task of the judge to balance these two conflicting elements. Chief Justice Warren came down firmly on the side of change, leading the effort to enable the law to cope with societal change. Warren rejected judicial restraint because he believed that it thwarted effective performance of the Court's constitutional role. In Warren's view, the Court functioned to ensure fairness and equity, particularly in cases where they had not been secured by other governmental processes. Where a constitutional requirement remained unenforced due to governmental default, the Court had to act. The alternative, as Warren saw it, was an empty Constitution, with essential provisions unenforced.

The *Brown* desegregation decision was a direct consequence of the failure of political processes to enforce the guarantee of racial equality. Before *Brown*, it had become constitutional cliché that the guarantee had not succeeded in securing equality for African-Americans; that situation largely resulted from governmental default. For Warren, the years of legislative inaction made it imperative for the Court to intervene. The alternative would leave untouched a practice that flagrantly violated both the Constitution and the ultimate human values involved.

The bases of the major Warren decisions were fairness and equality. For the Chief Justice, the technical issues traditionally fought over in constitutional cases always seemed to merge into larger questions of fairness. His concern was expressed in the question he so often asked at argument: "But was it fair?" When Warren concluded that an individual had been treated unfairly, he would not let rules or precedents stand in the way.

Even more important was the notion of equality. If one great theme recurred in the Warren decisions, it was equality before the law—equality of races, of citizens, of rich and poor, of prosecutor and defendant. The result was that seeming oxymoron: "a revolution made by judges." Without the Warren Court decisions giving ever-wider effect to the right to equality, most of the movements for equality that have permeated American society might never have gotten started.

Perhaps Warren as a judge will never rank with the consummate legal craftsmen who have fashioned the structure of Anglo-American law over the generations. But Warren was never content to deem himself a mere vicar of the common-law tradition. He was the epitome of the "result-oriented" judge, who used his power to secure the result he deemed right. Employing judicial authority to the utmost, he never hesitated to do whatever he thought necessary to translate his conceptions of fairness and equality into the law of the land.

For Warren, principle was more compelling than precedent. The key decisions of the Warren Court overruled decisions of earlier Courts. Those precedents had left the enforcement of constitutional rights to the political branches. Yet the latter had failed to act. In Warren's view, this situation left the Court with the choice either to follow the precedent or to vindicate the right. For the Chief Justice, there was never any question as to the correct alternative.

When all is said and done, Warren's place rests not on his opinions, but on his decisions. In terms of impact on the law, few occupants of the bench have been more outstanding. To criticize Warren, as some have done, for lack of scholarship or judicial craftsmanship seems petty when we consider the contributions he made as leader in the greatest judicial transformation of the law since Marshall.

4. Joseph Story

Joseph Story (1779–1845), at thirty-two, was the youngest Justice ever appointed as well as the most learned scholar to sit on the Supreme Court. He also enjoyed a reputation as a minor poet. He had composed a lengthy poem, "The Power of Solitude," referring to it in a letter as "the sweet employment of my leisure hours." Story rewrote the poem, with additions and alterations, and published it with other poems. One who reads the extracts contained in his son's biography quickly realizes that it was no great loss to literature when Story decided to devote his life to the law. Story himself apparently recognized this, for he later bought up and burned all copies of the work he could find.

On the Marshall Court, Story supplied the one thing the great Chief Justice lacked—legal scholarship. Story's scholarship was, indeed, prodigious. "Brother Story here . . . can give us the cases from the Twelve Tables down to the latest reports," Marshall once said. Story reveled in legal research. His opinions were long and learned and relied heavily on prior cases and writers.

Not only that; Story was a leading writer on whom judges and lawyers relied. By the end of his career, he had published nine treatises (in thirteen volumes) on subjects ranging from constitutional to commercial law. They confirmed the victory of the common law in the United States and presented the courts with authoritative guides.

Story's best-known work—his three-volume *Commentaries on the Constitution of the United States* (1833)—was a restatement of the Marshall constitutional doctrines in textual form. The Story volumes showed through virtual clause-by-clause analysis that the Marshall jurisprudence was the "correct" constitutional doctrine. With the Story work, the national view of governmental power was firmly established. It could now serve as the basis for the harmonization of the law with the newly emerging economic forces.

In the Supreme Court also, Justice Story became the principal supporter of Marshall's constitutional doctrines. But it was not as a junior Marshall that Story left his main imprint. If Marshall was the prime molder of early American public law, Story was his Supreme Court counterpart for private law. Our commercial and admiralty law were largely the creation of Story's decisions. Important Story opinions blended the law of trusts with the rudimentary law of corporations that had developed in England to produce the modern business corporation and enable it to conduct its affairs. The Story jurisprudence played a vital part in the development of the business corporation, which (as James Kent noted) was beginning to "increase in a rapid manner and to a most astonishing extent." By permitting corporations to operate as freely as individuals, Story played a crucial part in accommodating the corporate form to the demands of the expanding economy.

Economic progress, to Story, depended on the creation of a *uniform* commercial law on which businessmen could rely. Some of the most important Story opinions contributed to the establishment of such a law. Uniform commercial law, made by the federal judges without the interference of juries (merchants, as Story noted, "are not fond of juries") and according to accepted mercantile custom and convenience, was what the commercial community wanted.

Despite his Republican (Jeffersonian) origins, Story is usually considered a paradigm of the conservative judge. But his approach to private law—particularly in relation to commercial development—was a transforming one. "It is obvious," Story wrote, "that the law must fashion itself to the wants, and in some sort to the spirit of the age." It was Story, more than any Justice, who helped ensure that our private law would have a common-law foundation and one that would be adapted to the conditions of the new nation. With his work, the law was now so clearly presented that the energies of the courts could be devoted to applying the new principles to concrete cases.

5. William J. Brennan, Jr.

Oliver Wendell Holmes is usually considered the most influential Justice to have sat on the Supreme Court. As we saw, it was Holmes, more than any other legal thinker, who set the agenda for modern constitutional jurisprudence.

Nevertheless, as Judge Richard A. Posner points out, "the primary vehicles of Holmes's innovations were dissenting opinions that, often after his death, became and have remained the majority position." The Holmes dissents may have sounded the theme of the coming era. But they did not really influence our law until after his death.

If we look at Justices for their role in the decision process, William J.

Brennan, Jr. (b. 1906), was the most influential. He was the catalyst for some of the most significant decisions during his tenure. More important, the Brennan jurisprudence set the pattern for American legal thought toward the end of this century. So pervasive was Brennan's influence that the English periodical the *Economist* headed its story on his retirement, "A lawgiver goes."

The *Economist*'s characterization is not an exaggeration. Dennis J. Hutchinson, an editor of the *Supreme Court Review*, in a review of my Warren biography, declared that to call it the "Warren Court" is a misnomer: "it was 'the Brennan Court.'" This assertion unduly denigrates Warren's leadership. Still, it is hard to argue with Hutchinson's conclusion, in another portion of his review that "[W]hen the public record is added to Schwartz's behind-the-scenes examples, Brennan emerges clearly as the most important justice of the period."

After Chief Justice Warren's retirement, Brennan was no longer the trusted insider. Yet even under Chief Justice Warren E. Burger, Brennan was able to lead a majority in important cases. In the Rehnquist Court, too, Brennan secured notable victories, particularly in the areas of abortion, separation of church and state, freedom of expression, and affirmative action. He was primarily responsible for the decisions toward the end of his tenure that the First Amendment protected flag burning and that congressional authority in the field of affirmative action should be upheld.

Before his 1956 appointment, Brennan had been a judge in New Jersey, rising from the state trial court to its highest bench. On the Supreme Court, Brennan proved a surprise to those who regarded him as a moderate, since he became a firm adherent of the activist philosophy. Brennan had been Justice Frankfurter's student at Harvard Law School; yet if Frankfurter expected the new Justice to continue his pupilage, he was soon disillusioned. After Brennan had joined the Court's activist wing, Frankfurter quipped, "I always encourage my students to think for themselves, but Brennan goes too far!"

Brennan's forte was his ability to lead the Justices to the decisions he favored, even at the cost of compromising his own position. More than any Justice, Brennan was the strategist behind Supreme Court jurisprudence—the most active lobbyist (in the nonpejorative sense) in the Court, always willing to take the lead in trying to mold a majority for the decisions that he favored. "In case after case," Hutchinson writes about my Warren biography, "Schwartz documents . . . how Brennan would accommodate his own drafts and views in order to preserve an opinion of the Court that was tumbling toward a plurality or worse."

With the retirement of Chief Justice Warren, many expected the Court to tilt away from its activist posture. If the Warren Court had made a legal revolution, a counter-revolution was seemingly at hand. It did not turn out that way. If anything, the intended counter-revolution served only as a confirmation of Warren Court jurisprudence. The Warren concept of the Court continued unabated under Brennan's leadership. Indeed, as Anthony Lewis summed it up, "We are all activists now."

In the end, of course, the underlying question comes down to how we resolve the already stated antinomy: the law must be stable, yet it cannot stand still. Justice Brennan is a prime example of the judge who has not taken stability as his polestar. He has been the leading opponent of the view that constitutional construction must be governed only by the Framers' original intention. Throughout his tenure, Brennan rejected "original intention" jurisprudence. To him, the meaning of the Constitution is to be found in today's needs, not in a search for what was intended by its eighteenth-century draftsmen.

To Justice Brennan, then, the outstanding feature of the Constitution is its plastic nature: rules and doctrines are malleable and must be construed to meet the changing needs of different periods. Brennan's tenure bears ample witness to his success in giving effect to the concept of a flexible law constantly adapted to contemporary needs. Above all, Brennan's jurisprudence was based on what he termed "the constitutional ideal of human dignity." This is what led him to his battle against the death penalty, which he considered a cruel and unusual punishment. The battle to outlaw capital punishment was a losing one for Brennan, but it was the only major one he did lose in his effort to ensure what he said was "the ceaseless pursuit of the constitutional ideal." The ultimate Brennan legacy was that no important decision of the Warren Court was overruled while the Justice sat on the Burger and Rehnquist Courts.

6. Louis D. Brandeis

Louis D. Brandeis (1856–1941), like Holmes, added a new dimension to legal thought—one that emphasized the facts to which the law applied, "In the past," Brandeis wrote, "the courts have reached their conclusions largely deductively from preconceived notions and precedents. The method I have tried to employ . . . has been inductive, reasoning from the facts."

Brandeis's method was inaugurated by his brief in *Muller v. Oregon* (1908)—the generic type of a new form of legal argument, ever since referred to as the Brandeis Brief. To persuade the Court to uphold an

Oregon law prohibiting women from working in factories for more than ten hours a day, Brandeis marshaled an impressive mass of statistics to demonstrate, in the brief's words, "that there is reasonable ground for holding that to permit women in Oregon to work . . . more than ten hours in one day is dangerous." The Brandeis Brief in *Muller* was devoted almost entirely to the facts: it contains 113 pages. Only 2 contain argument on the law.

Brandeis was appointed to the Supreme Court in 1916 and was confirmed over bitter opposition. On the bench, Brandeis continued to use the new approach he had developed in *Muller*—emphasizing the facts, particularly those underlying regulatory legislation. For him, the search of the legal authorities was the beginning, not the end, of research. The Brandeis emphasis on facts created what Justice Frankfurter called "a new technique" in jurisprudence. Until Brandeis, said Frankfurter, "social legislation was supported before the courts largely *in vacuo*—as an abstract dialectic between 'liberty' and 'police power,' unrelated to a world of trusts and unions, of large-scale industry and all its implications." With Brandeis, all this changed. In Brandeis's briefs and opinions, Frankfurter summed it up, "the facts of modern industry which provoke regulatory legislation were, for the first time, adequately marshaled before the Court."

The Brandeis method was used for a particular purpose. The Justice completely rejected the prevailing notion that the law was to be equated with laissez-faire. Brandeis urged that regulation was a necessary aspect of modern law: "We have long curbed the physically strong, to protect those physically weaker. More recently we have extended such prohibitions to business. . . . [T]he right to competition must be limited in order to preserve it."

If twentieth-century law has enabled the society to move from laissez-faire to the welfare state, that has been true because it has accepted the Brandeis approach. Emphasis on the facts has led to increasing understanding of the reality that led to interventions in the economy. "The small man," wrote Brandeis, "needs the protection of the law"; but, under the laissez-faire conception, "the law becomes the instrument by which he is destroyed."

To prevent that result, Brandeis urged, "business must yield to the paramount needs of the community." The Brandeis jurisprudence was a major factor in leading the law to adopt a more benign attitude to economic regulation. The Brandeis technique helped persuade jurists that the legal conception of "liberty" should no longer be synonymous with immunity from regulation. Instead, the law has come to believe with Brandeis that "[r]egulation . . . is necessary to the preservation and best development of liberty." That in turn has led to the rejection of laissez-faire as the foundation of our constitutional law.

7. Charles Evans Hughes

When Chief Justice William Howard Taft resigned in 1930, Charles Evans Hughes (1862–1948) was appointed to succeed him. Hughes was almost sixty-eight—the oldest man chosen until then to head the Court. However, he undertook his new duties with the vigor of a much younger person. In addition, his distinguished career endowed him with prestige that few in the highest judicial office had had.

As a leader of the Court, Hughes must be ranked with the great Chief Justices. "To see [Hughes] preside," Justice Frankfurter was to write, "was like witnessing Toscanini lead an orchestra." The Hughes leadership abilities were precisely what the Court needed to confront its most serious crisis in a century. Before Hughes's appointment, the Court's conservative core had carried its laissez-faire interpretation of the Constitution to the point where there was, in the famous Holmes phrase, "hardly any limit but the sky to the invalidating of [laws] if they happen to strike a majority of the Court as for any reason undesirable."

When Chief Justice Hughes ascended the bench in early 1930, the country was deep in our most serious economic crisis. The crisis only became worse as the Hughes term went on—putting the country and the Court to a severe test. The new Chief Justice had to meet the test with a Court composed almost entirely of Justices who had served under his predecessor. Despite this, Hughes was able to persuade a bare majority that the Constitution should no longer be treated as a legal sanction for laissez-faire. Writing in 1941, Justice Robert H. Jackson asserted, "The older world of *laissez-faire* was recognized everywhere outside the Court to be dead." It was Hughes who ensured that the recognition penetrated the Marble Palace.

Justice Frankfurter once said that Chief Justice Hughes "was, in fact, the head of two courts, so different . . . was the supreme bench in the two periods of the decade during which Hughes presided over it." The first Hughes Court sat from the Chief Justice's appointment to 1937. The period was dominated by decisions that both nullified the most important New Deal legislation and restricted state regulatory power. In both respects, the Court confirmed the laissez-faire jurisprudence of its predecessors.

The grim economic background, however, indicated how unrealistic reliance on laissez-faire was. Giant industries prostrate, nationwide crises in production and consumption, the economy in virtual collapse—the choice was between government action and chaos. A system of constitutional law that required the latter could hardly endure.

Hughes was responsible for the reversal in jurisprudence that occurred in 1937—a reversal so great that its effects justify the characterization of "constitutional revolution." In March 1937, Hughes announced a decision upholding a minimum-wage law, similar to one the Court had previously held beyond governmental power. The Chief Justice himself led the Court to repudiate the earlier case. The Court to which Hughes came contained four of the conservative Justices who had decided that case. It also contained three liberal Justices who were strongly in favor of overruling it. The remaining members were the Chief Justice and Justice Owen J. Roberts, who had taken his seat at the same time as Hughes. Roberts played the crucial "swing man" role in the Hughes Court.

It was Hughes who persuaded Roberts to vote with the new majority. Hughes himself fully realized the critical importance of Roberts's vote. He later recounted how, when the Justice told him that he would vote to sustain the minimum-wage law, he almost hugged him—which, coming from one with so great a reputation for icy demeanor, says a great deal.

Hughes's lead and his successful persuasion of Roberts made possible the decision upholding the minimum-wage law. Hughes also wrote the landmark opinion in *National Labor Relations Board v. Jones & Laughlin Steel Corp.* (1937)—the seminal decision in which the National Labor Relations Act was upheld. The act applied to industries throughout the nation, to those engaged in production and manufacture as well as to those engaged in commerce, literally speaking. This appeared to bring it directly in conflict with prior decisions limiting the scope of federal authority over interstate commerce, including some of the decisions of the 1934 to 1936 period on which the ink was scarcely dry. In *Jones & Laughlin*, these precedents were not followed. Instead, the Hughes opinion gave the federal commerce power its maximum sweep. Mines, mills, and factories—whose activities had formerly been decided to be "local" and hence immune from federal regulation—were now held to affect interstate commerce directly enough to justify congressional control.

Once again, there is no doubt that Hughes was primarily responsible for the *Jones & Laughlin* decision. The leading Hughes biography emphasizes the vigor and thoroughness with which the Chief Justice presented *Jones & Laughlin* at the conference. The biographer also states that Hughes told him that he had not "pleaded with Roberts to save the NLRB." The Hughes disclaimer should be taken with a grain of salt. Strong Chief Justices such as Hughes are noted for their success in persuading colleagues to follow their views. Hughes never denied that he had influenced Justice Roberts's vote. All he states in his *Autobiographical Notes* is, "I am able to say with definiteness that [Roberts's] view in favor of [*Jones & Laughlin*] would have been the same if [President Roosevelt's Court-packing] bill had never been proposed." Of course, it would, since it was the Chief Justice's persuasion, not the president's threat, that led to the Roberts vote.

8. Hugo Lafayette Black

During the second third of this century, two members of the Court were the paradigms of the new constitutional approach: Hugo Lafayette Black (1886–1971) and Earl Warren. Neither had a defined philosophy of law; neither was a founder, leader, or even follower of any school of jurisprudence. Yet each had an influence on legal thought greater than that of other judges. Their forte was one peculiar to the demands of the emerging society—not so much adaptation of the law to deal with changing conditions as a virtual transformation of the law to meet a quantum acceleration in societal change.

Chief Justice William H. Rehnquist has called Justice Black the "most influential of the many strong figures who have sat during . . . his Justiceship." During Black's tenure, he and Justice Felix Frankfurter were the polar opposites on the Court. A recent book about the two is titled *The Antagonists*. Yet the issue between them was more basic than personal antagonism. At the core, there was a fundamental disagreement over the proper role of the law in a period of unprecedented development. Frankfurter remained true to the Holmes rule of restraint. Black considered the restraint approach a repudiation of the judge's duty. As Black saw it, judicial abnegation came down to abdication by the Court of its essential role. To Black, the judicial function meant that the judge was to decide on the basis of his own independent judgment, however much it differed from that of the legislature or prior law on the matter.

The Black approach was the basis for the two positions that the Justice most forcefully advocated: the absolutist view of the First Amendment; and the incorporation of the Bill of Rights in the due process clause of the Fourteenth Amendment.

To students of the Court, Black stands primarily for the absolutist literal interpretation of the First Amendment. When the amendment says that no laws abridging speech or press shall be made, it means flatly that *no* such laws shall, under any circumstances, be made.

Black's absolutist view has never been accepted by the Court. Countless cases hold that the fact that speech is protected by the First Amendment does not necessarily mean that it is wholly immune from governmental regulation. That did not, however, deter Black from following the view of law that he deemed correct. The same was true of the Black assertion that the framers of the Fourteenth Amendment sought to change the rule limiting application of the Bill of Rights to federal action alone. The Bill of Rights, Black urged, was incorporated in the due process clause of the Fourteenth Amendment. This meant that all the Bill of Rights guarantees were binding on the states as well as on the federal government.

Black had been a populist senator and on the bench he employed judicial power to make social policy that would favor individuals and protect them against the governmental and corporate interests that the law had fostered. From this point of view, a Frankfurter satiric portrayal of Justice Black acting as though he were "back in the Senate" contained some truth.

In the end, however, it was Black, not his great rival, who ranks as a prime molder of twentieth-century legal thought. History has vindicated the Black approach, for it has helped protect personal liberties in an era of encroaching public power.

Black's absolutist advocacy was a prime mover in First Amendment jurisprudence. The absolutist view may not have been accepted; but the "firstness" of the First Amendment has been firmly established. If today, as Black stated in an opinion, "[f]reedom to speak and write about public questions . . . is the heart" of the constitutional scheme, that has in large part been due to his own evangelism on the matter.

Similarly, Black's incorporation position may never have commanded a Court majority. Under Black's prodding, nevertheless, the Justices increasingly expanded the scope of the Fourteenth Amendment's due process clause. Although the Court continued to hold that only those rights deemed "fundamental" are included in due process, the meaning of "fundamental" became flexible enough to absorb one by one almost all the guarantees of the Bill of Rights. By the end of Black's tenure, the rights that had been held binding on the states under the Fourteenth Amendment included all the rights guaranteed by the Bill of Rights, except the rights to a grand jury indictment and to a civil jury trial. Black may have appeared to lose the Bill of Rights incorporation battle, but he really won the due process war.

It was Justice Black as much as anyone who changed the very way we think about constitutional law. If the focus of judicial inquiry has shifted from duties to rights, if personal rights have been elevated to the preferred plane, that has in large part been the result of Black's jurisprudence. Nor has his impact been limited to the Black positions that the Court has accepted. It is found in the totality of today's judicial awareness of the Bill of Rights and the law's new-found sensitivity to liberty and equality.

9. Stephen J. Field

If influence on the law is a criterion of judicial greatness, there were few Justices who deserve inclusion in this list more than Stephen J. Field (1816–1899). Toward the end of the nineteenth century, Justice Frankfurter tells us, the Justices "wrote Mr. Justice Field's dissents into the opinions of the Court." It was Field who was largely responsible for the expansion of substantive due process, which became the major theme of constitutional jurisprudence during the Gilded Age.

Field himself was one of the most colorful men ever to sit on the Court. He began his legal career in his brother's New York office. A few years later, he joined the gold rush to California, becoming a frontier lawyer and carrying a pistol and bowie knife. He was involved in a quarrel with a judge, during which he was disbarred, sent to jail, fined, and embroiled in a duel. His feud with another judge, David Terry, Chief Justice of the California Supreme Court, led to a threat to shoot Field. Years later, in 1889, when Field had long been a Supreme Court Justice, Terry assaulted him and was shot by a federal marshal. The marshal was indicted for murder, but the Supreme Court held the killing justified.

Field's years on the Court saw the law responding to the demands of burgeoning capitalism by insulating business from governmental interference. Field was the leader in inducing the Court to employ the due process clause to protect property rights. He served in an influential capacity on the Court for more than thirty-four years—the longest tenure before that of Justice William O. Douglas. While on the Court, Field wrote 620 opinions, then a record.

Field's most important opinions were dissents, but as Frankfurter tells us, they were ultimately written into Supreme Court jurisprudence. In *Allgeyer v. Louisiana* (1897), to quote Frankfurter again, the Court "wrote Mr. Justice Field's dissents into the opinions of the Court." In *Allgeyer*, for the first time, a regulatory law was set aside because it infringed on the "liberty" guaranteed by due process. Thenceforth, all governmental action—whether federal or state—would have to run the gantlet of substantive due process.

For Field and the Court that adopted his approach, substantive due process was used for a particular purpose—to invalidate legislation that conflicted with the laissez-faire doctrine that then dominated thinking. Due process became the rallying point for judicial resistance to efforts to control the excesses of the rising industrial economy.

A century later, the Field laissez-faire approach appears too extreme. But it set the tone for constitutional law for over half a century. Justice Field's own view on the matter is shown by his opinion in the Income Tax Case (*Pollock v. Farmers' Loan & Trust Co.*, 1895), in which the Court struck down a federal income tax law. Counsel opposing the statute argued that the income tax was "a doctrine worthy of a Jacobin Club," the "new doctrine of this army of 60,000,000—this triumphant and tyrannical majority—who want to punish men who are rich and confiscate their property."

Such an attack on the income tax (though, technically speaking, irrelevant) found a receptive ear. "The present assault upon capital," declared Justice Field, "is but the beginning. It will be but the stepping-stone to others, larger and more sweeping, till our political contests will become a war of the poor against the rich; a war constantly growing in intensity and bitterness." If the Court were to sanction the income tax law, "it will mark the hour when the sure decadence of our present government will commence."

A judge who felt this way about a tax of 2 percent on annual incomes above $4000 was the Justice who furnished the newly fashioned tool of substantive due process by which the law was made into an instrument for judicial protection of private enterprise.

10. Roger Brooke Taney

How can the Chief Justice who presided over the most discredited decision in Supreme Court history be placed on a list of the greatest Justices? The answer is that one judicial blunder, however great it may be, should not destroy the accomplishments of the judge who, apart from the decision in *Dred Scott v. Sandford* (1857), infra p.70, was second only to Marshall in laying our constitutional law foundation.

Roger Brooke Taney (1777–1864) was the first Chief Justice to wear trousers; his predecessors had always given judgment in knee breeches. There was something of portent in his wearing democratic garb beneath his robe, for under Taney and the new majority appointed by President Andrew Jackson, the Supreme Court for the first time mirrored the Jacksonian emphasis on public power as a counterweight to the property rights stressed by the Federalists and then the Whigs.

It was the Taney Court that developed the seminal concept of the police power—the most important constitutional instrument by which property rights may be limited. Under Taney, the Court first gave to the police power something like its modern connotation. "But what," Taney asked in an 1847 case, "are the police powers of a State? They are nothing more or less than the powers of government . . . to punish offenses, or to establish courts of justice, or requiring certain instruments to be recorded, or to regulate commerce within its own limits . . . the power of sovereignty, the power to govern men and things within the limits of its dominion."

Of course, such a broad conception of state power over internal government may be inconsistent with the exertion of individual rights. Taney's chief contribution was to recognize and articulate the superior claim, in appropriate cases, of public over private rights. Community rights were thus, in Taney's words, ruled "paramount to all private rights . . . , and these last are, by necessary implication, held in subordination to this power, and must yield in every instance to its proper exercise."

The police power was a necessary complement to the expansion of governmental power during the Jacksonian period. At that time, Edward S. Corwin tells us, "the demand went forth for a large governmental programme: for the public construction of canals and railroads, for free schools, for laws regulating the professions, for anti-liquor legislation." In the police power concept, the law developed the constitutional theory needed to meet the public demand. Government was given what Taney called the "power of accomplishing the end for which it was created." Through the police power a state might, Taney wrote, "for the safety or convenience of trade, or for the protection of the health of its citizens," regulate the rights of property and person. Thenceforth, a principal task of the Supreme Court was to be determination of the proper balance between individual rights and the police power.

It is customary to point to the drastic change that occurred when Taney succeeded Marshall. Such an approach is incorrect. "It is not true," wrote Justice Felix Frankfurter, "that Taney accomplished a wholesale reversal of Marshall's doctrines." The Taney Court did not translate wholesale the principles of Jacksonian democracy into constitutional law. Instead, paradoxical though it may seem, the erstwhile Jacksonian politician did as much as Marshall and his colleagues to promote economic development.

Chief Justice Taney may have had the strong Jacksonian bias against what Jackson called "the multitude of corporations with exclusive privileges which [the moneyed interest] have succeeded in obtaining in the different States," but it was the Taney opinions in cases like *Charles River Bridge v. Warren Bridge* (1837) and *Bank of Augusta v. Earle* (1839) that opened the door to the greatest period of corporate expansion in our history. Before Taney, only $50 million was invested in manufacturing; that figure had grown to $1 billion by 1860.

The Taney Court did tend to give the benefit of the doubt, in close cases, to state power; but this is far from saying that Taney and his confrères were ready to overturn the edifice of effective national authority constructed by their predecessors. When the occasion demanded, Taney could assert federal power in terms characterized by Chief Justice Charles Evans Hughes as "even more `national' than Marshall himself." This shows how difficult it is to pigeonhole Justices like Taney. His states'-rights heritage did not blind him to the need for effective governmental power. His distrust of corporations did not make him disregard the practical possibilities of the corporate device and its utility in an expanding economy. Indeed, it was Taney, Frankfurter tells us, "who adapted the Constitution to the emerging forces of modern economic society."

Henry Clay, who had led the fight against Taney's confirmation, was later to tell the Chief Justice that "no man in the United States could have been selected, more abundantly able to wear the ermine which Chief Justice Marshall honored." The judgment of history has confirmed Clay's estimate. The pendulum has shifted from the post–*Dred Scott* censures to the more sober estimate of Justice Frankfurter: "The devastation of the Civil War for a long time obliterated the truth about Taney. And the blaze of Marshall's glory will permanently overshadow him. But the intellectual power of his opinions and their enduring contribution to a workable adjustment of the theoretical distribution of authority between two governments for a single people, place Taney second only to Marshall in the constitutional history of our country."

The Also-Rans—Justices on Other Lists

I am, of course, not alone in my attempt to draw up a list of the greatest Justices. The most recent effort of this type is contained in *Great Justices of the U.S. Supreme Court* (1993), written by two political scientists. Their work was based on a survey sent to scholars, lawyers, judges, and students. The list of great Justices, according to a combined list of all the respondents surveyed, contains four names not included in my list: Benjamin N. Cardozo,

Felix Frankfurter, William O. Douglas, and William H. Rehnquist.

Why were these four not included in my list of Supreme Court all-stars?

Benjamin N. Cardozo

Without a doubt, Benjamin Cardozo is one of the great names in law. He was the outstanding common-law jurist of the century, who showed how the common law could be used to serve present needs—how the judge could be innovative while remaining true to the experience of the past. By doing so, he helped to move the law closer to the goal of making the law an effective instrument of social welfare.

All the same, the Cardozo place in jurisprudence is not based on his service on the Supreme Court. Cardozo's judicial contribution was made on the New York Court of Appeals, the state's highest court, where he spent most of his judicial career. During the Cardozo years, that court was recognized as the strongest in the country, and its judgments had a decisive influence on American law. Cardozo, however, was able to serve on the Supreme Court only six years—scarcely long enough for him to make the substantial contribution to its jurisprudence that his judicial ability warranted.

Felix Frankfurter

Few members of the Supreme Court have been of greater interest both to the public and to Court specialists than Felix Frankfurter. In large measure, that has been true because his career has posed a puzzle. Before his appointment, he was known for his interest in libertarian causes, and it was expected that, on the Court, he would continue along a liberal path. Yet if one thing is certain, it is that it is risky to make predictions of how new appointees to the Court will behave. Frankfurter seemed altogether different as a Justice than he had been off the bench. From academic eminence behind the New Deal to leader of the conservative Court cabal—that was the way press and public tended to tag Justice Frankfurter.

On the Court, Frankfurter's unfailing adherence to judicial restraint appeared increasingly anomalous. In an era of encroaching public power, the deference doctrine did not provide enough protection for personal liberties. Judicial restraint no longer appeared adequate to ensure the "Blessings of Liberty" in a world that had seen so clearly the consequences of their denial.

For Frankfurter himself, no matter how he tried to clothe his opinions with the Holmes mantle, there was an element of shabbiness in the results reached by him in too many cases. After Frankfurter delivered his opinion upholding a compulsory flag salute, he was talking about the opinion over cocktails at the Roosevelt home in Hyde Park. Eleanor Roosevelt, in her impulsive way, declared that, regardless of the Justice's learning and legal skills, there was something wrong with an opinion that forced little children to salute a flag when such a ceremony was repugnant to their consciences. To critics, there was only hypocrisy in Frankfurter's constant insistence that he could not reach judgments on the bench that he would readily have favored as a private citizen.

With all his intellect and legal talents, Frankfurter's judicial career remained a lost opportunity. As far as the law was concerned, he may well have had more influence as a professor than as a Justice. There is no doubt that Frankfurter expected to be the intellectual leader of the Court, as he had been of the Harvard law faculty. As it turned out, the leadership role was performed first by Justice Black, and then by Chief Justice Warren and Justice Brennan.

William O. Douglas

William O. Douglas's place on other lists is a reflection less of his contribution as a member of the Court than of his public image. To outside observers, Douglas seemed the personification of the last frontier—the down-to-earth Westerner whose granite-hewed physique always seemed out of place in Parnassus. But the real Douglas was different from his public image. Douglas was the quintessential loner who personified the lover of humanity who did not like people.

Douglas may have had a brilliant mind, but he was erratic. He could whip up opinions faster than any of the other Justices. In fact, he wrote both the majority and dissenting opinions in one case. (Justice Charles E. Whittaker, who had been assigned the Court opinion was unable to write it, and Douglas sent him a draft within an hour after learning this.) Yet his opinions were too often unpolished, as though he lacked the interest for the sustained work involved in transforming first drafts into finished products. Although Chief Justice Warren came to appreciate Douglas's supporting votes, he felt that the peripatetic Justice spent too much time writing nonlegal books and doing things not related to the Court. With all his potential, Douglas made little significant contribution to jurisprudence; in Supreme Court history, he is now remembered primarily as Justice Black's auxiliary among the Justices.

William H. Rehnquist

The inclusion of William H. Rehnquist, says the introductory commentary of *Great Justices of the U.S. Supreme Court*, "marks the first appearance of one of the current members of the Court on a list of great justices."

To be sure, Rehnquist has been a more effective Chief Justice than his predecessor. Nevertheless, his elevation to the list of Supreme Court greats appears unwarranted. That is true not because of disagreement with his conservative posture (after all, Justice Field's even more conservative views did not bar him), but because the Rehnquist contribution to constitutional jurisprudence does not begin to bear comparison with those of the Justices on my list.

Although Rehnquist has led the Court's recent tilt toward the right, he has not been able to carry out the goals he had on his appointment. Rehnquist came to the Court with an agenda that included dismantling of the Warren jurisprudential structure—to see, as he said in an interview, that the "Court has called a halt to a number of the sweeping rulings that were made in the days of the Warren Court." The Rehnquist agenda was not carried out. Instead, his intended counter-revolution has served only as a confirmation of most of the Warren jurisprudence.

When he became Chief Justice, Rehnquist indicated that he had more ambitious goals. Inside the Court, the Chief Justice has urged even more extreme views on civil rights than have appeared in his published opinions. In *Patterson v. McLean Credit Union* (1990), the Court heard argument on "[w]hether or not . . . *Runyon v. McCrary* [a leading 1976 decision expanding civil-rights protection] . . . should be reconsidered." At the post-argument conference, Rehnquist declared that *Runyon* was wrong and the Court should overrule it. The Chief Justice did not, however, stop with his recommendation to overrule *Runyon*. He also told the *Patterson* conference that the Court should overrule *Jones v. Alfred H. Mayer Co.* (1968), an even more important civil-rights case, as well.

The Rehnquist attempt to overrule the two leading civil-rights decisions failed. *Jones v. Alfred H. Mayer Co.* was not questioned in any published opinion, and in *Patterson v. McLean Credit Union*, the Court expressly refused to overrule *Runyon v. McCrary*. In the *Patterson* conference, though some of the Justices agreed with Rehnquist's view that *Runyon* had been wrongly decided, they refused to go along with the Chief Justice and overrule that case.

Another Rehnquist bête noire has been *Roe v. Wade* (1973), where he had been one of the two dissenters. In *Webster v. Reproductive Health Services* (1989), the Chief Justice actually circulated a draft opinion of the Court that would have relegated *Roe* to virtual constitutional limbo. However, the Rehnquist *Webster* opinion lost its majority when Justice Sandra Day O'Connor refused to join and the Chief Justice had to issue it only as a plurality opinion. Since then, though Rehnquist has dissented in cases following *Roe*, he has not succeeded in securing a Court to follow him in overruling it.

A Chief Justice who cannot persuade a Court to give effect to his judicial agenda can scarcely be considered a great Chief Justice. For, as we now see, influence on the law is the primary criterion for elevation to the judicial pantheon.

Greatness and Influence

The 1993 survey of great Justices lists the criteria used to establish a Justice as "great" that were mentioned by those who responded to the survey. These are summarized as follows: "While writing and intellectual ability seem to be common criteria for the different groups, protection of individual rights is a criterion used frequently by only two of the groups, attorneys and students. Similarly, leadership appears to be a concern for two of the groups, judges and scholars, while not getting much attention from either attorneys or students."

To me, however, Supreme Court greatness is virtually synonymous with influence on the law. This results in the elimination of Justices who did not serve long enough to have had a substantial impact on jurisprudence. I have already given the example of Justice Cardozo who was one of the greatest judges in our history, but whose tenure on the high bench was too brief for him to make the contribution on the Court that his ability warranted.

All the Justices on my list served on the Court long enough to enable them to make major contributions. The shortest term among them was that of Chief Justice Hughes. Yet even he served for eleven years (almost twice the Cardozo tenure), and, more important, he led the Court during the crucial 1937 revolution in constitutional law. There is truth in Holmes's observation that Marshall's "greatness consists in his being there"—that he led the Court when our constitutional law was being formed. Chief Justice Hughes, too, was *there* at a crucial juncture in Supreme Court history.

But the greatness of a Chief Justice consists in more than his being *there*. If Chief Justice William Howard Taft, Hughes's predecessor, had continued to preside, it is doubtful that the 1937 constitutional revolution would have occurred. Not only was Hughes *there*, but he seized the opportunity to lead the Court to its recognition that the pre-1937 jurisprudence (in the words of a 1992 opinion) "rested on fundamentally false . . . assumptions" and that that "warranted the repudiation of the old law."

The same is true of Chief Justice Warren's great accomplishment in securing the unanimous *Brown* decision. Chief Justice Fred M. Vinson,

Warren's predecessor, was also *there* for *Brown*; he was the Court head when *Brown* came to the Court. However, had he been able to preside during the entire *Brown* decision process, the result would have been a fragmented decision that would have upheld segregation. According to a contemporary memo by Justice Douglas, under Vinson "the vote would be five to four in favor of the constitutionality of segregation." It was the Warren leadership that produced the unanimous decision striking down segregation. And it was Warren also who was the catalyst for this century's second revolution in constitutional jurisprudence. If Vinson had continued to head the Court during the Warren years, he would have been *there*, but the constitutional corpus would have been very different from that produced under Warren.

In my view, then, it all comes down to influence on the law. The Justices on my list are there because each changed the course of Supreme Court jurisprudence: Marshall laid the foundation of both our public law and the Supreme Court's role as the fulcrum of the constitutional system. Story led the early movement to adjust the common law to the needs of the new nation. Taney led his Court in molding the Marshall constitutional edifice to recognize both public power and the burgeoning corporate expansion. Field shifted the emphasis to private rights, in the process shielding business from regulatory power. Holmes set the theme for twentieth-century law and the need to adapt it to the "felt necessities of the time." Brandeis laid the juristic foundation for the welfare state, in the process developing a new method for the decision of cases. Hughes led the Court in the repudiation of the Field jurisprudence and the upholding of broad governmental power. Black tilted the constitutional balance toward protection of personal rights. Warren led a new activism that has made the Court the vital center of the constitutional system. Brennan ensured that "[w]e are all activists now" and that his concept of a "living Constitution" would dominate contemporary jurisprudence.

No other Justice in Court history has had an influence on the law comparable to that of these ten. All of them employed their authority to mold constitutional jurisprudence to meet what they deemed the needs of the nation during their tenure. All were activists who did not hesitate to use judicial power to adapt the law to the time's necessities. Not all of them were masters of the common law or consummate judicial craftsmen. But all employed the authority of the ermine to the utmost. This, in the end, is what makes them great. More than any other Justices, they seized the occasion to alter constitutional jurisprudence by their transforming touch.

2

TEN

WORST

SUPREME COURT

JUSTICES

We are told by the writer James Weldon Johnson that "every nation should be judged by the best it has been able to produce, not by the worst." The same is doubtless true of the Supreme Court. Yet this *Book of Legal Lists*, which lists the greatest Supreme Court Justices, would scarcely be complete without inclusion of their polar opposites—the worst Justices in the Court's history. The Marshalls and Holmeses who have dominated the Court's roster should not make us forget that the great Justices, like their counterparts elsewhere, are comparatively rare.

Most members of the Court have not risen above the level of "average." The Justices have generally been respectable judges—though too many of them without sign or promise of distinction. What Justice Holmes wrote of a colleague can be said of most Justices: "He had not wings and was not a thunderbolt, but he was a very honest hard working Judge."

Compared with the Justices on this list, however, the average Justice almost shines. Here we are dealing with the Supreme Court failures—those of whom we can say, with John Randolph of Roanoke, that "[n]ever were abilities so much below mediocrity so well rewarded; no, not when Caligula's horse was made Consul." The most remarkable thing about these Justices is that, in James Bryce's phrase, "being so commonplace they should have climbed so high."

— ★ — ★ — ★ —

— ★ — ★ — ★ —

Ten Worst Supreme Court Justices

1. Alfred Moore (1755–1810), Justice, United States Supreme Court, 1799–1804

2. Charles E. Whittaker (1901–1973), Justice, United States Supreme Court, 1957–1962

3. Fred M. Vinson (1890–1953), Chief Justice of the United States, 1946–1953

4. James C. McReynolds (1862–1946), Justice, United States Supreme Court, 1914–1941

5. Rufus W. Peckham (1838–1909), Justice, United States Supreme Court, 1895–1909

6. Samuel Chase (1741–1811), Justice, United States Supreme Court, 1796–1811

7. Philip P. Barbour (1783–1841), Justice, United States Supreme Court, 1836–1841

8. Salmon P. Chase (1808–1873), Chief Justice of the United States, 1864–1873

9. Pierce Butler (1866–1939), Justice, United States Supreme Court, 1922–1939

10. Sherman Minton (1890–1965), Justice, United States Supreme Court, 1949–1956

1. Alfred Moore

"Alfred Moore," begins a biographical sketch of the Justice, "must surely be one of the most unnoticed men ever to sit on the Supreme Court. . . . Moore's career made scarcely a ripple in American judicial history."

It is not, however, only the fact that Alfred Moore (1755–1810) is all but unknown that warrants his place at the head of this list. Moore himself may have been a man of some ability. He had been active in the Revolutionary struggle and became a leader of the North Carolina bar (arguing the first case holding a law unconstitutional) and of the effort to have his state ratify the Constitution.

On the Supreme Court, however, Moore was less than a nonentity. Although he served as a Justice for five years, he authored only one opinion. With Justice Thomas Johnson, Moore holds the record for having delivered the fewest opinions, and Johnson was on the Court for only one year. The Moore opinion, issued in 1800, was only about a page in length; it accepted the view that the United States and France were then at "war" and that France was, therefore, an "enemy" within the meaning of a federal statute. Two other Justices delivered more substantial opinions emphasizing that no full state of war existed, but only a "limited, partial war." The decision confirmed the Federalist insistence that there was a state of war with France and was bitterly attacked by the Jeffersonian press, which called for the impeachment of "every Judge who asserted we were in a state of war, contrary to the rights of Congress to declare it."

Not only did Justice Moore write only one opinion,but he managed to be absent from every significant case decided during his Court tenure. Most important, he missed the argument in *Marbury v. Madison* (1803) because of a delay in traveling to Washington and hence could not participate in the decision. He had fought against judicial review in the leading pre-*Marbury* state case, and might well have expressed disagreement with Chief Justice Marshall's *Marbury* opinion had he been part of the Court that decided the case. Instead, he had to remain silent as Marshall announced his opinion. In the end, Moore's career on the Court was a story of missed opportunities.

2. Charles E. Whittaker

Charles E. Whittaker (1901–1973) may have been the dumbest Justice ever appointed. Justice Potter Stewart once told me that Whittaker "used to come out of our conference literally crying. You know Charlie had gone to night law school, and he began as an office boy and he'd been a farm boy and he had inside him an inferiority complex, which . . . showed and he'd say, 'Felix used words in there that I'd never heard of.'"

There is not one Whittaker opinion that decides an important case or stands out from the humdrum. The difficulty the Justice had in writing is shown by the case of *Meyer v. United States* (1960). Whittaker had been assigned the majority opinion. He told Justice William O. Douglas, who had already written a dissent, that he had tried but was simply unable to get started on his opinion. Douglas asked if he would like him to draft the majority opinion. "Would you please?" Whittaker replied. This was one case (hopefully the only one) in which the majority and dissenting opinions were written by the same Justice.

In addition, Whittaker, more than any other Justice, found it difficult to make up his mind; his indecisiveness became legend in the Warren Court. Justice Stewart said to me, "That was Charlie Whittaker's great problem, you know. He was a very, very conscientious man and a fine man, but he just didn't have the power of decision." According to Douglas, "In Conference, Whittaker would take one position when the Chief or Black spoke, change his mind when Frankfurter spoke, and change back again when some other Justice spoke." Then, after the conference, Whittaker would agonize and agonize over decisions, swinging back and forth in key cases, which would make it most difficult for the others. This was particularly true in close cases. Thus in the important Expatriation Cases (1958), as well as in the landmark case of *Baker v. Carr* (1962), Whittaker switched his votes several times and ultimately abstained in *Baker*.

After he retired from the Court, Whittaker took a highly paid legal post with General Motors. He then delivered widely reported attacks on the Court's decisions, notably in a 1964 speech before the American Bar Association. When he heard about Whittaker's criticism, Chief Justice Warren used to say, "Charlie never could make up his mind about decisions until he left the Court."

To me, the incident that best illustrates why Whittaker is on this list occurred during the 1957 term when Justice Frankfurter circulated the following satirical mock opinion in a movie censorship case:

No. 372.—October Term, 1957.

Times Film Corporation, Petitioner,
v.
City of Chicago, Richard J. Daley
and Timothy J. O'Connor

The Court of Appeals in this case sustained the censorship, under an Illinois statute, of a motion picture entitled, "The Game of Love." The theme of the film so far as it has one, is the same as that in Benjamin Franklin's famous letter to his son, to the effect that the most easing way for an adolescent to learn the facts of life is under the tutelage of an older woman. A judgment that the manner in which this theme was conveyed by this film exceeded the bounds of free expression protected by the Fourteenth Amendment can only serve as confirmation of the saying, *"Honi soit qui mal y pense."*

After he read this, Whittaker wrote back,

> Dear Felix:
>
> No. 372—Times Film Corporation,
> Petitioner v. City of Chicago, et al.
>
> I join in your *per curiam* in this case.

Frankfurter had to send Whittaker a written note explaining, "This was intended as a joke."

3. Fred M. Vinson

"This is the first indication that I have ever had that there is a God."

This caustic comment to two former law clerks was Justice Felix Frankfurter's reaction to Chief Justice Fred M. Vinson's (1890–1953) death just before reargument was scheduled in *Brown v. Board of Education*. Vinson's death prevented him from presiding over the Court that decided the *Brown* school segregation case. Had Vinson still been Chief Justice when the Court decided *Brown*, the result would have been a divided decision. More than that, according to a confidential memo written by Justice William O. Douglas at the time, the decision would have upheld segregation by a bare majority. In a letter just after the unanimous *Brown* decision was announced, Frankfurter wrote, "That would have been catastrophic."

Instead of the clarion call to end segregation sounded by Chief Justice Earl Warren after he had succeeded Vinson, the latter indicated to the Justices that he was in favor of upholding segregation. A decision the other way, he told the first conference discussing *Brown*, meant, "We face the complete abolition of the public school system in the South."

Vinson's handling of *Brown* was symptomatic of his ineffectiveness as Chief Justice. In fact, he was, in my opinion, the least effective Court head in history. His appointment was due primarily to his close friendship, even cronyism, with President Harry Truman, who hoped that his skill at getting along with people would enable him to restore peace to a Court that had become splintered. Throughout his career, Vinson had been known for his ability to smoothe ruffled feathers. But his hearty bonhomie was not enough to enable him to lead the Court effectively. The Justices looked down on Vinson as the possessor of a second-class mind. Even Justice Stanley Reed, the least intellectually gifted of the Roosevelt appointees, could dismiss the dour-faced Chief, in a comment to Justice Frankfurter, as "just like me, except that he is less well-educated."

As it turned out, Vinson failed completely in his mission to unify the Court. He was inept in perhaps the most important function of a Chief Justice—that of leading the conference. According to Frankfurter's diary, Vinson presented cases in a shallow way. He "blithely hits the obvious points . . . disposing of each case rather briefly, by choosing, as it were, to float merely on the surface of the problems raised by the cases."

When Vinson did lead the Court, it was often to the wrong decisions. His opinions invariably elevated governmental power over individual rights—notably in *Dennis* v. United States (1951), affirming the most important sedition convictions since the infamous Sedition Act of 1798, as well as in cases upholding Cold War restrictions such as loyalty oaths. In the Steel Seizure Case (*Youngstown Sheet & Tube Co. v. Sawyer, 1952*), where the Court imposed limitations on Presidential power, Vinson wrote a strong dissent in defense of broadside executive authority.

Even the Vinson opinions upholding the right of blacks to attend white graduate schools (usually considered important steps on the road to *Brown*) are deceptive. Counsel had urged the Court to invalidate segregation, but Vinson successfully urged at the conferences that segregation itself was not at issue. More than that, according to Justice Douglas's conference notes, he told the Justices that he "can't say that schools shouldn't be separate" and that he "can't distinguish professional and elementary schools"—the key distinction on which the Court ultimately decided. The Vinson conference view is, however, understandable when we realize that he indicated, according to Douglas, that "[h]e inclines to think he would affirm" the exclusion of the black applicant. Presumably, he changed his mind after all the others voted the other way, though his opinion of the Court did mirror his conference avoidance of the segregation issue.

What Richard Kluger calls the "testament . . . to Vinson's failure as Chief Justice" is the fact that the Vinson Court was the most fragmented in the Court's history. During the last Vinson term, only 19 percent of the cases were decided unanimously—a record low. Vinson himself averaged thirteen dissents per term—a record for a Chief Justice.

Vinson's record supports what Washington wags said when he supported Justice Tom Clark's appointment—that it was because he wanted someone on his Court who knew less law than he did. Throughout his tenure, the Justices would openly display their contempt for their Chief. As a law clerk recalls it, several of Vinson's colleagues "would discuss in his presence the view that the Chief's job should rotate annually and . . . made no bones about regarding him—correctly—as their intellectual inferior."

Perhaps the most devastating comment on Vinson was that by Phillip Elman, who had clerked for Frankfurter and was one of the most knowledgeable Court watchers. Elman wrote to the Justice about "the C.J." from the Solicitor General's Office: "What a mean little despot he is. Has there ever been a member of the Court who was deficient in so many respects as a man and as a judge. Even that s.o.b. McReynolds, despite his defects of character, stands by comparison as a towering figure and powerful intellect . . . this man is a pygmy, morally and mentally. And so uncouth."

4. James C. McReynolds

James C. McReynolds (1862–1946) was undoubtedly the least lovable person ever to sit on the Supreme Court. Justice Holmes called him "insolent" and "arrogant"; he certainly was, in *Time*'s phrase, "intolerably rude . . . savagely sarcastic." When Justice Harlan F. Stone said to him of an attorney's brief, "That was the dullest argument I ever heard in my life," McReynolds rudely replied, "The only duller thing I can think of is to hear you read one of your opinions."

Time also called McReynolds "anti-Semitic." His anti-Semitism was as pronounced as it has been in any American public figure. He wrote to Holmes, on a case where Justice Brandeis was in dissent, "that for four thousand years the Lord tried to make something out of Hebrews, then gave it up as impossible and turned them out to prey on mankind in general—like fleas on the dog for example." He used to leave the conference room when Brandeis spoke and, while Justice Cardozo was being sworn in, he ostentatiously scanned a newspaper.

McReynolds's prejudices were scarcely limited to "the two Hebrews who are on our bench." He hated women lawyers. When one appeared in the courtroom, McReynolds would mutter, "I see the female is here again," or a similar negative remark. He also displayed a definite racism, calling blacks "ignorant, superstitious, immoral and with but small capacity for racial improvement." All in all, as Chief Justice Taft wrote, McReynolds was "fuller of prejudice than any man I have ever known."

The McReynolds character had a direct effect on his Court work. In the 1930s, the Court began to display an increasing liberalism in racial cases. Justice McReynolds, almost alone, refused to go along with the trend. In a lone dissent, he stated that possible racial prejudice, "whatever that may be," on the part of a juror in the trial of a black for murder would not justify a reversal. He also disagreed with the reversal in the celebrated Scottsboro Cases (*Powell v. Alabama, 1932; Harris v. Alabama, 1935*), where due process had been violated as flagrantly as it had been in any case, as well as with the holding that a Texas primary law that denied the franchise to African-Americans was invalid. He also dissented in *Missouri ex rel. Gaines v. Canada* (1938) (a direct precursor of *Brown v. Board of Education*), which required Missouri to admit a black to its state law school. McReynolds rejected the notion that the Court should overturn the state's settled policy in not allowing blacks to attend the all-white institution, asserting, "the state should not be unduly hampered through theorization inadequately restrained by experience."

Justice McReynolds is, however, now best remembered as the most extreme (and certainly the most virulent) of the Four Horsemen—charitably characterized by Chief Justice Rehnquist as "the four whose legal philosophy was least sympathetic to sustaining New Deal measures." It was McReynolds who delivered the bitterest harangues against the New Deal measures to deal with the Great Depression. McReynolds actually voted against more New Deal laws than any of the other Justices. Between 1933 and his 1941 resignation, he wrote 146 dissents, 119 of them from 1937 to 1941, after the Court had begun to uphold New Deal legislation.

McReynolds had displayed a similar approach throughout his tenure. He dissented from the 1919 decision upholding a workmen's compensation law, calling it "a measure to stifle enterprise, produce discontent, strife, idleness, and pauperism." The Court's doctrine, he proclaimed, "is revolutionary and leads straight towards destruction of our . . . system of government." When he read this hyperbole, Harold J. Laski wrote to Holmes, "Was it meant seriously? Is it just a bad joke?"

To Justice McReynolds, the decisions starting with *National Labor Relations Board v. Jones & Laughlin Steel Corp.* (1937), upholding regulatory measures, were certainly no joke, and he strongly dissented from all of them. But his most extreme dissent was in the Gold Clause Cases (*Norman v. Baltimore & Ohio Railroad Co.; Nortz v. United States; Perry v. United States, 1935*), which upheld congressional power to go off the gold standard. "Shame and humiliation are upon us . . . anarchy and despotism are at the door," McReynolds declared. "Moral and financial chaos may confidently be expected. . . . Here we have a monetary system the extent—I almost said wickedness—of which is almost beyond comprehension." The McReynolds announcement from the bench concluded with the wail, "The Constitution is gone."

The more one considers McReynolds, both as a person and as a judge, the more one wonders that he was elevated to the bench by one of our best presidents. The easy explanation of contemporary gossip was that Wilson appointed him to the Court because he could no longer stand his abrasive personality in Cabinet meetings. Perhaps the best conclusion is that of Harold J. Laski: "McReynolds and the theory of a beneficent deity are quite incompatible."

5. Rufus W. Peckham

More than any other judge, Rufus W. Peckham (1838–1909) was the exemplar of the conservative jurist at the beginning of the twentieth century. His decisions were prime applications of the dominant legal thought of the day—using the law as the barrier against interferences with operation of the economic system. If laissez-faire was read into the Constitution, that was true in large part because of Justice Peckham's opinions.

A young law clerk once asked Justice Holmes, "What was Justice Peckham like, intellectually?" "Intellectually?" Holmes replied, puzzlement in his voice. "I never thought of him in that connection. His major premise was, 'God damn it!'" A few years later, after making the same comment, Holmes explained that he meant "thereby that emotional predilections governed him on social themes."

Peckham's opinions bear witness to the Holmes observation. The "emotional predilections" that governed Peckham's decisions were based on fear of changes in the existing order. "When socialism first began to be talked about," Holmes tells us, "the comfortable classes of the community were a good deal frightened. I suspect that this fear has influenced judicial action both here and in England." It certainly influenced the Peckham jurisprudence.

At the same time, few can doubt Justice Peckham's importance in helping to translate laissez-faire into the law of the land. It was Peckham who wrote the opinions in both *Allgeyer v. Louisiana* (1897), in which liberty of contract was first relied on by the Court, and *Lochner v. New York* (1905), where the liberty-of-contract tide reached its crest. The *Allgeyer* opinion struck down a state law prohibiting an individual from contracting with an out-of-state insurance company for insurance of property within the state: "Has not a citizen of a State, under the provisions of the Federal Constitution above mentioned, a right to contract outside of the State for insurance on his property—a right of which state legislation cannot deprive him?" The Peckham opinion gave the broadest construction to the "liberty" protected by due process.

That liberty, Peckham wrote, "is deemed to embrace the right of the citizen to be free in the enjoyment of all his faculties; to be free to use them in all lawful ways; to live and work where he will; to earn his livelihood by any lawful calling; to pursue any livelihood or avocation, and for that purpose to enter into all contracts . . . carrying out to a successful conclusion the purposes above mentioned."

Peckham's jurisprudence reached its culmination in *Lochner v. New York*, where the Peckham opinion pushed freedom of contract to its zenith. *Lochner* was, however, merely illustrative of the Peckham jurisprudence, founded as it was on what he called "the most sacred rights of property and the individual liberty of contract." Any effort to interfere with them "should [not] be indulged in." Economic abuses, declared a Peckham opinion, should be dealt with not by a law, which "will not, as seems to me plain, even achieve the purposes of its authors," but by "the general laws of trade [and] the law of supply and demand."

What made the Peckham jurisprudence so important is that it both reflected and set the tone for the dominant legal thought of his day. It was Justice Peckham as much as anyone who made the law the businessman's first line of defense. Behind it, corporate power could operate free from legal interference. In the Peckham approach, the negative conception of law reached its judicial climax. The Justices now saw their task not as one of making law to meet changing needs, but of stabilization and formalization. The law itself had become the great bulwark against economic and social change.

6. Samuel Chase

Samuel Chase (1741–1811) has an important place in Supreme Court history as the only Justice to have been impeached. That is not, however, why he is included in this list. Chase had been a leader in Maryland in the fight for independence and had legal ability. But his extreme political partisanship made him the epitome of all that a Justice should not be. In 1800, the Court could not sit because of the absence of a quorum. During that time, Chase was busy in his state working for President Adams's reelection. This led to attacks in the press that condemned "the suspension of the highest court . . . to permit Chase to make electioneering harangues in favor of Mr. *Adams*." Even Adams's son wrote to his cousin that Chase was "too much engaged in electioneering."

After Adams's defeat by Jefferson, Chase used the bench as a pulpit for bitter attacks against the new administration. In a charge to the Baltimore grand jury (Supreme Court Justices then also sat on circuit in lower courts), Chase asserted that Jeffersonian principles would "take away all security for property and personal liberty . . . and our republican constitution will sink into a mobocracy."

Chase also presided at the trials of several defendants prosecuted under the notorious Sedition Act of 1798, which made it a crime to publish writings that discredited the government, president, or Congress. During the trials, Irving Dilliard tells us, Chase's "performance as a judge was almost indistinguishable from that of the prosecution." This was particularly true in the trial of James Callender, a leading Jeffersonian editor, who had published a strong attack against President Adams. Riding to the trial, Chase was told that Callender had once been arrested as a vagrant. "It is a pity," replied Chase, "that they had not hanged the rascal." During the Callender trial, Chase openly displayed his bias against the defendant, giving substance to Dilliard's assertion. Chase's conduct, concludes Raoul Berger in the leading work on impeachment, demonstrated his "evident disposition to play the hanging judge." Certainly, Chase's patent display of partisanship was scarcely proper judicial conduct, particularly for a member of the highest Court.

The impeachment of Justice Chase was based on his partisan behavior in his grand jury charge and in trials such as Callender's under the Sedition Act. The fact that Chase was acquitted in his impeachment trial does not change the fact that the Justice constantly engaged in nonjudicial conduct so flagrant as to justify his inclusion on this list. He may have been a man whose intellect should have made him at least an average Justice. "But," Dilliard sums up Chase, "he also was unrestrained, autocratic, violent, and headstrong. He was more the advocate than the judge. . . . District Judge Richard Peters of Pennsylvania spoke for many others as well as himself when he said: 'I never sat with him without pain, as he was forever getting into some intemperate and unnecessary squabble.' And he aided and abetted the police state era of the Alien and Sedition Acts, that 'reign of witches,' as Jefferson called the dark and ugly years."

Dilliard's conclusion pithily explains Chase's place on this list: "One Samuel Chase on the Supreme Court of the United States may be said to have been enough."

7. Philip P. Barbour

In rating Supreme Court Justices, we must distinguish between those who are merely unknowns and those who were failures. In pre–Civil War days, the Justices (except for Chief Justice Taney and Justice Benjamin R. Curtis, who wrote the famous dissent in *Dred Scott v. Sandford)* were not even ordinary. Almost all of those who served on the Taney Court have remained ciphers in Supreme Court history.

When we think of the Presidents between Jackson and Lincoln we must ask, with James Bryce, "who now knows or cares to know anything about the personality of James K. Polk or Franklin Pierce?" The same is true of most of the Justices chosen by our pre–Civil War presidents. Almost all of them, too, have been relegated to the obscurity reserved for the Tylers, Buchanans, and other lesser lights who failed to measure up to what those in their high positions should be.

These Justices in the Taney Court undoubtedly included one or more who deserve mention on this list. But almost all of them were such nonentities and many of them served such brief terms that they are too unimportant even to be listed among the worst Justices. At the same time, this list should contain one of the pre–Civil War Justices — at least as representative of the less than mediocre men who then served.

Who should be chosen from what may have been (despite the abilities of Chief Justice Taney and Justice Curtis) the worst Court in our history? At first, I thought of James M. Wayne, Justice from 1835 to 1867, because he persuaded the Justices to decide the crucial constitutional issues in *Dred Scott,* when the case could easily have been disposed of on another ground without consideration of those issues. Yet, aside from his *Dred Scott* role, Wayne was a competent, if not sparkling, Justice. Then I considered Henry Baldwin, who sat from 1830 to 1844, and who had an approach to constitutional law followed by no other Justice (Baldwin himself referred to his "peculiar views"). He may even have been incompetent during much of his tenure; Justice Story wrote that, "he is partially deranged." Still, on the principle that mental incapacity absolves a person of responsibility, Baldwin has been passed over.

Instead, I have chosen Philip P. Barbour (1783–1841), who was described by Senator Thomas Hart Benton "as a Virginia country gentleman, after the most perfect model of that class." On his appointment, a newspaper noted Barbour's "inflexible and uncompromising State-Rights principles." This was an unhappy portent. On the bench, Justice Barbour was a rigid representative of the Virginia school of strict construction in favor of states' rights. In his diary, John Quincy Adams referred to him as a "shallow-pated wild-cat, . . . fit for nothing but to tear the Union to rags and tatters."

Like most of his confreres, Justice Barbour wrote boringly stiff opinions. More important, as the leading work on the Taney Court puts it, "Barbour pushed logical distinctions to the point of wearisome sterility." A newspaper critic complained in 1838 that "such small lights . . . have been recently placed on the bench—such shallow metaphysical hairsplitters as P. P. Barbour."

A year earlier, the most important Barbour opinion had been delivered—the opinion of the Court in *New York v. Miln*, where a state law required ship masters to make detailed reports on all passengers brought into New York. Bonds had to be given for each foreigner brought in, and the masters had to remove at their own expense any foreigners likely to become public charges. Counsel for New York urged, "as a fact worthy of notice that, although [defendant was] a stranger among us, he has undertaken to teach us constitutional law."

He did not teach constitutional law to Justice Barbour. His opinion not only upheld the state law, but went out of its way to magnify state authority at the expense of the federal commerce power. As Barbour stated it, "a State has the same undeniable and unlimited jurisdiction over all persons and things within its territorial limits, as any foreign nation." Further, "in relation to these, the authority of a State is complete, unqualified and exclusive."

The opinion did not, however, stop there. According to Justice Barbour, the state law was not even a regulation of commerce. That was true, he said, because it regulated persons rather than goods: "the goods are the subject of commerce, the persons are not." Of persons, Barbour wrote, "[t]hey are not the subject of commerce; and, not being imported goods, cannot fall within . . . a power given to Congress to regulate commerce."

This Barbour holding cast doubt on *Gibbons v. Ogden* (1824), where Chief Justice Marshall delivered the classic opinion on the Commerce Clause. That case involved steamboat transportation of passengers, and, even in the pre-1937 decisions that restricted the scope of the federal commerce power, it was never doubted that persons as well as goods were subjects of commerce. Fortunately, starting with the Passenger Cases (*Smith v. Turner; Morris v. Boston*, 1849), the Court came to abandon the Barbour position that persons were not subjects of commerce.

Writing about the Taney Court, Daniel Webster deplored the fact that the Court did not have "a strong and leading mind." Certainly this was true of almost all the Justices at the time. As indicated, several of those Justices are candidates for bottom ranking. Justice Barbour does not stand alone in this respect, but he has been chosen because his extreme view of the commerce power would have gutted federal authority and undone Marshall's formative work.

8. Salmon P. Chase

It may appear paradoxical that Salmon P. Chase (1808–1873), who had held more high governmental posts and positions of political leadership than anyone previously appointed, should be on this list. Only William Howard Taft in later Courts had held higher office. However, Taft desired appointment as Chief Justice more than the presidency; the Chief Justiceship was to him the ultimate compensation for the unhappiness of his White House years. Chase's sole ambition, though, was the White House.

While President Lincoln was considering Chase's appointment, Gideon Welles wrote in his famous diary, "The President sometimes does strange things, but this would be a singular mistake." The Welles assessment proved accurate, and not primarily because Chase lacked legal learning. More important was the overriding fact that (as Lincoln put it) Chase "had the Presidential maggot in his brain, and he never knew anybody who once had it to get rid of it." Certainly, Chase did not get rid of his ambition merely because of his appointment to the highest judicial position. As Chief Justice, said Henry Adams, "[h]e loved power as though he were still a Senator" and throughout his judicial career still nourished the hope that the presidential mantle would at last descend on him. "In my judgment," wrote Chase's successor, Morrison R. Waite, "my predecessor detracted from his fame by permitting himself to think he wanted the Presidency. Whether true or not it was said that he permitted his ambitions in that direction to influence his judicial opinions." His confreres on the bench, like the rest of the country, felt that Chase's judicial actions were governed primarily by political considerations. The inevitable result was, to quote Lincoln again, "impairing the strength & impartiality of the Judiciary."

And so it happened. The leading history of the Chase Court concludes, "In much of what was done in [the Court's] labors he seems to have taken no deep interest." To one whose every thought was on the White House (Chase wrote in his diary), "[w]orking from morning till midnight and no result, except that John Smith owned this . . . property instead of Jack Robinson; I caring nothing . . . about the matter."

Except for John Rutledge (who suffered from what John Adams called "accelerated and increased . . . Disorder of the Mind" while he served one interim term) and Fred M. Vinson, Chase was the worst Chief Justice. When he led his Court (or at least delivered its opinions), it was, more often than not, to unfortunate decisions. That in *Hepburn v. Griswold* (1870) would, had it not been overruled the next year, have had devastating economic effects. Equally unfortunate was the descision in *Ex Parte McCardle* (1869), where Chase's opinion upheld congressional power to curtail the Supreme Court's jurisdiction. *McCardle* has served as the basis for efforts in Congress to deny Court jurisdiction in cases involving segregation, school prayer, and other areas.

Chase not only was an ineffective Chief Justice, but saw fit to dissent from some of his Court's best decisions. He, of course, dissented in the Legal Tender Cases (*Knox v. Lee; Parker v. Davis*, 1871) from the Court's correction of his *Hepburn v. Griswold* blunder. But he also disagreed with the landmark *Ex Parte Milligan* (1866), immunizing civilians from military justice; the Chase dissent asserted military power to try civilians in a state far removed from the war. Chase also dissented from a decision striking down loyalty oaths—as pernicious in his day as they were a century later during the McCarthy era—as well as from one holding that state courts have no jurisdiction over federal officers and agencies, a holding essential for the federal supremacy proclaimed by the Constitution.

All in all, Chase was one of the Court's striking failures. He turned out as Lincoln had predicted when he hesitated over appointing Chase as Chief Justice: "If he keeps on with the notion that he is destined to be President of the United States, and which in my judgment he will never be, he will never acquire . . . fame and usefulness as Chief Justice."

9. Pierce Butler

Supreme Court historians generally include all the Four Horsemen (Justices James McReynolds, Willis Van Devanter, George Sutherland, and Pierce Butler) among the worst Justices. Yet two of them, however hostile they may have been to the New Deal Era measures, do not deserve inclusion on the list. Justice Sutherland was the intellectual leader of the four and a better than average spokesman for his conservative views. As for Justice Van Devanter, it cannot be denied that his opinions are mostly pedestrian. But while he was afflicted with what a Justice once called "pen paralysis," he was a trusted adviser to his colleagues, who relied heavily on his conference statements and what Chief Justice Hughes called his common sense.

The same cannot be said of Justice Pierce Butler (1922–1939), who was, in most ways, a nonirascible McReynolds clone. Butler joined with his ill-tempered colleague in virtually every significant case—particularly in those striking down regulatory power. He voted consistently to narrow the concept of "businesses affected with a public interest," which alone were then subject to governmental authority. Butler also shared McReynolds's restrictive approach to the rights of African-Americans. He wrote the Court opinion upholding a poll tax and joined the dissenters in the Scottsboro Cases, as well as in the decisions striking down an all-white primary and ordering a black admitted to a state law school. In addition, Butler opinions upheld laws restricting property rights of Japanese and their access to citizenship.

During the crucial 1935 term, when the Court decided the last of its cases striking down New Deal measures (notably *Carter v. Carter Coal Co.* [1936]), Justice Butler voted with the other Four Horsemen in every case involving governmental power. In particular, he wrote the last opinion following *Adkins v. Children's Hospital* (1923). The Butler language there was, if possible, even more extreme than that in *Adkins*: "The state is without power by any form of legislation to prohibit, change or nullify contracts between employers and . . . workers as to the amount to be paid." Hence any law that deprives employers and workers of freedom to agree on wages is unconstitutional. Well might an article on the Justice conclude, "Butler's decisions throughout his years on the Court reveal an almost unrelenting conservatism."

Yet Butler is not on this list because of his conservatism, but because of the rigidity of his jurisprudence. Except for Justice McReynolds, he was the most inflexible of the Justices who rejected the New Deal legislation. According to Merlo J. Pusey's biography of Chief Justice Hughes, "Butler was the most difficult man on the court." Butler's philosophy was still one of complete laissez-faire, his world one of either/or, black or white—a world in which dogma could never be sacrificed to changing needs. The Butler opinions are simplistic, reflecting complete assurance in their author's rightness, if not righteousness.

Once, after a lengthy conference debate, Justice Butler's position was adopted with only Justice Holmes dissenting. Butler then turned to Holmes and said, "I am glad we have finally arrived at a *just* decision." Holmes came back, "Hell is paved with *just* decisions." Holmes later characterized Butler with a single word—"a monolith," adding, "there are no seams the frost can get through. He is of one piece."

10. Sherman Minton

Sherman Minton (1890–1965) was such a nonentity on the Supreme Court that he may well be best remembered as the last to use the spittoon provided for each Justice behind the bench, which always upset the fastidious Justice Harold H. Burton, who sat next to him. Minton was the worst of the Justices appointed by Truman; by any standard, he ranks near the bottom on any list of Justices.

Minton had the build of a heavyweight boxer (he had excelled in sports in college) and was noted for the saltiness of his tongue. He reacted to decisions reversing judgments against workers in cases under the Federal Employers' Liability Act with a typical letter to Justice Frankfurter. The decisions, Minton wrote, "seem to have reached the position in the law of negligence where a railroad employee has an urgent call of nature the railroad company is negligent if the railroad company does not furnish him with a safe gondola car to crap in—to your credit you are still dissenting to this kind of law."

Justice Minton's first important opinion, in 1950, denied due process to the German-born wife of a World War II veteran. An editorial complained that this was "a pretty raw deal to hand a soldier's bride." A Minton letter replied that Congress had authorized the bride's exclusion without any hearing, writing that he had "always believed that this Court has no power to legislate." Hence, the exclusion had to be upheld.

This set the theme for the Minton jurisprudence, which invariably came down in favor of congressional and other governmental power against claims of individual right. In this respect, he was a junior Vinson, voting with the Chief Justice in supporting claims against government in less than 15 percent of the cases. Minton joined both the Vinson dissent in the Steel Seizure Case and his Court opinion in *Dennis v. United States.* He invariably voted for government in the national security cases of the Cold War period—including those dealing with alleged subversion and loyalty programs. It was the Minton opinion in *Adler v. Board of Education* (1952) that upheld loyalty oaths for teachers and their discharge for belonging to an organization designated subversive. In the decade that he served on the Warren Court, Minton dissented from most of that Court's decisions moving away from the Vinson Court's pro-government jurisprudence.

The one exception was in racial discrimination cases. From the beginning of the *Brown* decision process, Minton strongly asserted segregation's unconstitutionality. But this is a situation where the exception does not change the rule. In all other cases, Minton was below mediocrity as a Justice. His opinions, relatively few for his tenure, are less than third-rate, characterized by their cavalier approach to complicated issues.

The shallowness of the Minton approach to constitutional issues is shown by his reaction to a 1959 decision striking down New York's attempt to ban the film *Lady Chatterley's Lover*. After the decision, Minton wrote to Frankfurter, "Adultery has been outlawed since Moses brought the tablets down from the Mountain. . . . To say that this policy cannot be carried out by N.Y. preventing the teaching of adultery as a way of life because the Constitution makes teaching adultery something protected by it seems ridiculous to me—I suppose a gangster school set up to teach crime would be protected!"

With all this, it should be said that his colleagues considered the earthy Hoosier most congenial to work with. "Minton," wrote Frankfurter, "will not go down in history as a great jurist, but he was a delightful colleague." Then he plaintively asked, "Why are most lawyers dull company?"

Bottom of the Barrel?

A list of Supreme Court worsts is even more subjective than one of greats. After all, everyone agrees that, starting with John Marshall, certain Justices belong in the judicial pantheon. But who now has heard of, much less knows anything about, Justices Moore, Barbour, and the other anonymities who burdened the bench in the nineteenth century? And if more recognize the names of the two Chases, it is only because the first was the defendant in the only Supreme Court impeachment trial and the second played an important part in nonjudicial history. True, the names of those on the list who served in this century may spark more recognition, but only because they are closer to us in time.

Except for Justices Moore and Whittaker, the Justices listed stood for legal doctrines that have since been repudiated. Samuel Chase partisanly enforced the Sedition Act, which is now considered a byword for an infamous law. Barbour's constitutional approach would have undone much of Marshall's contribution. Salmon Chase was responsible for one of the worst Supreme Court decisions and on the wrong side in most of the other important cases during his tenure. Peckham led the Court in making the Constitution the bulwark against social and economic change. McReynolds and Butler carried the Peckham jurisprudence to the extremes of the anti–New Deal decisions. Vinson and Minton upheld restrictions on civil liberties, including even the Cold War excesses censured by most observers.

If rejected jurisprudence is the criterion, it may be asked why these Justices are listed and not Justice Stephen J. Field, whose opinions furnished the foundation for the Court's hostility to governmental interference in economic matters. Field's jurisprudence, however, served the needs of his day when the law gave burgeoning business the room it needed to complete the transition to the new industrial economy. More than that, Field furnished the rationale for due process as a substantive restriction on governmental power. The need for the substantive due process guarantee was well stated by the second Justice Harlan: "Were due process merely a procedural safeguard it would fail to reach those situations where the deprivation of life, liberty or property was accomplished by legislation which . . . could, given even the fairest possible procedure . . ., nevertheless destroy the enjoyment of all three." The Justice who provided what Harlan called the "bulwarks against arbitrary legislation" certainly stands on a higher plane than those who carried this concept to what we now consider ridiculous extremes.

The Justices whom I have ranked as the Supreme Court's worst are listed not so much because of their jurisprudence, but because each was almost a travesty of what a judge, much less one on the high bench, should be. The Chief Justices on the list did not lead or, when they did, steered the Court to disastrous decisions. The two Chases, moreover, acted as political partisans, which inevitably brought the Supreme Court itself into disrepute. The others were bigoted, rigid, and simplistic in their jurisprudence, anonymities in judicial history, and just plain dumb. They well deserve their place at the bottom of the judicial barrel.

3

TEN

GREATEST

SUPREME COURT

DECISIONS

"The history of the United States," says Charles Warren at the outset of his now classic history of the Supreme Court, "has been written not merely in the halls of Congress, in the Executive offices and on the battlefields, but to a great extent in the chambers of the Supreme Court of the United States." The decisions of the Court reflect our history in all its manifold aspects. Every important decision has had its impact on the nation, from the founding of the Republic to the internal stresses of the society two centuries later.

What are the most important Supreme Court decisions? My answer is contained in two lists. The first, in this chapter, lists the greatest Supreme Court decisions, starting with *Marbury v. Madison*, which laid the foundation of American constitutional law. The second list, in the following chapter, contains the worst decisions of the high bench, starting with that in the *Dred Scott* case, usually considered the Court's greatest self-inflicted wound.

— ★ — ★ — ★ —

— ★ — ★ — ★ —

Ten Greatest Supreme Court Decisions

1. *Marbury v. Madison*, 1 Cranch 137 (U.S. 1803)

2. *Brown v. Board of Education*, 347 U.S. 483 (1954)

3. *McCulloch v. Maryland*, 4 Wheat. 316 (U.S. 1819)

4. *Gibbons v. Ogden*, 9 Wheat. 1 (U.S. 1824)

5. *Ex Parte Milligan*, 4 Wall. 2 (U.S. 1866)

6. Granger Cases, 94 U.S. 113 (1876)

7. *National Labor Relations Board v. Jones &
   Laughlin Steel Corp.*, 301 U.S. 1 (1937)

8. *United States v. Nixon*, 418 U.S. 683 (1974)

9. *Baker v. Carr*, 369 U.S. 186 (1962)

10. *Charles River Bridge v. Warren Bridge*,
    11 Pet. 420 (U.S. 1837)

1. *Marbury v. Madison*

If Chief Justice John Marshall ranks as the greatest American judge, his decision in *Marbury v. Madison* (1803) ranks as the greatest handed down by the Supreme Court. It was that decision that established judicial review as the foundation of the constitutional system.

Marbury v. Madison arose out of the passage of the Judiciary Act of 1801 during the last days of President John Adams's Federalist administration. That law provided for the appointment of a large number of federal judges by the outgoing president. The Senate confirmed the appointees, and Adams signed their commissions. Because of the pressure of last-minute business, however, some of the commissions, including William Marbury's, were not delivered. The new president, Thomas Jefferson, ordered his secretary of state, James Madison, not to deliver them. Marbury then brought an action to order Madison to deliver his commission. The action was brought directly in the Supreme Court under section 13 of the Judiciary Act of 1789, which gave the Court original jurisdiction in such cases against federal officials.

The Marshall opinion ruled that section 13 of the Judiciary Act was unconstitutional. Since the original jurisdiction conferred on the Supreme Court by the Constitution was exclusive, it could not be enlarged by Congress. To reach that decision, the Court decided that it had the power to review the constitutionality of acts of Congress. As Charles Warren tells us, "the significance of Marshall's opinion lies in its establishment of the power of the Court to adjudicate the validity of an Act of Congress—the fundamental decision in the American system of constitutional law."

Marbury v. Madison is *the* great case in American constitutional law because it was the first case to establish the Supreme Court's power to review constitutionality. To be sure, *Marbury* merely confirmed a doctrine that was part of the American legal tradition, derived from both the colonial and Revolutionary experiences. That does not, however, detract from *Marbury*'s importance. The great Chief Justice, like Jefferson in writing the Declaration of Independence, may have merely set down in clear form what had already been declared. Yet as Marshall's biographer Albert J. Beveridge observes, Thomas Jefferson and John Marshall as private citizens of Charlottesville and Richmond might have written declarations and opinions all their lives, and today none but the curious student would know that such men had ever lived. It is the authoritative positions that those two Americans happened to occupy that have given immortality to their enunciations. If Marshall's achievement in *Marbury v.*

Madison was not transformation but only articulation, what made it momentous was that it was magisterial articulation in terms so firm and clear that review power has never since been legally doubted.

In Marshall's *Marbury* opinion, the authority to declare constitutionality flows inexorably from the judicial duty to determine the law: "It is emphatically the province and duty of the judicial department to say what the law is. . . . If two laws conflict with each other, the courts must decide that case conformably to the law, disregarding the constitution; or conformably to the constitution, disregarding the law; the court must determine which of these conflicting rules governs the case. This is of the very essence of judicial duty." One may go further and say that judicial review, as declared in *Marbury v. Madison*, has become the sine qua non of the American constitutional machinery: draw out this particular bolt, and the machinery falls to pieces.

Addressing the court in the Five Knights' Case (1627) in England, the attorney general, arguing for the Crown, asked, "Shall any say, The King *cannot* do this? No, we may only say, He will not do this." It was precisely to ensure that in the American system one would be able to say, "The state *cannot* do this," that the people enacted a written Constitution containing basic limitations on the powers of government. Of what avail would such limitations be, however, if there were no legal machinery to enforce them? Even a constitution is naught but empty words if it cannot be enforced by the courts. It is judicial review that makes constitutional provisions more than mere maxims of political morality, and it was *Marbury v. Madison* that made judicial review the cornerstone of our constitutional law.

2. *Brown v. Board of Education*

Brown v. Board of Education (1954) stands at the head of cases decided since *Marbury v. Madison*. In many ways, indeed, *Brown* was the watershed constitutional case of the twentieth century. Justice Stanley Reed told one of his law clerks that "if it was not the most important decision in the history of the Court, it was very close." When *Brown* struck down school segregation, it signaled the beginning of effective enforcement of civil rights in American law.

Brown, like *Marbury* itself, dramatically illustrates the crucial role of the Chief Justice. The case first came before the Court under Chief Justice Fred M. Vinson. At the *Brown* conference, Vinson sounded what can most charitably be described as an uncertain trumpet, instead of the clarion needed to deal with the issue that had become an incubus on American society. Vinson urged the Court to uphold segregation and the Justices were sharply split. According to a confidential memorandum by Justice William O. Douglas, "the vote would be five to four in favor of . . . segregation." Such a fragmented decision would have been, in Justice Felix Frankfurter's phrase in a letter to Justice Stanley Reed, "catastrophic."

That result was avoided when the decision was postponed until reargument the following year. In the interim, Chief Justice Vinson died and Earl Warren was appointed in his place. The new Chief Justice was to play the crucial role in fashioning the unanimous *Brown* decision. At the *Brown* conference, Warren set a completely different tone from that of his predecessor. "I don't see," Warren told the conference, "how in this day and age we can set any group apart from the rest and say that they are not entitled to exactly the same treatment as all others. To do so would be contrary to the [Constitution]. . . . Personally, I can't see how today we can justify segregation based solely on race."

Warren's *Brown* presentation stated the question in moral terms. Segregation, he told the Justices, could be justified only by belief in the inherent inferiority of blacks, and, if we uphold it, we have to do it on that basis. Warren's words went straight to the ultimate human values involved. The proponents of segregation were placed in the awkward position of appearing to subscribe to racist doctrine.

This time, except for Justice Reed, the Justices indicated that they could support the new Chief Justice's position. Warren now worked at ensuring a unanimous decision striking down segregation. In the end, he was able to secure the concurrence of the others, including Reed, who had been prepared to dissent.

The *Brown* opinion was written by the Chief Justice himself. It was written in the typical Warren style: short, nontechnical, well within the grasp of the average reader. The opinion, Warren wrote, was "prepared on the theory that the opinions should be short, readable by the lay public, non-rhetorical, unemotional, and, above all, non-accusatory."

May 17, 1954—decision day in *Brown v. Board of Education*—was one of the most dramatic in Supreme Court history. Chief Justice Warren read the unanimous opinion striking down segregation to a packed courtroom that eagerly anticipated the decision. After stating the case and the background of segregation, Warren came to the crucial question: "Does segregation of children in public schools solely on the basis of race, even though the physical facilities and other 'tangible' factors may be equal, deprive the children of the minority group of equal educational opportunities?"

Until then, with the opinion two-thirds finished, the Chief Justice had not indicated the outcome. Now, in the next sentence, he did. Answering the critical question, he asserted, "We believe that it does." That was true because, "[t]o separate [schoolchildren] from others of similar age and qualifications solely because of their race generates a feeling of inferiority as to their status in the community that may affect their hearts and minds in a way unlikely ever to be undone."

The prior law had been based on the assumption that segregation did not suppose the inferiority of blacks. Warren declared that segregation did mean their inferiority: "Whatever may have been the extent of psychological knowledge [when segregation was upheld], this finding is amply supported by modern authority. Any language . . . contrary to this finding is rejected." This statement was supported by footnote 11 of the opinion, which listed seven works by social scientists and was to become the most famous note in a Supreme Court decision.

The Chief Justice then stated the Court's far-reaching conclusion: "We conclude that in the field of public education the doctrine of 'separate but equal' has no place. Separate educational facilities are inherently unequal."

Brown sounded the death knell of all legally enforced segregation. In the years after *Brown*, the Court ruled segregation invalid in all public buildings, housing, transportation, and recreational and eating facilities. The Court, following Warren's lead, struck down every segregation law challenged before it. By 1963, an opinion could declare categorically: "[I]t is no longer open to question that a State may not constitutionally require segregation of public facilities."

Four decades after the case, *Brown* has taken its place in the very forefront of historic decisions. In the light of what Justice Arthur J. Goldberg once termed the American commitment to equality and its part in helping to fulfill the commitment, *Brown* will occupy a paramount position comparable only to the great decisions of the Marshall Court at the outset of our constitutional development.

3. *McCulloch v. Maryland*

For Chief Justice Marshall, judicial review, like law itself, was a means, not an end. The end was the goal intended by the Framers—an effective national government endowed with vital substantive powers, the lack of which had rendered the Articles of Confederation sterile. Judicial review was the tool that enabled Marshall to translate this goal into legal reality.

To Marshall, the overriding end to be served was nationalism in the broad sense of that term. The law was to be employed to lay down the doctrinal foundation of an effective nation. That object was attained through a series of now classic decisions that had two principal aims: to ensure that the nation possessed the powers needed to enable it to govern effectively, and to ensure federal supremacy vis-à-vis state powers.

The key case in this respect was *McCulloch v. Maryland* (1819). It established the doctrine of implied powers in our constitutional law, resolving in the process the controversy between those who favored a strict and those who favored a broad construction of the necessary and proper clause of the Constitution. That clause, after enumerating the specific powers conferred on Congress, authorizes it "to make all laws which shall be necessary and proper for carrying into execution the foregoing powers, and all other powers vested by this Constitution in the government of the United States." Conflicting approaches had been taken to the clause by Jefferson and Hamilton. Jefferson had adopted a strict view, emphasizing the word "necessary" in the clause: it endowed the federal government with only those powers indispensable for the exercise of its enumerated powers. The broader Hamilton view maintained that to take the word in its rigorous sense would be to deprive the clause of real practical effect.

In *McCulloch v. Maryland*, Marshall adopted the broad Hamiltonian approach. The case presented the same issue on which Jefferson and Hamilton had differed—the constitutionality of the Bank of the United States, established by Congress to serve as a depository for federal funds and to print bank notes. Maryland had imposed a tax on the bank's Baltimore branch and then brought suit in a state court against James William McCulloch, the branch's cashier, when he refused to pay the Maryland tax.

To decide whether the Maryland tax law was constitutional, the Court had to determine whether Congress had the power to charter the bank. In giving an affirmative answer, Marshall gave a broad construction to the necessary and proper clause. If the establishment of a national bank would aid the government in the exercise of its granted powers, the authority to set one up would be implied.

McCulloch put to rest the view that the necessary and proper clause extended only to laws that were indispensably necessary. The clause, Marshall ruled, embraces "all means which are appropriate" to carry out "the legitimate ends" of the Constitution, unless forbidden by "the letter and spirit of the constitution."

As so construed, the necessary and proper clause has been the source of vast federal authority. Practically every power of the federal government has been expanded by the clause. Thus the authority of Congress under the clause has been held to include power to enact laws to carry out treaties, to utilize all appropriate means for collecting revenue, to acquire property by eminent domain, to make treasury notes legal tender, to create corporations, to exclude and deport aliens, to determine maritime law, and to enact the federal Criminal Code. None of these is among the powers specifically delegated to Congress.

Marshall used *McCulloch v. Maryland* not only to ensure that the nation had the powers needed to govern effectively, but also to cement the federal supremacy declared in Article VI. Having decided, as just seen, that Congress had the power to charter the Bank of the United States, the Court then had to determine whether Maryland might tax the bank. The Marshall opinion answered the question with a categorical negative. The national government, it declared, "is supreme within its sphere of action. This would seem to result necessarily from its nature." National supremacy is utterly inconsistent with any state authority to tax a federal agency. Federal supremacy, to Marshall, meant "that the states have no power, by taxation or otherwise, to retard, impede, burden, or in any manner control, the operations" of the federal government or its agencies and instrumentalities. More than that, federal action, if itself constitutional, must prevail over all inconsistent state action. State laws otherwise valid must give way to federal laws with which they conflict.

4. *Gibbons v. Ogden*

The third of Marshall's landmark opinions gave a broad construction to the commerce clause. The clause is deceptively simple. Congress, it reads, shall have power "[t]o regulate Commerce with foreign Nations, and among the several States, and with the Indian Tribes." Yet this brief clause is the fount and origin of vast power. It is, indeed, the direct source of the federal government's most significant powers. The authority of Congress to enact regulatory laws stems almost entirely from the commerce clause.

The need to federalize regulation of commerce was one of the principal needs that motivated the Constitutional Convention of 1787. Yet the delegates there were interested mainly in the negative aspects of such regulation, concerned as they were with curbing state restrictions that had interfered with the commerce of the nation. It was Marshall, in *Gibbons v. Ogden* (1824), who first construed the commerce power in a positive manner, enabling it to be fashioned into a formidable federal regulatory tool.

The *Gibbons* case resulted directly from Robert Fulton's invention of the steamboat. Early in the nineteenth century, Fulton and Robert Livingston, American minister in Paris when the inventor had demonstrated his steamboat in France in 1803, secured from the New York legislature a monopoly of steam navigation on the waters of that state. The partners licensed Aaron Ogden to operate ferryboats between New York and New Jersey. When Thomas Gibbons began to run steamboats in competition with Ogden and without New York permission (though he had a coasting license from the federal government), Ogden sued to stop Gibbons.

The case became a sensational battle between the two men and almost wrecked them both. (One man who prospered was young Cornelius Van Derbilt, Gibbons's skipper, who got his start by running his craft in defiance of Ogden's attempts to halt him.) Gibbons was a southern planter noted for his belligerence. His litigation with Ogden, a former governor of New Jersey and United States senator, became a personal vendetta in which Gibbons spared no expense. He hired the top lawyers of the day, including Daniel Webster and Attorney General William Wirt, and made a provision of $40,000 in his will to carry on the case if he died before it was finished. During the litigation, Gibbons went to Ogden's home with a challenge to a duel. Instead of fighting, Ogden sued for trespass and won a $5000 verdict. It was to prove of slight satisfaction. Before he was through, the case wrecked a fortune that he had accumulated in legal practice.

The Supreme Court decision nullifying Ogden's monopoly was more than the settling of a quarrel between two combative men. Marshall seized the opportunity to deliver an opinion on the breadth of Congress's authority under the commerce clause. The clause vests in Congress the power "to regulate commerce." The noun "commerce" determines the subjects to which congressional power extends. The verb "regulate" determines the types of authority that Congress can exert. Both the noun and the verb were defined most broadly in Marshall's opinion.

"Commerce," in Marshall's view, covered all economic intercourse—a conception comprehensive enough to include within its scope all business dealings: "It describes the commercial intercourse between nations, and parts of nations, in all branches." Marshall then proceeded to take an equally liberal view of the meaning of the verb "regulate." "What is this power?" he asked. "It is the power to regulate; that is, to prescribe the rule by which commerce is to be governed. This power, like all others vested in congress is complete in itself, may be exercised to its utmost extent."

The Supreme Court has said that, in *Gibbons*, "Marshall described the federal commerce power with a breadth never yet exceeded." So interpreted, the commerce clause was to become the source of the most important powers the federal government exercises in time of peace. If in recent years it has become trite to point out how regulation from Washington controls Americans from the cradle to the grave, that is true only because of the Marshall emphasis at the outset on the embracing and penetrating nature of the federal commerce power.

5. *Ex Parte Milligan*

In 1976, the daughter of Billy Martin, the New York Yankees manager, was convicted by a military tribunal in Colombia on a drug charge. Such a case could not take place in this country because the Constitution erects a wall of separation between the civil and the military. That this wall is breached by the use of military tribunals to punish civilians was the holding in what Chief Justice Earl Warren called the "landmark decision in this field"—*Ex Parte Milligan* (1866).

Milligan was a leading Copperhead during the Civil War who had been arrested in Indiana during the war and tried, convicted, and sentenced to be hanged by a military commission. The Court stated the constitutional question presented by Milligan's trial and conviction as follows: "Milligan, not a resident of one of the rebellious states, or a prisoner of war, but a citizen of Indiana for twenty years past, and never in the military or naval service, is, while at his home, arrested by the military power of the United States, imprisoned, and, on certain criminal charges preferred against him, tried, convicted, and sentenced to be hanged by a military commission, organized under the direction of the military commander of the military district of Indiana. Had this tribunal the *legal* power and authority to try and punish this man?"

The Court answered with a categorical negative. According to it, a civilian like Milligan could not, consistently with the Constitution, be tried by military tribunal "where the courts are open, and in the proper and unobstructed exercise of their jurisdiction."

Thus was declared the celebrated "open court" rule of the *Milligan* case. As summarized by Chief Justice Warren, *Milligan* "established firmly the principle that when civil courts are open and operating, resort to military tribunals for the prosecution of civilians is impermissible." *Milligan* holds that the military lacks any constitutional power in war or in peace to substitute its tribunals for civil courts that are open and operating in the proper and unobstructed exercise of their jurisdiction. Only if a foreign invasion or civil war were actually to close the courts and render it impossible for them to administer criminal justice could martial law validly be invoked to suspend their functions.

Above all, *Milligan* ensures that the courts will rebuff military attempts to exercise jurisdiction over civilians. After the Japanese attack on Pearl Harbor on December 7, 1941, martial law was proclaimed in Hawaii, and government (including administration of justice) was taken over by the military. There is little doubt that the Pearl Harbor attack was an "invasion" justifying the proclamation of martial law. What was true of Hawaii when Pearl Harbor was bombed was, however, not necessarily true of Hawaii after the danger of invasion had passed. Despite this, military justice was continued in Hawaii until almost the end of 1944.

In the case of *Duncan v. Kahanamoku* (1946), the Supreme Court followed *Milligan* and decided that the trials and convictions of civilians by military tribunals in Honolulu in mid-1942 and 1944 were unconstitutional. While martial law could be declared after the attack on Pearl Harbor, the Court denied that this gave the armed forces the power to substitute military for judicial trials after the Japanese "invasion" of Hawaii had long ended. At the time of the convictions, the courts could not be superseded by military tribunals in their enforcement of the ordinary criminal law.

If, in this hemisphere, the United States has been almost unique in avoiding rule by the military throughout its history, that has been true because of the wall of separation between the civil and the military. *Duncan v. Kahanamoku* shows that *Milligan* is still *the* great case ensuring that the wall is not breached while civil government is capable of carrying on its functions.

6. Granger Cases

The greatest decisions are not always by the greatest judges or the greatest courts. One of the landmark Supreme Court decisions—that in the so-called Granger Cases—was handed down in 1877, when the Court was headed by Chief Justice Morrison R. Waite. He was a little-known Ohio lawyer chosen to head the Court after President Grant had failed to secure the appointment of several cronies. Certainly, Waite had nothing of the grand manner, the spark that made Marshall and Taney what they were. A humdrum, pedestrian lawyer, he remains a dim figure in our constitutional history. "I can't make a silk purse out of a sow's ear," wrote

Justice Samuel F. Miller a year after Waite's appointment. "I can't make a great Chief Justice out of a small man."

Yet it was Chief Justice Waite who wrote the key opinion in the Granger Cases. "Judged by any standards of ultimate importance," wrote Justice Felix Frankfurter, Waite's ruling in the Granger Cases "places it among the dozen most important decisions in our constitutional law." It upheld the power of the states to regulate the rates of railroads and other businesses—a holding, never since departed from, that has served as the basis on which governmental regulation has rested.

The Granger Cases arose out of the abuses that accompanied the post–Civil War growth of railroads. Highly speculative railroad building, irresponsible financial manipulation, and destructive competitive warfare resulted in monopolies, fluctuating and discriminatory rates, and inevitable public outcry. The grievances against the railroads were especially acute in the Midwest, where farmers depended on them for moving crops, as well as on the grain elevators in which those crops were stored. The farmers' resentment led to the Granger movement, which swept through the Midwest in the early 1870s. The Grangers sought to correct these abuses through state regulation. They secured state laws regulating railroads and grain elevators and limiting the prices they could charge. These were the laws at issue in the Granger Cases. In the principal case before the Court, an Illinois law fixed the maximum prices to be charged by grain elevators in Chicago; four companion cases involved state statutes regulating railroad rates.

The Court sustained all these laws against due process attacks on the ground that "property . . . become[s] clothed with a public interest when used in a manner to make it of public consequence, and affect the community at large." Such property may "be controlled by the public for the common good, to the extent of the interest . . . thus created."

Under the Granger approach, for a business to be subject to regulation, it need only be one that affects the community. "Waite's reference to property 'clothed with a public interest,' " Justice Frankfurter tells us, "surely meant no more than that the Court must be able to attribute to the legislature the fulfillment of a public interest." In this sense, a business affected with a public interest becomes nothing more than one in which the public has come to have an interest. This rationale enables governmental regulatory power to be asserted over business far beyond what was previously thought permissible. As a Justice once pointed out, "There is scarcely any property in whose use the public has no interest." Thus stated, Waite's rationale has furnished the constitutional foundation for the ever-broader schemes of business regulation that have become so prominent a feature of the society.

7. *National Labor Relations Board v.*
Jones & Laughlin Steel Corp.

During the first part of the twentieth century, the Supreme Court drastically restricted the reach of federal regulatory power. This was especially the case during the early years of the Franklin D. Roosevelt administration, when the Court invalidated most of the important New Deal legislation on the ground that the manufacturing, mining, and agriculture regulated by them were not within the federal commerce power. Congress was rendered powerless to deal with problems in those fields, however pressing they might become.

However, if ever there was a need for exertion of federal power, it was during the Great Depression. The market and the states had found the crisis beyond their competence. The choice was between federal action and chaos. A system of constitutional law that required the latter could hardly endure. The New Deal decisions, the Supreme Court itself was later to concede, "produced a series of consequences for the exercise of national power over industry conducted on a national scale which the evolving nature of our industrialism foredoomed to reversal."

For the government in Washington to be able to exercise regulatory authority on the necessary national scale, it was essential that the Court liberalize its construction of the Constitution. The required liberalization took place in 1937. The key case was *National Labor Relations Board v. Jones & Laughlin Steel Corp.* In it, the constitutionality of the National Labor Relations Act of 1935 was upheld. Justice Robert H. Jackson termed the decision the most far-reaching victory ever won on behalf of labor in the Supreme Court. This was no overstatement, for the 1935 act was the Magna Carta of the American labor movement. It guaranteed the right of employees to organize collectively in unions and made it an unfair labor practice prohibited by law for employers to interfere with that right or to refuse to bargain collectively with the representatives chosen by their employees.

The labor act was intended to apply to industries throughout the nation, to those engaged in production and manufacture as well as to those engaged in commerce, literally speaking. But this appeared to bring it directly in conflict with the decisions drastically limiting the scope of the federal government's authority over interstate commerce, including some of the decisions of the early New Deal period. This was particularly true of the Court's decision nullifying the National Industrial Recovery Act, which had denied power in Congress to regulate local business activities, even though they affected interstate commerce. In *Jones & Laughlin*, these precedents were not followed: "These cases," laconically stated the Court, "are not controlling here."

Instead, the Court gave the federal power over interstate commerce its maximum sweep. Mines, mills, and factories, whose activities had formerly been decided to be "local" and hence immune from federal regulation, were now held to affect interstate commerce directly enough to justify congressional control. There is little doubt that, as the dissenting *Jones & Laughlin* Justices protested, Congress in the labor act exercised a power of control over purely local industry beyond anything theretofore deemed permissible.

The *Jones & Laughlin* decision was the foundation of what turned out to be a virtual constitutional revolution. The decision marked a definite break with the restricted view that most industries were beyond the federal commerce power. *Jones & Laughlin* itself removed the immunity from the commerce power that manufacturing had come to enjoy. But the Court soon extended *Jones & Laughlin* to other productive industries, sustaining laws regulating the coal industry and agriculture that were similar to those that had been condemned.

Since *Jones & Laughlin*, the Court has upheld virtually all regulations of business. No longer must production be treated as a purely "local" activity, immune from congressional control regardless of the impact it may have. The law has come back to the *Gibbons v. Ogden* conception of commerce as an organic whole, with the commerce clause embracing all commerce that concerns more than one state. Under that conception, federal power is not limited to commerce that actually moves across state lines. It includes all activities that affect interstate commerce, though such activities, taken alone, might be considered "local." The whole point about the post–*Jones & Laughlin* law is that these activities can no longer be considered alone. If they have an effect on interstate commerce, they concern more than one state and come within the commerce clause. With effect on commerce as the test, the radius of federal power becomes as broad as the economic life of the nation.

8. *United States v. Nixon*

United States v. Nixon (1974) belongs on this list because it subjected the president to the rule of law that is binding on all other officials. The case itself was, in many ways, the culmination of the Watergate scandal, which dominated the news during President Richard M. Nixon's shortened second term. The case arose from a motion filed by the Watergate special prosecutor for a subpoena that directed President Nixon to produce certain tape recordings and documents relating to his conversations with aides and advisers. Following the return of an indictment against top White House aides and others for crimes arising out of the Watergate scandal, the special prosecutor determined that the tapes and documents in the president's possession were relevant evidence in the criminal trial and sought their production through the subpoena.

The tapes themselves, it was widely believed, contained the "smoking gun" evidence sought by the special prosecutor and congressional investigators of President Nixon's participation in a felonious coverup of illegal acts. The president had maneuvered politically and had fought legally to maintain possession of the tapes. He had even indicated that if the Supreme Court ordered him to give them up, he might refuse.

After he was served, President Nixon moved to quash the subpoena, asserting that conversations between a president and his close advisers were privileged and that the doctrine of separation of powers precluded judicial review of his privilege claim. The president's claim—characterized by the Supreme Court as "a claim of absolute Presidential privilege against inquiry by the coordinate Judicial Branch"—would have immunized even patent misuses of executive power from all judicial scrutiny.

The Nixon assertion was put to the constitutional test and found wanting. The Court refused to quash the subpoena to the president issued by the Watergate special prosecutor. The opinion of Chief Justice Warren E. Burger recognized that there may be presumptive privilege for presidential communications based on the expectation of a president to confidentiality of his conversations and correspondence. The presumptive privilege is, however, only a qualified one. It must give way here. A claim of privilege based only on the generalized interest in confidentiality cannot prevail over the demonstrated specific need for evidence in a pending criminal trial. Hence the president was subject to the subpoena to produce information relevant to an ongoing criminal prosecution.

The *Nixon* case rejected the claim of an absolute immunity in the president based on the separation of powers. It is for the courts "to say what the law is" in any case involving the legality of claims relating to exercises of power by the executive and legislative branches. The "judicial Power" vested in the courts by Article III can no more be shared with the executive than the president can share with the judiciary the veto power. Any other conclusion would be contrary to the basic concepts of separation of powers and checks and balances.

Just before he died, Earl Warren, hospitalized by a heart attack, was visited by Justice William J. Brennan. The man Brennan fondly called "Super Chief" had avidly followed politics and the law since his retirement as Chief Justice. He was eager to hear the latest on the *Nixon* case, then before the Supreme Court.

The case had provoked a "lively discussion" at the conference, Brennan said. "It was very quickly apparent," he told Warren, "that the President would be treated like any other person."

When the Justice told Warren the news, the old Chief lifted himself from the pillows. "Thank God, thank God, thank God!" Warren declared fervently. "If you don't do it this way, Bill, it's the end of the country as we have known it."

Soon thereafter, the *Nixon* decision was announced and the opinion summarized by Chief Justice Burger in a packed courtroom. Seventeen days later, the president resigned.

9. *Baker v. Carr*

Earl Warren wrote in his memoirs that *Baker v. Carr* (1962) "was the most important case of my tenure on the Court." It was *Baker* that led to the requirement of equality in legislative apportionments, resulting in a major shift in political power from rural areas to the urban and suburban concentrations in which most Americans now live. In an interview just after he retired as Chief Justice, Warren declared, "I think the reapportionment . . . of representative government in this country is perhaps the most important issue we have had before the Supreme Court."

Baker v. Carr arose out of an action by a Tennessee voter for a judgment that the 1901 law under which seats in the state legislature were apportioned violated the Fourteenth Amendment. He claimed that voters from urban areas had been denied equal protection "by virtue of the debasement of their votes," since a vote from the most populous district had only a fraction of the weight of one from the least populous district. The population ratio for the most and least populous districts was over nineteen to one.

Before *Baker*, the Court had held that an action challenging a legislative apportionment might not be brought because it would embroil the Court in issues "of a peculiarly political nature . . . not meet for judicial determination." It was in the leading pre-*Baker* case that Justice Frankfurter made his often quoted statement: "Courts ought not to enter this political thicket."

Baker v. Carr overruled these earlier cases and held that the federal courts were competent to entertain an action challenging legislative apportionments as contrary to equal protection. The Brennan opinion of the Court supplied the rationale for discarding the earlier cases and holding that attacks on legislative apportionments may be heard and decided by the federal courts.

The *Baker* opinion supports the characterization in my list of great Justices of William J. Brennan as the Associate Justice who had the most influence on the Court's decision process during his tenure. *Baker* is the paradigmatic case to illustrate the Brennan juristic approach. We saw that Justice Frankfurter, Brennan's former teacher, had warned against courts entering "this political thicket." The *Baker v. Carr* opinion replied, "The mere fact that a suit seeks protection of a political right does not mean that it presents a political question." That, commented the English periodical the *Economist*, was the Brennan watchword.

What has *Baker v. Carr* meant in practice? That became apparent when, in 1964, *Reynolds v. Sims* applied *Baker* to lay down the rule that "the Equal Protection Clause requires that both houses of a state legislature be apportioned on a population basis." The "basic constitutional principle of representative government" was "equality of population among districts."

Chief Justice Warren himself never had doubts about the reapportionment decisions. He maintained that if their "equal population" principle had been laid down years earlier, many of the nation's legal sores would never have festered. "If *Baker v. Carr* had been in existence fifty years ago," he later insisted, "we would have saved ourselves acute . . . troubles. Many of our problems would have been solved a long time ago if everyone had the right to vote, and his vote counted the same as everybody else's. Most of these problems could have been solved through the political process rather than through the courts. But as it was, the Court had to decide."

The Chief Justice was well aware that the reapportionment decisions were the political death warrant for undetermined numbers of rural legislators, whose seats would now be reapportioned out of existence. Soon after the decision, Warren flew to his home state to hunt with his sons and some old friends. One of them was asked to invite the Chief Justice to go with some state senators on a trip to hunt quail. When Warren was asked if he wanted to drive down and join them, he looked incredulous. "All those *senators*?" he inquired in mock horror. "With *guns*?"

10. *Charles River Bridge v. Warren Bridge*

John Marshall's great decisions laid the foundations of our constitutional law. In the Supreme Court, too, however, there were also brave men after Agamemnon. The first of them, as far as the greatest decisions are concerned, was Chief Justice Roger B. Taney, who had just taken his place as Marshall's successor.

The Marshall Court had been concerned with strengthening the power of the fledgling nation so that it might realize its political and economic destiny. Like the Framers themselves, it stressed the need to protect federal power and property rights as the prerequisite to such realization. To Jacksonians like Taney, private property, no matter how important, was not the be-all and end-all of social existence. "While the rights of property are sacredly guarded," declared the new Chief Justice in his first important opinion, "we must not forget that the community also have rights, and that the happiness and well being of every citizen depends on their faithful preservation." The opinion was delivered in *Charles River Bridge v. Warren Bridge* (1837), a case that was a cause célèbre in its day, both because it brought the Federalist and Jacksonian views on the place of property into sharp conflict and because stock in the corporation involved was held by Boston's leading citizens and Harvard College.

The Charles River Bridge had been operated as a toll bridge by a corporation set up under a charter obtained by John Hancock and others in 1785. Each year, £200 was paid from its profits to Harvard. The bridge, opened on a day celebrated by Boston as a "day of rejoicing," proved so profitable that the value of its shares increased tenfold. The bridge became a popular symbol of monopoly, and, in 1828, the legislature incorporated the Warren Bridge Company to build and operate another bridge near the Charles River Bridge. The second charter provided that the new bridge would be a free bridge. This would, of course, destroy the business of the first bridge, and its corporate owner sued to enjoin construction, alleging that the contractual obligation contained in its charter had been impaired.

The new Chief Justice delivered the opinion of the Court. Taney's opinion refused to hold that there had been an invalid infringement on the first bridge company's charter rights. There was no express provision in the charter making the franchise granted exclusive or barring the construction of a competing bridge, and the basic principle is "that in grants by the public, nothing passes by implication." Since there was no express obligation not to permit a competing bridge nearby, none might be read in.

In deciding as it did, the Taney Court laid down what has since become a legal truism: the rights of property must, where necessary, be subordinated to the needs of the community. The Taney opinion declined to rule that the charter to operate a toll bridge granted a monopoly in the area. Instead, the charter should be construed narrowly to preserve the rights of the community: where the rights of private property conflict with those of the community, the latter must be paramount.

Justice Story, who delivered a characteristically learned 35,000-word dissent, declared that the Court, by impairing the sanctity of property rights, was acting "to alarm every stockholder in every public enterprise of this sort, throughout the whole country." Yet, paradoxical though it may seem, it was the Taney decision, not the Story dissent, that ultimately was the more favorable to the owners of property, particularly those who invested in corporate enterprises.

Although in form the *Charles River Bridge* decision was a blow to economic rights, it actually facilitated economic development by providing the legal basis for public choices favoring technological innovation and economic change, even at the expense of vested interests. The case arose when the corporate form was coming into widespread use as an instrument of capitalist expansion. The Marshall Court had ruled the privileges in corporate charters to be contracts and, as such, beyond impairment by government. The Marshall approach here would have meant the upholding of the first bridge company's monopoly. Such a result would have had most undesirable consequences, for it would have meant that every bridge or turnpike company was given an exclusive franchise that might not be impaired by newer forms of transportation. To read monopoly rights into existing charters would be to place modern improvements at the mercy of existing corporations and defeat the right of the community to the benefits of scientific progress.

Daniel Webster wrote to Story that Taney and the majority had virtually "overturned . . . one great provision of the Constitution." The truth, of course, is that Taney had only interpreted the contract clause in a manner that coincided with the felt needs of the era of economic expansion on which the nation was entering. Because of the Taney decision, that expansion could proceed unencumbered by inappropriate legal excrescences. By 1854, a Justice could confidently assert, with regard to the *Charles River Bridge* decision, "No opinion of the court more fully satisfied the legal judgment of the country, and consequently none has exerted more influence upon its legislation."

Coda

To be sure, all the lists in this book are as personal as a sports writer's choices for an all-star team. Without a doubt, there are different decisions that others would include on a list of Supreme Court greats—decisions such as (to take only the past three decades) *Miranda v. Arizona* (1966), giving criminal suspects key rights; *New York Times Co. v. United States* (1971), the Pentagon Papers case invalidating prior restraints against the press; *Roe v. Wade* (1973), upholding the constitutional right to an abortion; *Regents of the University of California v. Bakke* (1978), the affirmative action case; *INS v. Chadha* (1983), striking down the so-called legislative veto; *Bowsher v. Synar* (1986), invalidating congressional exercises of executive power; and *Cruzan v. Director* (1990), the "right to die" case on withdrawal of life support from a patient in a vegetative state.

These are all important decisions, but none of them had the impact on the law and the society of the cases on my list. Once again, influence on the law is my criterion that determines greatness. From that point of view, the decisions chosen are eminently *great* decisions—the greatest decided by the Supreme Court. All of them made a difference, not only in the law, but in the history of the nation itself.

The Marshall decisions on my list laid the foundation of our constitutional law: *Marbury v. Madison* established the judicial power to review constitutionality, guaranteeing effective enforcement of the Constitution; *McCulloch v. Maryland* expanded federal power to allow the exercise of implied powers not enumerated in the Constitution and affirmed federal supremacy vis-à-vis state authority; and *Gibbons v. Ogden* gave a broad scope to the most important federal power, enabling it to serve as the tool for national regulation of the economy. The decision in *Charles River Bridge v. Warren Bridge* subordinated property rights to the needs of the community, ensuring at the same time that economic change could not be blocked by vested corporate interests. *Ex Parte Milligan* erected a wall of separation between the civil and the military, which may not be breached by exercises of military power over civilians. The Granger Cases upheld public power to regulate businesses, serving as the foundation for pervasive economic regulation. The *Jones & Laughlin* decision rejected the narrow conception of the commerce power that prohibited federal regulation of most businesses, permitting the extensive regulation from Washington that has become so prominent a feature of the polity. *Brown v. Board of Education* marked the beginning of effective enforcement of civil rights, signaling a crucial turning point in this respect for both the law and the society. *Baker v. Carr* worked a political change comparable to that effected more than a century earlier by the great English Reform Act of 1832. *United States v. Nixon* subjected the president to the same rule of law that governs other public officers; as such, it ensures that we have not reached the stage stated over a century ago by William H. Seward—that "[w]e elect a king for four years."

We can only imagine what our system would be like if these cases had not been decided or had been decided differently. Consider the consequences if *Brown* had been the decision upholding segregation by the fragmented Court that it would have been if the decision had been made under Chief Justice Vinson. The Jim Crow era would have continued, and the racial transformation that has taken place in both the law and the society might never have happened. The other decisions may not have had so crucial an impact, but all of them did make a major difference. Think of our system with the courts relegated to the role of judges enforcing a doctrine like parliamentary supremacy, federal authority limited to the powers specifically enumerated and regulatory power virtually stillborn, military authority exercised over civilians, political power dominated by a "rotten borough" franchise, and the president above the law. The mind boggles at how different our system would be if these cases had not been decided as they were.

4

TEN

WORST

SUPREME COURT

DECISIONS

From the sublime, we turn to the ridiculous. This is a list of the worst Supreme Court decisions. They range from what Shakespeare calls "the bottom of the worst"—in our list the *Dred Scott* case, that ill-starred decision (to use Chief Justice William H. Rehnquist's term) that helped to bring on the Civil War—to decisions not as well known, which had less baneful consequences.

— ★ — ★ — ★ —

— ★ — ★ — ★ —

Ten Worst Supreme Court Decisions

1. *Dred Scott v. Sandford,* 19 How. 393 (U.S. 1857)

2. *Plessy v. Ferguson,* 163 U.S. 537 (1896)

3. *Lochner v. New York,* 198 U.S. 45 (1905)

4. *Hammer v. Dagenhart,* 247 U.S. 251 (1918)

5. *Adkins v. Children's Hospital,* 261 U.S. 525 (1923)

6. *Korematsu v. United States,* 323 U.S. 214 (1944)

7. *Bradwell v. Illinois,* 16 Wall. 130 (U.S. 1873)

8. *Buck v. Bell,* 274 U.S. 200 (1927)

9. *Carter v. Carter Coal Co.,* 298 U.S. 238 (1936)

10. *Hepburn v. Griswold,* 8 Wall. 603 (U.S. 1870)

1. *Dred Scott v. Sandford*

Dred Scott v. Sandford (1857) stands first in any list of the worst Supreme Court decisions—Chief Justice Hughes called it the Court's greatest self-inflicted wound.

The case arose out of an action by Dred Scott, a slave, against his owner. Scott claimed that his service in Illinois and in the Wisconsin Territory, from which slavery had been excluded by Congress, made him a free man. Defendant pleaded that Scott could not bring the action based on diversity of citizenship because a black could not be a citizen.

As presented to the Court, the case highlighted the two key issues in the slavery controversy. First was the power of Congress to prohibit slavery in the territories, which slavery opponents hoped would confine the institution to the existing slave states. Even more important was the question posed by defendant's plea: whether even a free black could be a citizen. Legislative power to eliminate slavery would be empty form if those freed could not attain citizenship. If even the free black would have to remain beyond the pale, the northern majority who hoped that slavery would gradually disappear was doomed to disappointment. Extralegal means would be needed to end the degraded status of the enslaved race.

The *Dred Scott* decision was an attempt to resolve in the judicial forum the basic controversy tearing the nation apart. In *Dred Scott*, the Supreme Court fell a victim to its own success. The power and prestige built up under Chief Justice Marshall, and continued under Chief Justice Taney, had led men to expect too much of judicial power. The Justices themselves acted on the notion that judicial power could succeed where political power had failed. Their decision contained two main points. First, it ruled that blacks were not and could not become citizens within the meaning of the Constitution. In addition, it rejected the claim that Scott had become a free man (and hence eligible for citizenship) by residence in a territory from which slavery had been excluded by Congress. This was true because "the act of Congress which prohibited a citizen from holding and owning property of this kind in the territory . . . is not warranted by the Constitution, and is therefore void."

There was more, of course, in the turgid opinion of Chief Justice Taney, as well as in the seven other opinions rendered in the case. But what burst with such dramatic impact was the fact that the Court had denied both the right of blacks to be citizens and the power of Congress to interfere with slaveholding in the territories. Acquiescence in such rulings was fatal to the hopes of those who sought to confine slavery to an ever-smaller minority in an expanding nation. Instead, slavery was a national institution, and Congress could not abolish it in the territories. In a concurring *Dred Scott* opinion, Justice James Moore Wayne referred to the controversies involved in the case and affirmed that "the peace and harmony of the country required the settlement of them by judicial decision." Seldom, it has been said, has wishful thinking been so spectacularly wrong.

Dred Scott had two direct results,though they were exactly the contrary of those intended. In the first place, the storm of abuse that burst over the majority decision cast a dark shadow over the highest bench itself. No decision in our history has done more to injure the reputation of the Court. For the better part of a generation thereafter, that tribunal was to remain in the shade, playing a diminished role in the governmental structure. From an immediate point of view, even more important was the case's effect upon the political polarization of the nation. If anything, the decision had the opposite effect from that intended by those who had hoped that a Supreme Court pronouncement would quell the sectional strife that threatened to destroy the Union. Far from accomplishing this goal, *Dred Scott* proved a catalyst that helped precipitate the civil conflict that soon followed.

Mention should also be made of the fact that *Dred Scott* was ultimately overruled, though not by the Court itself. Despite *Dred Scott*, in 1862 Congress passed a law expressly prohibiting slavery in the territories, and the Thirteenth Amendment mooted the issue by outlawing slavery altogether. In addition, the Fourteenth Amendment overruled the *Dred Scott* holding on black citizenship. Under it, all persons born or naturalized in the United States are citizens regardless of race.

2. *Plessy v. Ferguson*

Plessy v. Ferguson (1896) was the seminal decision that, for more than half a century, made equal protection only a hortatory slogan for African-Americans. While the Court, toward the end of the nineteenth century, developed the Fourteenth Amendment's due process clause as the principal safeguard of property rights, its *Plessy* decision ensured that the amendment was of little value to the blacks for whose benefit it had primarily been adopted.

Homer Plessy, a Louisiana resident, was one-eighth black. In 1892, while riding on a train out of New Orleans, he was ejected from a car for whites and directed to a coach assigned for nonwhites. A Louisiana statute provided for separate railway carriages for whites and blacks. Plessy claimed that the statute was contrary to the equal protection requirement. The Supreme Court rejected Plessy's contention, holding that segregation alone did not violate the Constitution.

As summarized by the Court in 1992, *Plessy* held that "racial segregation . . . works no denial of equal protection, rejecting the argument that racial separation enforced by the legal machinery of American society treats the black race as inferior." Instead, the *Plessy* Court stated, "Laws permitting, and even requiring their separation in places where they are liable to be brought into contact do not necessarily imply the inferiority of either race to the other." If blacks felt discriminated against, said the Court, it was "not by reason of anything found in the act, but solely because the colored race chooses to put that construction upon it."

The Court's rationale, however, overlooked reality. The device of holding a group separate—whether by confinement of Jews to the ghetto, by exclusion of untouchables from the temple, or by segregation of blacks—is a basic tool of discrimination.

Plessy v. Ferguson gave the lie to the American ideal "that all men are created equal." Upon the "separate but equal" doctrine approved by the Court was built a whole structure of racial discrimination. Jim Crow replaced equal protection, and legally enforced segregation became a dominant fact.

To the present-day observer, of course, the "separate but equal" doctrine is all wrong. All the same, perhaps one should not be too harsh in judging the Court for a decision that mirrored its own time and place. Living in an era that has witnessed a virtual egalitarian revolution, we find it all too easy to censure the *Plessy* Court for its reliance on doctrine that we deem outmoded. But that Court—a reflection of the less tolerant society in which it sat—could hardly hope to lift itself (by its own bootstraps as it were) above the ingrained prejudices of its day.

In addition, we should recognize that, inadequate though the *Plessy* decision may have been, it was the language in *Plessy* requiring equality of treatment for the separate races that was to prove significant in the movement for racial legal equality. Indeed, it was precisely the requirement of equality of treatment articulated in the *Plessy* opinion that was half a century later to provide the opening wedge for the ultimate overruling of the *Plessy* holding itself—an overruling that came in 1954 in *Brown v. Board of Education*.

3. *Lochner v. New York*

According to Chief Justice William Rehnquist, *Lochner v. New York* (1905) "may be fairly described as one of the most ill-starred decisions that [the Supreme Court] ever rendered." Indeed, in any list of discredited decisions, *Lochner* stands not far behind *Dred Scott.*

Lochner set the theme for the Court's interpretation of due process as a substantive restraint. Substantive due process is essentially a prohibition against arbitrary governmental action. Arbitrary action is synonymous with unreasonable action, and due process becomes a test of reasonableness.

In *Lochner,* the Court indicated that reasonableness under due process must be determined as an objective fact by the judge's independent judgment. In holding invalid a law prescribing maximum hours for bakers, the Court substituted its judgment for that of the legislature and decided for itself that the statute was not reasonably related to the ends for which governmental power might validly be exercised. "This case," asserted the celebrated dissent of Justice Holmes, "is decided upon an economic theory which a large part of the country does not entertain." It was because the *Lochner* Court disagreed with the economic theory on which the legislature had acted that it struck down the statute as unreasonable.

What made *Lochner* so important was that its approach meant more than control in the abstract of the wisdom of legislation. Court control was directed to a particular purpose—the invalidation of state laws that conflicted with the laissez-faire thinking that prevailed at the turn of the century. To a Court that adopted the *Lochner* approach, the "liberty" protected by the Fourteenth Amendment became synonymous with governmental hands-off in economic affairs. Any legislative encroachment on the existing economic order became suspect. "For years," the Supreme Court itself conceded in 1952, "the Court struck down social legislation when a particular law did not fit the notions of a majority of Justices as to legislation appropriate for a free enterprise system."

All this has, however, changed. Starting in the late 1930s, our law has seen what the Court in 1992 termed "the demise of *Lochner.*" The *Lochner* Court had struck down the regulatory law because it disagreed with the economic theory on which the legislature had acted. This was precisely the approach to judicial review that has been rejected. There may, in the given case, be economic arguments against a challenged regulatory law. To the Court now, however, such arguments are properly addressed to the legislature, not to the judges. The present posture was summarized in

1985 by Justice John Paul Stevens: "When the Court repudiated . . . *Lochner v. New York*, it did so in strong language that . . . seemed to foreclose forever any suggestion that the due process clause of the fourteenth amendment gave any power to federal judges to pass on the substance of the work product of state legislatures."

4. *Hammer v. Dagenhart*

"The only class which is arrayed against the court . . . is organized labor," wrote Chief Justice William Howard Taft in 1922. During the first part of the twentieth century, labor had good cause for complaint against the Supreme Court, for the Justices then served as the virtual censors of legislative attempts to enact regulatory laws, particularly those protecting labor. Among the decisions we now consider erroneous in striking down such laws was *Hammer v. Dagenhart* (1918), usually known as the Child Labor Case. Commentators place that case with *Lochner v. New York* on the list of discredited Supreme Court decisions.

In the Child Labor Case, a federal statute prohibited transportation in interstate commerce of goods made in factories that employed children. Although the statute did not in terms regulate local manufacturing, its purpose was to suppress child labor in the production of goods. With goods produced by children denied their interstate market, child labor could not continue on a widespread scale. To the majority of the Court, the congressional purpose rendered the law invalid. Congress was seeking primarily to regulate the manner in which manufacturing was carried on; such manufacturing under the restrictive meaning of the Court before the *Jones & Laughlin* case was not commerce that could be reached by federal authority. Congress could not, even by a law whose terms were specifically limited to regulation of commerce, use its commerce power to exert authority over matters like manufacturing, which were not, within the Court's restricted pre–*Jones & Laughlin* notion, commerce.

Justice Holmes wrote just after the decision that he thought it "ill timed and regrettable." This led him to deliver a dissent that stands among the greatest ever delivered. Holmes explained his dissent in a letter: "I said that as the law unquestionably regulated interstate commerce it was within the power of Congress no matter what its indirect effect on matters within the regulation of the states, or how obviously that effect was intended."

Most important at the time was the distressing effect of the Child Labor decision. As Chief Justice Rehnquist's book on the Court points out, the decision was a body blow to child-labor laws; it made effective regulation of child labor all but impossible. In a country like the United States, if a practice like child labor is to be dealt with effectively, it must be by national regulation. But the Court, Rehnquist tells us, "held that the condition of labor at factories within the states was a matter for regulation by the states rather than for regulation by Congress." By rigidly excluding Congress from exercising regulatory authority, the Child Labor Case virtually decreed that child labor should be left only to whatever controls were afforded by the workings of unrestrained laissez-faire. The United States alone, among nations, was precluded from taking effective action against an evil so widely censured by civilized opinion.

However, the Child Labor decision, like most on the list of worst decisions, has been overruled by the Court. That occurred in 1941 in *United States v. Darby*, where the Court upheld the federal law that prohibited the shipment in interstate commerce of products made by employees whose wages were less than the prescribed minimum or whose hours were greater than the prescribed maximum. The employer relied on the Child Labor Case, but the Court stated laconically, "*Hammer v. Dagenhart* has not been followed." Instead, *Darby* specifically refused to accept the Child Labor view that a federal law's "effect to control in some measure the use or production within the states of the article thus excluded from the commerce can operate to deprive the [law] of its constitutional authority."

5. *Adkins v. Children's Hospital*

In a 1992 opinion, the Supreme Court stated that the "line of cases identified with *Lochner v. New York*" was "exemplified by *Adkins v. Children's Hospital* [1923]." The decision in *Adkins* was the most extreme of those following the *Lochner* approach.

In *Adkins*, as the 1992 opinion summarized it, "this Court held it to be an infringement of constitutionally protected liberty of contract to require the employers of adult women to satisfy minimum wage standards." The opinion, in *Adkins*, like that in *Lochner*, was based on rigid reliance on freedom of contract. The law in question, said the Court, "forbids two parties having lawful capacity . . . to freely contract with one another in respect of the price for which one shall render service to the other in a purely private employment where both are willing, perhaps anxious, to agree." Nor did the protection of women justify the added burden imposed on employers: "[T]o the extent that the sum fixed exceeds the fair value of the services rendered, it amounts to a compulsory exaction from the employer."

In *Adkins*, the protection of freedom of contract reached its apogee. As stated by *Adkins*, "[F]reedom of contract is . . . the general rule and restraint the exception; and the exercise of legislative authority to abridge it can be justified only by the existence of exceptional circumstances."

The effect of *Adkins* on social legislation was as devastating as that of *Lochner*. The decision, Justice Frankfurter wrote, "struck the death knell not only of this legislation, but of kindred social legislation because it laid down as a constitutional principle that any kind of change by statute has to justify itself, not the other way around."

Like other decisions on this list, *Adkins* has now had its day. The Great Depression, the 1992 opinion tells us, taught "the lesson that seemed unmistakable to most people by 1937, that the interpretation of contractual freedom protected in *Adkins* rested on fundamentally false factual assumptions about the capacity of a relatively unregulated market to satisfy minimal levels of human welfare." The result was the decision in *West Coast Hotel Co. v. Parrish* (1937), which overruled *Adkins* and upheld a state minimum wage law for women. As the 1992 opinion put it, the Depression's "clear demonstration that the facts of economic life were different from those previously assumed warranted the repudiation of [*Adkins*]."

6. *Korematsu v. United States*

The case of Toyosaburo Korematsu is one that is unique in American law. As described in Justice Robert H. Jackson's dissent: "Korematsu was born on our soil, of parents born in Japan. The Constitution makes him a citizen of the United States by nativity and a citizen of California by residence. No claim is made that he is not loyal to this country. There is no suggestion that apart from the matter involved here he is not law-abiding and well disposed. Korematsu, however, has been convicted of an act not commonly a crime. It consists merely of being present in the state whereof he is a citizen, near the place where he was born, and where all his life he has lived."

Had Korematsu been of Italian, German, or English ancestry, his act would not have been a crime. His presence in California was made a crime solely because his parents were Japanese. For him, the difference between innocence and crime resulted not from anything he did, said, or even thought, but only from his racial stock. For Korematsu was a victim of what a *Harper's* article was to term "America's Greatest Wartime Mistake"—the evacuation of those of Japanese ancestry from the West Coast after the attack on Pearl Harbor.

Acting on the belief that they posed a security threat, the military issued orders excluding "all persons of Japanese ancestry, both alien and non-alien" from the western part of the country. Those excluded were evacuated to what were euphemistically termed Relocation Centers in interior states, in which they were detained until almost the end of the war. Under this evacuation program, over 112,000 persons of Japanese ancestry were herded from their homes on the West Coast into the Relocation Centers—which, had they been set up in any other country, we would not hesitate to call by their true name of concentration camps.

In *Korematsu v. United States* (1944), the Court upheld the evacuation of the Japanese. Korematsu had been convicted for remaining in a military area contrary to the exclusion order. Such an order, said the Court, could validly be issued by the military because of the situation confronting them after Pearl Harbor. In the face of a threatened Japanese attack, citizens of Japanese ancestry could rationally be set apart from those who had no particular associations with Japan; in time of war, residents having ethnic affiliations with an invading enemy may be a greater source of danger than those of a different ancestry.

The record of the Government in dealing with the West Coast Japanese during the war is hardly one that an American can contemplate with satisfaction. As the Court has eloquently declared, "Distinctions between citizens solely because of their ancestry are by their very nature odious to a free people whose institutions are founded upon the doctrine of equality." Yet it cannot be gainsaid that those who, like Toyosaburo Korematsu, were forced into the Relocation Centers were deprived of their freedom merely because they were the children of parents whom they did not choose and belonged to a race from which there was no way to resign. Under the evacuation program, in the words of one Justice, "no less than 70,000 American citizens have been placed under a special ban and deprived of their liberty because of their particular racial inheritance. In this sense it bears a melancholy resemblance to the treatment accorded to members of the Jewish race in Germany and in other parts of Europe."

Korematsu has not been specifically overruled, but its racist approach is plainly inconsistent with the whole thrust of the law since *Brown v. Board of Education*. Under *Brown* and its progeny, the Court said in 1958, "law and order are not . . . to be preserved by depriving the Negro of their constitutional rights." Important though it may be to deal with a war emergency, it cannot be accomplished by practices that involve the blatant racial discrimination involved in *Korematsu*. Hence, Justice Ginsburg tells us in a 1995 opinion, "A *Korematsu*-type classification . . . will never again survive scrutiny." Perhaps the best comment on the matter was made by Earl Warren, who, as attorney general and governor of California, had strongly supported the Japanese evacuation. Years later, the Chief Justice told Justice Arthur J. Goldberg, "You know, in retrospect, that's one of the worst things I ever did."

7. *Bradwell v. Illinois*

According to the famous English epigram, "A woman can never be outlawed, for a woman is never in law." Until recently, American law displayed a similar attitude. The first decision under the Fourteenth Amendment denied the right of women to practice law. The case was brought by Myra Bradwell, who had studied law and established the *Chicago Legal News*, the pioneer western legal periodical. It was not denied that she possessed the necessary qualifications; indeed, the Illinois court stated expressly: "Of the ample qualifications of the applicant we have no doubt." Nevertheless, that court denied her application for admission to the bar solely because she was a woman. The Supreme Court affirmed, ruling that the Fourteenth Amendment did not restrict state power to limit practice of law to males.

Under *Bradwell v. Illinois* (1873), women were scarcely included in the legal concept of equality. Instead, the decision confirmed what Alexis de Tocqueville had termed "that great inequality of man and woman which has seemed . . . to be eternally based in human nature." The same view was expressed by Justice Joseph P. Bradley in *Bradwell*: "The civil law, as well as nature herself, has always recognized a wide difference in the respective spheres and destinies of man and woman. Man is, or should be, woman's protector and defender. The natural and proper timidity and delicacy which belongs to the female sex evidently unfits it for many of the occupations of civil life. The constitution of the family organization, which is founded in the divine ordinance, as well as in the nature of things, indicates the domestic sphere as that which properly belongs to the domain and functions of womanhood."

Although the equal protection clause, by its own terms, is applicable to "any person," *Bradwell* held that it protects only men. Justice Bradley contrasted "those energies and responsibilities, and that decision and firmness which . . . predominate in the sterner sex" with "the peculiar characteristics, destiny, and mission of women." Indeed, Bradley asserted, "The paramount destiny and mission of woman are to fulfill the noble and benign offices of wife and mother. This is the law of the Creator."

A century later, of course, the law of the Creator is construed differently. The common-law jeremiad against women has been abandoned; virtually all legal disabilities based on sex have been eliminated, by either statute or judicial decision. Today women have the legal right not only to be members of the bar, but also to join any other profession or engage in any occupation or economic activity. The law has thoroughly repudiated what the Supreme Court in 1973 called the "gross, stereotyped distinctions between the sexes"—including, in Justice Sandra Day O'Connor's phrase, "the stereotyped view" of certain work "as exclusively [a man's or] woman's job." *Bradwell* has by now been completely discredited, referred to, if at all, only to show how the law has progressed during the twentieth century.

And what of Myra Bradwell herself, who was denied admission to the bar despite her "ample qualifications"? She continued to publish her legal periodical; its importance is shown by the fact that, in his diary, Justice Bradley himself noted that he sent copies of his opinions to Bradwell's *Chicago Legal News*. In 1882, Bradwell was instrumental in securing passage of an Illinois law granting women the right to practice any profession (Congress had passed a law allowing qualified women to practice before the Supreme Court in 1879). The Illinois court finally admitted Myra Bradwell to practice in 1885, and she was admitted to the United States Supreme Court bar in 1892.

8. *Buck v. Bell*

Even mighty Homer nods. Oliver Wendell Holmes, we saw, is considered second only to John Marshall among Supreme Court Justices. Yet it was Holmes who wrote the opinion of the Court in *Buck v. Bell* (1927), which plainly has its dishonored place on any list of the worst Supreme Court decisions. *Buck v. Bell* shows, in Erwin N. Griswold's recent words, "that great men, like the rest of us, have their failings from time to time."

As described in Holmes's opinion, "Carrie Buck is a feeble-minded white woman who was committed to the State Colony [for Feeble Minded]. She is the daughter of a feeble-minded mother in the same institution, and the mother of an illegitimate feeble-minded child." She had been ordered sterilized under a state law providing for the compulsory sterilization of "mental defectives."

The Court upheld the state law and the sterilization order. "It is," declared the opinion, "better for all the world, if instead of waiting to execute degenerate offspring for crime, or to let them starve for their imbecility, society can prevent those who are manifestly unfit from continuing their kind. The principle that sustains compulsory vaccination is broad enough to cover cutting the Fallopian tubes." And then Holmes made the oft-quoted pithy statement. "Three generations of imbeciles are enough."

Both the *Buck* decision and the Holmes opinion are so repugnant that they can scarcely be reconciled with basic constitutional values. Perhaps the only explanation is that, as a Holmes biography states, "The American public was at the time caught up in a eugenics craze . . . the idea that selective breeding could vastly improve the composition of the human race." Holmes, like so many others then, "was a true believer" and had written that "eugenics . . . was the true beginning, theoretically, of all improvement." After the *Buck* decision, the Justice wrote that in the case, "I . . . felt that I was getting near the first principle of real reform."

Today, of course, we look at such things differently. The eugenic theories on which *Buck* was based bear a disquieting resemblance to those upon which the racist laws of Nazi Germany were grounded. In fact, the Nazi law under which millions were sterilized contains language similar to that in the *Buck* sterilization law. Both were based on the Model Eugenical Sterilization Law proposed by the American eugenicist Harry Laughlin, and *Buck v. Bell* itself was cited by defendants in the Nuremberg trials.

We now recognize that the eugenics that Holmes supported was based on theories that may be termed scientific only in the euphemistic sense. They were, as J. B. S. Haldane once so pithily put it, "as much justified by science as were the proceedings of the Inquisition by the Gospels."

The Supreme Court itself has come to realize this. The decision in *Skinner v. Oklahoma* (1942) struck down a compulsory sterilization law. Such legislation, said *Skinner*, "involves one of the basic civil rights of man. . . . The power to sterilize, if exercised, may have subtle, farreaching and devastating effects. In evil or reckless hands it can cause races or types which are inimical to the dominant group to wither and disappear. There is no redemption for the individual whom the law touches. . . . He is forever deprived of a basic liberty."

Skinner did not expressly overrule *Buck* but, in the words of one commentator, "distinguished the case out of existence" when it invalidated what Justice Robert H. Jackson said was a "plan to sterilize the individual in pursuit of a eugenic plan to eliminate from the race characteristics that are only vaguely identified and which in our present state of knowledge are uncertain as to transmissibility." *Skinner* rejects the view that, in Jackson's words, "a legislatively represented majority may conduct biological experiments at the expense of the dignity and personality and natural powers of a minority."

More recent investigation provides what amounts to a suggestive footnote to *Buck v. Bell*. It may well be that "three generations of imbeciles" were not really involved in the case. After her sterilization, Carrie Buck left the mental institution. During the rest of her life, according to a 1985 article, "she regularly displayed intelligence and kindness that belied the 'feeblemindedness' and 'immorality' that were used as an excuse to sterilize her. She was an avid reader, and even in her last weeks was able to converse lucidly, recalling events from her childhood. Branded by Holmes as a second generation imbecile, Carrie provided no support for his glib epithet throughout her life."

The same was true of Carrie Buck's daughter. "Although she lived barely eight years," states the same article, "she too disproved Holmes's epigram. In her two years of schooling, she performed quite well, at one point earning a spot on the school 'Honor Roll.'"

Despite the Holmes aphorism, there may not have been even one "generation of imbeciles" involved in the case.

9. *Carter v. Carter Coal Co.*

"During the past half century," asserted President Franklin D. Roosevelt in 1937, "the balance of power between the three great branches of the Federal Government, has been tipped out of balance by the Courts in direct contradiction of the high purposes of the framers of the Constitution." FDR's complaint was triggered by the Supreme Court decisions invalidating the most important early New Deal measures. Those decisions culminated in *Carter v. Carter Coal Co.* (1936). At issue was a federal law regulating the coal industry by price fixing, proscription of unfair trade practices, and prescription of labor conditions. In declaring this law, and particularly its labor provisions, invalid, the majority of the Court relied directly on the narrowed notion of federal regulatory power that prevailed prior to 1937.

The *Carter* decision rests on the proposition that mere manufacturing or mining does not constitute commerce. The effect of the labor provisions of the challenged law, said the Court, falls on production, not commerce. Commerce was a thing apart from the employer–employee relation, which in all producing occupations was said to be purely local in character. And, in *Carter's* view, it made no difference that labor practices in the gigantic coal industry clearly had an effect on interstate commerce. To the Court, this effect was not "direct" enough; the direct effect was on production, and, then, the production itself affected commerce.

Carter's restrictive interpretation was catastrophic in its consequences. Elimination of manufacturing, mining, agriculture, and other productive industries from the reach of the commerce clause rendered Congress powerless to deal with problems in those fields, however pressing they might become. And so, as Justice Robert H. Jackson stated, in characterizing the effect of *Carter*, "a national government that has power, through the Federal Trade Commission, to prohibit the giving of prizes with penny candy shipped by the manufacturer from one state to another, was powerless to deal with the causes of critical stoppages in the gigantic bituminous coal industry."

This comment drew special pertinence from the grim economic background in *Carter*. Giant industries prostrate, crises in production and consumption throughout the country, the economy in a state of virtual collapse—if ever there was a need for exertion of federal power, it was after 1929. If federal power was not to be as broad as that need, it meant that the nation was helpless in the face of economic disaster.

Under *Carter*, all this was irrelevant. If there was no "direct" effect on commerce, in the narrow sense in which the Court used the term "commerce," there was no federal power to regulate—regardless of the size of the industry or the magnitude of the problems involved. "If the production by one man of a single ton of coal intended for interstate sale and shipment, and actually so sold and shipped, affects interstate commerce indirectly," asserted *Carter*, "the effect does not become direct by multiplying the tonnage, or increasing the number of men employed, or adding to the expense or complexities of the business, or by all combined."

This was the veritable reductio ad absurdum of the Court's restrictive approach. Under it, the matter of degree had no bearing on the question of federal power: there was no difference between the mining of 1 ton of coal and 10 million tons of coal, as far as the effect on commerce was concerned. Production was purely local. Even though there was a production crisis throughout the country, it could not be dealt with on a national level.

Cases such as *Carter* presented a disturbing paradox. As industry became more and more interstate in character, the power of Congress to regulate was given a narrower and narrower interpretation. For the coal industry in *Carter*, national intervention had become a necessity. The market and the states had found the industry's problems beyond their competence. The choice was between federal action and chaos. As the Court expressed it in 1948, *Carter* and similar decisions, "embracing the same artificially drawn lines, produced a series of consequences for the exercise of national power over industry conducted on a national scale which the evolving nature of our industrialism foredoomed to reversal."

The reversal came with *National Labor Relations Board v. Jones & Laughlin Steel Corp.* Although *Jones & Laughlin* did not expressly overrule *Carter* and other restrictive decisions, the opinion there did state, "These cases are not controlling here." Plainly, the broad sweep given in *Jones & Laughlin* to federal regulatory power relegated *Carter* to constitutional limbo.

10. *Hepburn v. Griswold*

Not only is *Hepburn v. Griswold* one of the worst Supreme Court decisions, but nothing shows the inadequacy of "original intention" as the be-all and end-all of constitutional interpretation as well as that decision.

During the early history of the United States, federal paper currency, with notes issued as legal tender, did not exist. Instead, as John Kenneth Galbraith points out, "the money of the United States was precious metal. . . . The only paper currency was the notes of banks." During the Civil War, Congress was forced to make substantial changes to the currency system. In three Legal Tender Acts, it provided for the issuance of $450 million in United States notes (the so-called greenbacks) and provided that those notes were to be legal tender that had to be accepted at face value.

While the Civil War raged, the Supreme Court astutely avoided deciding the validity of the greenback laws. After the war, the issue could not be evaded. In *Hepburn v. Griswold* (1870), a bare majority ruled the Legal Tender Acts invalid. One of the main reasons that President Lincoln had appointed Salmon P. Chase as Chief Justice was to ensure a favorable decision on the laws, for Chase, as secretary of the treasury, had been their chief architect. But the new Chief Justice disappointed the presidential expectation. It was Chase who delivered the majority opinion in *Hepburn v. Griswold*, which held that Congress did not have the power to issue paper money and make it legal tender.

Hepburn v. Griswold was one case where the decision was in exact accord with the Framers' original intention. If there was any point on which the men of 1787 were agreed, it was the need to prevent a repetition of the Revolution's paper-money fiasco, when the expression "not worth a continental" was born. To prevent that, they determined to give the government they were establishing power to issue only a metallic currency.

This can be seen from both the constitutional text and the Framers' debates. They gave Congress the power "to coin Money," which clearly indicates their determination to authorize only a metallic currency. As Chief Justice Chase put it, "The power conferred is the power to coin money. . . . And we have been referred to no authority which at that time defined coining otherwise than as minting or stamping metals for money; or money otherwise than as metal coined for the purpose of commerce."

The available records of the Philadelphia Convention bear out Chase's view of the Framers' intent. The original constitutional draft gave Congress power to "emit Bills on the Credit of the United States." Gouverneur Morris moved to strike out those words. Except for one delegate, who said that he "was a friend to paper money," those who spoke on the matter supported the motion, which carried. As Luther Martin, a delegate at Philadelphia, explained it in November 1787, a "majority of the convention, being wise beyond every event, and being willing to risk any political evil, rather than admit the idea of a paper emission, in any possible event, refused to trust this authority to [the federal] government."

Yet if *Hepburn v. Griswold* was thus categorically correct in terms of original intention, it was plainly wrong as far as the needs of the nation were concerned. It is all but impossible to conceive of a functioning modern economy without paper money, in which the only currency is specie. As Judge Robert H. Bork strikingly puts it, "If a judge today were to decide that paper money is unconstitutional, we would think he ought to be accompanied not by a law clerk, but by a guardian."

As it turned out, *Hepburn v. Griswold* was not destined to achieve its harmful result, for it was overruled the next year by the so-called Legal Tender Cases (*Knox v. Lee; Parker v. Davis*). The decisions in those cases finally put to rest the controversy over congressional authority and ruled that the nation's fiscal powers included the authority to issue paper money vested with the quality of legal tender. This was one case where original intention had been tried and ultimately found wanting, even though the Framers' intent on the matter was as clear as it could possibly be.

"Beauts" Beautified

"When I make a mistake," Fiorello LaGuardia once said, "it's a beaut!" All the decisions in this chapter are "beauts." They may make us wonder whether we should continue to believe with those who, as Henry Adams wrote, "clung to the Supreme Court, much as the churchman still clings to his last rag of Right."

Nevertheless, Supreme Court history tells us that the decisions in this chapter are aberrations; they do not change the fact that, in the main, the Court has molded its decisions to meet what Justice Holmes called "the felt necessities of the time." As far as the "beauts" in this chapter are concerned, the bottom line is that they have all been repudiated—either by being overruled by later decisions or because societal and legal changes have relegated them to constitutional limbo.

More specifically, *Dred Scott v. Sandford* was overruled not by a decision of a court (unless we include that at Appomattox Courthouse), but by the Thirteenth and Fourteenth Amendments; *Hepburn v. Griswold* was overruled a year after it was decided by the Legal Tender Cases; *Bradwell v. Illinois* may never have been overruled, but it has been overtaken by more recent cases and statutes that have confirmed the right to engage in any profession, occupation, or economic activity regardless of sex; *Plessy v. Ferguson* was overruled by *Brown v. Board of Education*; what the Court in 1992 called "the demise of *Lochner [v. New York]*" has been signaled by the post–1937 decisions repudiating the *Lochner* approach; *Hammer v. Dagenhart* was overruled by *United States v. Darby*; *Adkins v. Children's Hospital* was overruled by *West Coast Hotel Co. v. Parrish*; *Buck v. Bell*, though not expressly overruled, was "distinguished out of existence" by *Skinner v. Oklahoma*'s invalidation of a compulsory sterilization law; *Carter v. Carter Coal Co.* was discarded, even if not specifically overruled, within a year by *National Labor Relations Board v. Jones & Laughlin Steel Corp.*; *Korematsu v. United States* was based on a racist approach that has been superseded by the post–*Brown v. Board of Education* law on racial discrimination.

Except for *Dred Scott*, all the decisions in the list of Supreme Court "worsts" were repudiated by the Court itself—two of them only a year after they were decided. In the other cases, to be sure, there was a judicial lag, which may be an inevitable concomitant of the system of judicial review established by *Marbury v. Madison*.

In assessing the Supreme Court in operation, one should bear constantly in mind James Bryce's famous truism a century ago that judges are only men (today we should, of course, say only human). And because of the manner in which judges are chosen and their tenure, they are men and women of the prior generation. The Supreme Court is almost never a really contemporary institution. The operation of life tenure in the Court, as against elections at short intervals in Congress, usually keeps the average viewpoint of the two institutions a generation apart. The Court is consequently the check of a preceding generation on the present one. That being the case, it is hardly surprising that there is at times a gap between public opinion and the decisions of the Supreme Court. The judges of that tribunal are, to be sure, only men and women who normally seek to keep in tune with the common sentiment of the community. Yet they are men and women whose roots are more in the past than those of most others in public life. Looking at the problems of the present through the distorting lenses of their generation's experience, they may be slower to accept drastic changes than those in the political departments.

Nor is the judicial lag in this respect necessarily an undesirable element in our system. If the limitations contained in the Constitution are to be given full effect, their enforcement must not be controlled by every shift in popular whims. A conservative (in the best sense of the word) institution that bends slowly is best suited to serve as the enforcing organ. That the Court may lag behind popular sentiment is exactly what was intended.

Judicial lag must not, all the same, prevent the law from adapting itself to changing needs. The decisions of yesterday may prove so out of line with the needs of today that they should be discarded even by a body normally wedded to precedent. Otherwise, the power of precedent becomes only, in Justice Cardozo's phrase, the power of the beaten track.

In all the cases on our list (except for *Dred Scott*, which was overruled by the Civil War itself), the Supreme Court recognized this and specifically corrected its erroneous decisions. Ultimately, the Court did not forget, in the words of Chief Justice John Marshall, that "it is a *constitution* we are expounding"—a living instrument that must be construed so as to meet the practical necessities of present-day government.

5

TEN

GREATEST

DISSENTING

OPINIONS

The first opinion in the very first case decided by the Supreme Court was a dissent, though not labeled as such. The case was *Georgia v. Brailsford* (1792), where Georgia was granted an injunction staying payment to others of a debt owed to the state. The Justices at that time followed the English practice of delivering their opinions one after another and the first opinion, delivered by Justice Thomas Johnson, disagreed with the majority and stated that "it is my opinion, that there is not a proper foundation for issuing an injunction." Soon thereafter, in *Wiscart v. D'Auchy* (1795), Justice James Wilson stated, at the beginning of his opinion, that it was a dissent. Thus it was established at the outset that Justices have the right to express their disagreement with the result reached by the Court.

Since then, the dissenting opinion has come to play an important role in the operation of the Supreme Court. "A dissent in a court of last resort," stated Chief Justice Hughes in an oft-quoted passage, "is an appeal to the brooding spirit of the law, to the intelligence of a future day, when a later decision may possibly correct the error into which the dissenting judge believes the court to have been betrayed." The great dissents not only have demonstrated the error of the Courts concerned, but also have successfully appealed to the future, which saw adoption of the dissenters' view. That was true of all the dissents listed, which may have spoken for only a minority in their day, but ultimately meant more for the development of the law than the quondam majority opinions.

— ★ — ★ — ★ —

Ten Greatest Dissenting Opinions

1. Curtis, J., in *Dred Scott v. Sandford*,
   19 How. 393, 564 (U.S. 1857)

2. Holmes, J., in *Lochner v. New York*,
   198 U.S. 45, 74 (1905)

3. Harlan, J., in *Plessy v. Ferguson*,
   163 U.S. 537, 552 (1896)

4. Holmes, J., in *Hammer v. Dagenhart*,
   247 U.S. 251, 277 (1918)

5. Holmes, J., in *Abrams v. United States*,
   250 U.S. 616, 624 (1919)

6. Brandeis, J., in *Whitney v. California*,
   274 U.S. 357, 372 (1927)

7. Brandeis, J., in *Olmstead v. United States*
   277 U.S. 438, 471 (1928)

8. Brandeis, J., in *New State Ice Co. v. Liebmann*,
   285 U.S. 262, 280 (1932)

9. Stone, J., in *United States v. Butler*,
   297 U.S. 1, 78 (1936)

10. Black, J., in *Adamson v. California*,
    332 U.S. 46, 68 (1947)

1. Curtis, J., in *Dred Scott v. Sandford*

Benjamin R. Curtis, like Benjamin N. Cardozo, did not serve long enough on the Supreme Court to be on the list of greatest Justices. Curtis resigned after only six years. Students of the Court, however, agree that had he, as a contemporary put it, "consented to devote the rest of his days to dispensing justice on the highest tribunal in the world," he would have become one of the Supreme Court greats. This consensus is based almost entirely upon his now classic dissent in *Dred Scott v. Sandford* (1857). If *Dred Scott* was the Court's worst decision, the Curtis dissent is rated by many as the greatest dissent in Supreme Court history.

The key issues in *Dred Scott* were those of black citizenship and congressional power to prohibit slavery in the territories. The Court opinion of Chief Justice Roger Taney denied both the right of blacks to be citizens and the authority of Congress to interfere with slaveholding in the territories. The Curtis dissent answered the Taney opinion on these rulings. Justice Curtis showed that citizenship for persons born within the United States was through the states and did not depend on national authority: "the citizens of the several States were citizens of the United States under the Confederation," and the same was true under the Constitution. Curtis cited both statutes and decisions to "show, in a manner which no argument can obscure, that in some of the original thirteen States, free colored persons, before and at the time of the formation of the Constitution, were citizens of those states." That, in turn, Curtis concluded, made them citizens of the United States.

Justice Curtis dealt with the issue of slavery prohibition by strongly reaffirming congressional authority over the territories. His dissent gave full effect to Article IV, section 3, which gives Congress power to make rules and regulations for the territories. According to Curtis, "An enactment that slavery may or may not exist there, is a regulation respecting the Territory." Hence it is within the power of Congress under the territories clause. The dissent referred with particular effect to the Northwest Ordinance prohibition against slavery in the Northwest Territory and the enactment in the First Congress that it should "continue to have full effect."

To us today, the most important part of the Curtis dissent was its refutation of Taney on the citizenship issue. It is now generally agreed that the materials relied on by Curtis showed conclusively that free blacks were citizens of at least some of the original thirteen states and hence citizens of the United States for purposes of the case. Curtis relied on constitutional and statutory provisions and decisions in five states to show that "free persons of color" had the right to vote and were consequently citizens of those states. This, to Curtis, disposed of the citizenship issue, since "it is only necessary to know whether any such persons were citizens of either of the States under the Confederation at the time of the adoption of the Constitution."

Dred Scott, to be sure, was never overruled by the Supreme Court. However, it was effectively nullified by an 1862 federal law prohibiting slavery in the territories, as well as by the Thirteenth and Fourteenth Amendments' outlawing of slavery and conferral of citizenship on all persons born or naturalized in this country.

History has, without a doubt, given the palm to the Curtis dissent. Few will disagree with this judgment, which has been based less on the technical law than on *Dred Scott*'s baneful effect. Even, if as some commentators assert, the Taney conclusion on citizenship had stronger support in the law than has been recognized, it must still be concluded that the *Dred Scott* decision was little short of disastrous. It meant that, without constitutional amendment, blacks were consigned to a permanent second-class status that could not be changed even if all the slaves were ultimately freed. More fundamentally, it gave the lie to the very basis of the American heritage: the notion of equality as the central theme of the Declaration of Independence—in Lincoln's words, "the electric cord in that Declaration that links the hearts of patriotic and liberty-loving men together." This disastrous result would have been avoided if the Curtis dissent had been followed by the Court. As it was, it took a bloody war and two constitutional amendments to undo *Dred Scott*'s pernicious effect.

2. Holmes, J., in *Lochner v. New York*

Aside from its use as the horrible example of what we now consider the wrong kind of judicial activism, *Lochner v. New York* (1905) is remembered today for its now classic dissent by Justice Oliver Wendell Holmes, celebrated for its oft-quoted aphorisms. Indeed, the Holmes's opinion in *Lochner* is, next to that in *Dred Scott*, the most famous dissent ever written. "There is a famous passage," Justice Cardozo wrote, "where Matthew Arnold tells us how to separate the gold from the alloy in the coinage of the poets by the test of a few lines which we are to carry in our thoughts." The flashing epigrams in Holmes's *Lochner* dissent do the like for those who would apply the same test to law.

The *Lochner* dissent contains one of Justice Holmes's most famous statements: "General propositions do not decide concrete cases." Yet the

Holmes dissent was based more on general propositions than on concrete rules or precedents. Indeed, Holmes began with a broad proposition: "This case is decided upon an economic theory which a large part of the country does not entertain." Holmes neither explained nor elaborated the charge. Instead, he went on to point out that the decision on economic grounds was not consistent with his conception of the judicial function. "If it were a question whether I agreed with that theory, I should desire to study it further and long before making up my mind. But I do not conceive that to be my duty, because I strongly believe that my agreement or disagreement has nothing to do with the right of a majority to embody their opinions in law."

The dissent then struck directly at the conception that then virtually equated the law with laissez-faire. That conception was stated by Holmes as a paraphrase of the British writer Herbert Spencer: "The liberty of the citizen to do as he likes so long as he does not interfere with the liberty of others to do the same." This led Holmes to his best-known aphorism: "The Fourteenth Amendment does not enact Mr. Herbert Spencer's Social Statics." This "general proposition" was supported by the "decisions cutting down the liberty to contract," such as the cases upholding a maximum-hours law for miners and prohibiting sales of stock on margin, as well as compulsory vaccination laws. According to Holmes, it was irrelevant whether the judges shared the "convictions or prejudices" embodied in these laws: "[A] constitution is not intended to embody a particular economic theory, whether of paternalism and the organic relation of the citizen to the State or of *laissez faire*."

Then Holmes stated his general approach to judicial review: "I think that the word liberty in the Fourteenth Amendment is perverted when it is held to prevent [legislation], unless it can be said that a rational and fair man necessarily would admit that the statute proposed would infringe fundamental principles as they have been understood by the traditions of our people and our law."

This was the theory of judicial restraint that Holmes was to urge throughout his tenure, and the approach to judicial review adopted after Holmes himself left the Court. To Holmes, the test to be applied was whether a reasonable legislator—the legislative version of the "reasonable man"—could have adopted a law like that at issue. Was the statute as applied so clearly arbitrary that legislators acting reasonably could not have believed it necessary or appropriate for public health, safety, morals, or welfare?

In *Lochner* itself, the law at issue did not fail to meet the Holmes standard. On the contrary, Holmes declared, "A reasonable man might think it a proper measure on the score of health." That is all that was necessary for the conclusion that the law should be sustained: "Men whom I certainly could not pronounce unreasonable would uphold it."

Judge Richard Posner asserts that the Holmes *Lochner* dissent would not have received a high grade in a law-school examination. Certainly, the Holmes opinion is utterly unlike the present-day judicial product—all too often the work of law clerks for whom the acme of literary style is the law-review article. The standard opinion style has become that of the law reviews: colorless, prolix, platitudinous, always erring on the side of inclusion, full of lengthy citations and footnotes—and, above all, dull.

The Holmes dissent is, of course, anything but dull. In fact, as Posner sums it up, it may not be "a *good* judicial opinion. It is merely the greatest judicial opinion of the last hundred years. To judge it by [the usual] standards is to miss the point. It is a rhetorical masterpiece."

3. Harlan, J., in *Plessy v. Ferguson*

Justice Frankfurter once wrote to a friend, "The present fashion to make old Harlan out a great judge is plumb silly." Despite Frankfurter's disparagement, most students of the Court list the first Justice John Marshall Harlan as one of the most important Justices. He was certainly one of the great dissenters in Supreme Court history; his frequent challenges to the majority led his colleagues, as he once wrote to Chief Justice Morrison R. Waite, to suggest that he suffered from "dis-sent-ery." Most important, Harlan's key dissents have in the main been affirmed in the court of history. A century later, his rejection of the narrow civil-rights view adopted by the Court majority has been generally approved.

On the bench, Harlan was the most serious of judges, who, Justice Frankfurter tells us, "wielded a battle-ax"; his dissents were vigorous, often impatient, sometimes bitter. Most notable among them was that in *Plessy v. Ferguson* (1896), now considered one of the greatest dissents.

The *Plessy* decision upheld the constitutionality of racial segregation. As we saw, it rejected the argument that separate facilities implied black inferiority, stating that if blacks felt that segregation implied inferiority, it was "solely because the colored race chooses to put that construction upon it." The Harlan dissent attacked this basic holding that segregation alone was not discriminatory. To Harlan, it was plain that segregation "proceed[s] on the ground that colored citizens are so inferior . . . that they cannot be allowed to sit [with] white citizens." The purpose, said Harlan, was that "of humiliating citizens . . . of a particular race." Indeed,

Harlan declared, segregation "is a badge of servitude inconsistent with . . . the equality before the law established by the Constitution."

Plessy v. Ferguson gave the lie to the American ideal, so eloquently stated in the Harlan dissent: "Our Constitution is color-blind, and neither knows nor tolerates classes among citizens." Nor was this changed by the supposed requirement of equality in facilities—a requirement that the courts would not even try to enforce for years. "The thin disguise of 'equal' accommodations for passengers in railroad coaches," movingly declared the Harlan dissent, "will not mislead anyone, nor atone for the wrong this day done."

To Harlan, "the judgment this day rendered will, in time, prove to be quite as pernicious as the decision made by this tribunal in the *Dred Scott* case." And so it turned out. Except for *Dred Scott,* no Court decision has harmed as many people as *Plessy.* To the present-day observer, of course, the merits of the case are all with Justice Harlan's dissent. As the Court stated in 1992, "we think *Plessy* was wrong the day it was decided." In particular, "the *Plessy* Court's explanation for its decision was . . . clearly at odds with the facts," since segregation "had just such an effect"—that is, "to stigmatize those who were segregated with a 'badge of inferiority.'"

In other words, Justice Harlan was correct in his reading of the humiliating effect of segregation and hence in his interpretation of the equal protection guarantee. Half a century after it was delivered, the Harlan dissent was finally elevated to the plane of accepted constitutional doctrine by the *Brown* desegregation decision.

4. Holmes, J., in *Hammer v. Dagenhart*

In Supreme Court history, Justice Holmes is known as the "great dissenter." A list of great dissents can be made up from the most important Holmes dissents, for they performed the most important function of the Supreme Court dissent—not only to demonstrate the error in the majority decision, but also to point the way to its correction by future Courts.

I have chosen what I consider the three greatest Holmes dissents for inclusion in my list: *Lochner v. New York,* where Holmes enunciated the theory of judicial restraint that was to take over the field—at least in review of regulatory laws; *Hammer v. Dagenhart* (1918), where Holmes took an expansive view of federal regulatory power; and *Abrams v. United States,* where Holmes laid the foundation for present-day First Amendment law.

The Holmes dissents not only demolished the majority decisions in these cases, but also are classic examples of appeals to the future that were heard. Indeed, in these opinions, Holmes sounded the clarion of the coming law. The views stated in the Holmes dissents were to be those followed by the Court itself as the century went on.

Hammer v. Dagenhart, the Child Labor Case, struck down a federal law that forbade the interstate shipment of goods manufactured by child labor. In doing so, the Court relied on a narrow conception of the congressional commerce power that excluded manufacturing and other production from the reach of federal authority, even though the goods involved were destined for an interstate market. The congressional purpose, the Court held, was to regulate manufacturing, and that made the law invalid even though, on its face, it reached only interstate shipment.

Holmes pithily summarized his Child Labor Case dissent in a letter to his famous English correspondent, Sir Frederick Pollock: "I said that as the law unquestionably regulated interstate commerce it was within the power of Congress no matter what its indirect effect on matters within the regulation of the states, or how obviously that effect was intended. I flatter myself that I showed a lot of precedent and also the grounds in reason."

Few today doubt that reason in the case was indeed with the Holmes dissent. Legally, to Holmes, the case was a simple one, controlled by the principle stated near the beginning of his opinion: "If an act is within the powers specifically conferred upon Congress, it seems to me that it is not made any less constitutional because of the indirect effects that it may have, however obvious it may be that it will have those effects, and that we are not at liberty upon such grounds to hold it void."

To Holmes, it was clear that the challenged law did not infringe on "anything belonging to the states," which remained free to regulate manufacturing within their borders. "But when they seek to send their products across the state line they are no longer within their rights. If there were no Constitution and no Congress their power to cross the line would depend upon their neighbors. Under the Constitution such commerce belongs not to the states but to Congress to regulate. It may carry out its views of public policy whatever indirect effect they may have upon the activities of the states."

In terms of constitutional reasoning, the Holmes argument seems unanswerable, though it took a quarter-century before the Court accepted it in its 1941 decision overruling *Hammer*. But Holmes did not stop with legal argument in his *Hammer* dissent. Instead, he made a moral argument as well, which led Max Lerner to term the Holmes dissent "one of the most moving from a humanitarian standpoint."

"If there is any matter upon which civilized countries have agreed . . . ," Holmes declared, "it is the evil of premature and excessive child labor." Congress had decided that that evil should be barred from interstate commerce. The Court should not intrude on the moral judgment: "It is not for this Court to pronounce when prohibition is necessary to regulation . . . to say that it is permissible as against strong drink but not as against the product of ruined lives."

5. Holmes, J., in
Abrams v. United States

The Holmes dissent in *Abrams v. United States* (1919) was the first opinion by the Justice really applying his "clear and present danger" test, stated by him a year earlier—a test that has served as the catalyst for broad protection of freedom of speech. Under the Holmes test, for speech to be restricted, it is not enough that the speech advocates unlawful action; there must also be a "clear and present danger" that the speech will actually result in unlawful action.

In *Abrams*, six factory workers had thrown leaflets from a loft window in downtown New York City urging a general strike to protest American intervention in Russia in 1917. They were convicted for having violated the Espionage Act's prohibition against advocating the curtailment of war production. The Supreme Court affirmed. The Holmes dissent did not assert that the Constitution provides for an absolute right of expression. To the contrary, Holmes's own famous example of the man falsely shouting "fire!" in a theater is simply the most obvious example of speech that can be controlled.

But the fire-in-a-theater example was a far cry from the facts presented in *Abrams*. There, Holmes argued, the "silly" leaflets thrown by obscure individuals from a loft window presented no danger of resistance to the American war effort.

Under the Holmes "clear and present danger" test, speech may be restricted only if there is a real threat—a danger, both clear and present, that the speech will lead to unlawful conduct that the legislature has the power to prevent. In the *Abrams* case, Congress had the authority to pass a law to prevent interferences with war production; but, said Holmes, there was no danger, clear and present, or even remote, that the leaflets would have had any effect on production. Not enough, Holmes concluded, "can be squeezed from these poor and puny anonymities to turn the color of legal litmus paper."

Roscoe Pound, then America's leading legal scholar, said at the time that the *Abrams* dissent would become a classic. And so it became, and not only because of Holmes's use of his "clear and present danger" test. The *Abrams* dissent contains the fullest expression of the Holmes concept of freedom of speech, itself a direct descendant of the ideas of John Milton and John Stuart Mill. Milton's *Areopagitica* argues for "a free and open encounter" in which "[Truth] and Falsehood grapple." The *Abrams* dissent sets forth the foundation of the First Amendment as "free trade in ideas," which through competition for their acceptance by the people would provide the best test of truth. Or as Holmes put it in a letter, "I am for aeration of all effervescing convictions—there is no way so quick for letting them get flat."

Like Milton and Mill, Holmes stressed the ability of truth to win out in the intellectual marketplace. For this to happen, the indispensable sine qua non was the free interchange of ideas. As the crucial passage of the *Abrams* dissent puts it, "when men have realized that time has upset many fighting faiths, they may come to believe even more than they believe the very foundations of their own conduct that the ultimate good desired is better reached by free trade in ideas—that the best test of truth is the power of the thought to get itself accepted in the competition of the market, and that truth is the only ground upon which their wishes safely can be carried out."

Those who govern, Holmes is saying, too often seek to "express [their] wishes in law and sweep away all opposition," including "opposition by speech." They forget that time may also upset their "fighting faiths" and that, in the long run, "truth is the only ground upon which their wishes safely can be carried out." That is the case because government is an experimental process. The Constitution itself "is an experiment, as all life is an experiment."

To make the experiment successful, Holmes concluded, room must be found for new ideas that will challenge the old, for "the ultimate good desired is better reached by free trade in ideas." Max Lerner has called this Holmes essay "the greatest utterance on intellectual freedom by an American, ranking in the English tongue with Milton and Mill."

Referring to Henry James, Harold J. Laski wrote to Holmes, "I said to Felix [Frankfurter] today that I'd rather have your dissent in *Lochner* or *Abrams* than all his damned novels put together." What is noteworthy about the Holmes dissents is that they are as much contributions to literature as they are to law. Indeed, one of the best articles on Holmes is by the literary critic Edmund Wilson. According to him, Holmes's legal writings "are so elegantly and clearly presented, so free from the cumbersome formulas and the obsolete jargon of jurists, that, though only an expert can judge them, they may profitably be read by the layman." As a legal stylist and phrasemaker, Holmes is second to none. He can be compared only with Voltaire in his ability to compress profound thoughts into epigrams and aphorisms, illuminating a topic with incomparable precision and brevity. Holmes proceeds directly to the point, the vital spot of an idea. We can hardly believe he was a lawyer, he is so concise and clear. Perhaps the best comment on the matter is that once made by Justice Frankfurter: to read "Holmes's writings is to string pearls."

6. Brandeis, J., in
Whitney v. California

When is a concurring opinion actually a dissent? When the opinion writer disagrees with the majority's rationale, but joins in the decision for technical reasons that have nothing to do with that rationale. That was the case in *Whitney v. California* (1927), where the Brandeis opinion, though labeled a concurrence, was really one of the greatest dissents delivered in the Supreme Court.

Next to Holmes himself, Justice Louis D. Brandeis was the greatest dissenter in Supreme Court history. Most of the time, the two voted together: Brandeis joined the Holmes dissents in *Lochner*, *Hammer*, and *Abrams*. Indeed, as Holmes wrote a year after *Whitney*, "There seems a preestablished harmony between Brandeis and me. He agrees with all my dissents and I agree with [his]." There has been no sounder currency in contemporary law than a Holmes–Brandeis dissent. In almost every case, their dissenting view has since been accepted by the Court. That was emphatically true of Brandeis's *Whitney* opinion, which was also joined by Holmes.

At issue in *Whitney* was the California Criminal Syndicalism Act, which made it a crime to advocate or teach crime, sabotage, violence, or terrorism as a means of accomplishing industrial or political change, or to organize or become a member of any organization advocating or teaching such criminal syndicalism. Defendant was convicted of having violated this law by organizing and being a member of the Communist Labor Party. The Court affirmed the conviction. As explained in *Brandenburg v. Ohio* (1969), "The Court upheld the statute on the ground that . . . 'advocating' violent means to effect political and economic change involves such danger to the security of the State that the State may outlaw it."

Justice Brandeis concurred in the decision on a technical ground: the claim that the statute, as applied, did not meet the "clear and present danger" test had not been raised in the lower court and the Supreme Court then strictly followed the rule that it would not correct even fundamental errors when the parties had not raised the issue below. But there is no doubt that the Brandeis opinion did not agree with the majority in their holding that, as he summarized it, "assembling with a political party, formed to advocate the desirability of a proletarian revolution . . . is not a right within the protection of the Fourteenth Amendment." From this point of view, as indicated, the Brandeis opinion in *Whitney* was a dissent, not a concurrence.

To Brandeis, the protection of expression and advocacy was deeply rooted. The Framers, his *Whitney* opinion declares, "believed that freedom to think as you will and to speak as you think are means indispensable to the discovery and spread of political truth; that without free speech and assembly discussion would be futile; that with them, discussion affords ordinarily adequate protection against the dissemination of noxious doctrine; that the greatest menace to freedom is an inert people; that public discussion is a political duty; and that this should be a fundamental principle of the American government."

Nor was it enough that the California law was motivated by fear of Communist advocacy: "Fear of serious injury cannot alone justify suppression of free speech and assembly. Men feared witches and burnt women. It is the function of speech to free men from the bondage of irrational fears." Hence, "the path of safety lies in the opportunity to discuss freely supposed grievances and proposed remedies; and . . . the fitting remedy for evil counsels is good ones." The alternative is "silence coerced by law—the argument of force in its worst form."

The proper approach in such a case, Brandeis urged, is the "clear and present danger" test. And "no danger flowing from speech can be deemed clear and present, unless the incidence of the evil apprehended is so imminent that it may befall before there is opportunity for full discussion. If there be time to expose through discussion the falsehood and fallacies, to avert the evil by the processes of education, the remedy to be applied is more speech, not enforced silence. Only an emergency can justify repression. Such must be the rule if authority is to be reconciled with freedom. Such, in my opinion, is the command of the Constitution."

The Supreme Court itself has come to agree with the Brandeis opinion. *Brandenburg v. Ohio* struck down a law similar to that upheld in *Whitney*, the Court saying, "*Whitney* has been thoroughly discredited by later decisions." *Brandenburg* ruled invalid such a criminal syndicalism law, "which, by its own words and as applied, purports to punish mere advocacy."

Brandeis's *Whitney* opinion was more than a successful appeal to future law. It is, next to Holmes's *Abrams* dissent, the greatest Supreme Court statement on freedom of expression. As Brandeis's principal biographer, Alpheus T. Mason, normally restrained in his comments, glowingly put it, "In 1927, Brandeis summarized in undying words the sanctity of the constitutional protection afforded freedom of . . . speech."

7. Brandeis, J., in
Olmstead v. United States

Justice Brandeis was noted for his weighty opinions. Filled with what Justice Holmes once called "the knowledge and thoroughness with which he gathers together all manner of reports and documents," the Brandeis product was often heavy going. After he had read one such Brandeis draft, Holmes sent it back with the following comment: "This afternoon I was walking on the towpath and saw a cardinal. It seemed to me to be the first sign of spring. By the way, I concur."

Holmes's reaction was, however, inappropriate as far as the great Brandeis dissenting opinions are concerned. Brandeis's *Whitney* opinion, like Holmes's dissents themselves, are contributions to literature as well as law. That is equally true of Brandeis's dissent in *Olmstead v. United States* (1928)—the Justice's most notable opinion. Brandeis himself is one of the fathers of the right of privacy, as it is protected in modern American law. It was he who, in 1890 (more than two and a half decades before his elevation to the highest bench), was the author of a seminal article, *The Right to Privacy*, that was to serve as the starting point for judicial recognition of the right.

What Brandeis was advocating in 1890 was a right of privacy against infringement by other individuals—a right that would be vindicated by the traditional tort action for damages and for an injunction. In his *Olmstead* dissent, Justice Brandeis went much further and was speaking not of a common-law right against private individuals, but of a constitutional right against government itself. The *Olmstead* defendants had been convicted of conspiring to violate the federal prohibition law. Evidence had been obtained by telephone wiretapping. The Court ruled that such wiretapping by law-enforcement officers did not contravene the Fourth Amendment.

The Brandeis dissent was an eloquent plea to adapt constitutional protection to a changing world. The fact that the challenged police acts in *Olmstead* involved an intrusion on privacy utterly beyond the contemplation of the Framers should not be determinative in dealing with a revolutionary new communications invention. To Brandeis, the Fourth Amendment protection is not limited to "searches and seizures" only in the literal meaning those words had in 1789. Instead, the Constitution erected a wall against unjustifiable governmental intrusions on privacy. The Framers "conferred, as against the government, the right to be let alone—the most comprehensive of rights and the right most valued by civilized men. To protect that right, every unjustifiable intrusion by the government upon the privacy of the individual, whatever the means employed, must be deemed a violation of the Fourth Amendment."

Above all, the Brandeis dissent urged, government should not be permitted to profit by its own wrong. "Our government is the potent, the omnipresent teacher. For good or for ill, it teaches the whole people by its example. . . . If the government becomes a lawbreaker, it breeds contempt for law." The Court "should resolutely set its face" against the "pernicious doctrine . . . that in the administration of the criminal law the end justifies the means—to declare that the government may commit crimes in order to secure the conviction of a private criminal."

Since *Olmstead*, of course, we have had a veritable technological revolution under which the crude wiretapping in *Olmstead* has given way to today's electronic eavesdropping techniques, which, as Justice William J. Brennan said in 1963, "permit a degree of invasion of privacy that can only be described as frightening." This, too, was foreseen in the *Olmstead* dissent: "The progress of science in furnishing the government with means of espionage is not likely to stop with wire tapping. Ways may some day be developed by which the government, without removing papers from secret drawers, can reproduce them in court, and by which it will be enabled to expose to a jury the most intimate occurrences of the home."

The *Olmstead* majority ignored all this and denied the modern means of communication the protection extended by the Fourth Amendment to the more traditional communication by letter. When one bears in mind the indispensable role of the telephone in present-day life, it is scarcely surprising that *Olmstead* caused such dissatisfaction that Congress overruled it by a 1934 statute making wiretapping a federal crime.

The law made it unnecessary for the Supreme Court specifically to overrule *Olmstead*. Its rationale was, however, repudiated in *Katz v. United*

States (1967). The Court there ruled that "bugging" (through an electronic device attached to the outside of a public telephone booth) was a search against which individuals were protected by the Fourth Amendment. The reach of the amendment, said the Court, can no longer "turn upon the presence or absence of a physical intrusion." That being the case, electronic eavesdropping, like the more traditional physical search, is no longer permissible unless authorized by a warrant—essentially the rule urged by Justice Brandeis in his *Olmstead* dissent.

8. Brandeis, J., in
New State Ice Co. v. Liebmann

Justices Holmes and Brandeis formed the most famous dissenting team in judicial history. Yet although they agreed on the proper approach to judicial review of regulatory laws, they differed on the merits of economic regulation. Justice Frankfurter once wrote that Holmes "privately distrusted attempts at improving society by what he deemed futile if not mischievous economic tinkering. But that was not his business." Yet it was emphatically Brandeis's business throughout his career.

Both on and off the bench, Brandeis was a leader in the movement to ensure that law mirrored society at large in its transition from laissez-faire to the welfare state. Before his Court appointment, Brandeis asserted, "Regulation . . . is necessary to the preservation and best development of liberty. . . . the right to competition must be limited in order to preserve it."

On the Supreme Court, the Brandeis approach to regulation was best expressed in his dissent in *New State Ice Co. v. Liebmann* (1932). A state law required a license (called a certificate of convenience and necessity) for entry into the business of manufacturing and selling ice. The licensing agency was forbidden to issue a license except upon proof of the necessity for a supply of ice at the place where it was sought to establish the business, and was to deny the application where the existing licensed facilities "are sufficient to meet the public needs therein."

The Court ruled invalid the licensing requirement for the ice business. The business of manufacturing and selling ice—like that of the grocer, the dairyman, the butcher, or the baker—was said to be an ordinary business, essentially private in its nature, and hence not so charged with a public interest as to justify the licensing restriction.

In his dissent, Justice Brandeis spelled out the legal and economic bases for licensing regulation such as the requirement at issue. Regulation, he contended, was necessary to ensure the proper working of the competitive system: "The introduction in the United States of the certificate of public convenience and necessity marked the growing conviction that under certain circumstances free competition might be harmful to the community, and that, when it was so, absolute freedom to enter the business of one's choice should be denied."

In this case, Brandeis asserted, the license requirement could be imposed because of the nature of the business involved: "The business of supplying ice is not only a necessity, like that of supplying food or clothing or shelter, but the Legislature could also consider that it is one which lends itself peculiarly to monopoly." Duplication of ice plants was wasteful and led "to destructive and frequently ruinous competition," which was "ultimately burdensome to consumers." There was a need of some remedy for the evil of destructive competition. "Can it be said in the light of these facts," asked the Brandeis dissent, "that it was not an appropriate exercise of legislative discretion to authorize the commission to deny a license to enter the business in localities where necessity for another plant did not exist?"

Here, too, the Brandeis approach was to be adopted in Supreme Court jurisprudence. The prevailing theme has become that stated in the Brandeis dissent: "Our function is only to determine the reasonableness of the Legislature's belief in the existence of evils and in the effectiveness of the remedy provided. In performing this function we have no occasion to consider whether all the statements of fact which may be the basis of the prevailing belief are well-founded; and we have, of course, no right to weigh conflicting evidence."

The Brandeis rationale for regulation in *New State Ice* has all but taken over the field during the past half-century. But the *New State Ice* dissent is now recalled even more because of the statement by Brandeis of the states as laboratories: "It is one of the happy incidents of the federal system that a single courageous state may, if its citizens choose, serve as a laboratory; and try novel social and economic experiments without risk to the rest of the country." The Brandeis concept here has become one of the foundations of what is compendiously called the New Federalism.

9. Stone, J., in *United States v. Butler*

From 1934 to 1936, the Supreme Court struck down the most important early New Deal regulatory measures. All these decisions were delivered over vigorous dissents by Justices Stone, Brandeis, and Cardozo—and, at times, Chief Justice Hughes. The outstanding opinion objecting to the restrictive New Deal decisions was Justice Harlan F. Stone's dissent in *United States v. Butler* (1936). At issue was the Agricultural Adjustment Act (AAA) of 1933. It sought to eliminate overproduction by paying farmers to curtail production. A processing tax was levied on agricultural commodities, and the proceeds were used to pay farmers who agreed to limit production. The AAA was ruled invalid because it attempted to regulate local production under the guise of an exercise of the taxing power. That power might not be used to accomplish regulation of agricultural production, which (under the decisions at that time) was beyond the scope of congressional commerce power.

In *Butler*, an otherwise valid exercise of the taxing power was condemned because of what the Court found to be the underlying purpose. As the Stone dissent put it, "[A] levy unquestionably within the taxing power of Congress [is] invalid because it is a step in a plan to regulate agricultural production and is thus a forbidden infringement of state power." The tax was void because it was actuated by an improper motive. "The present levy," said Stone, "is held invalid, not for any want of power in Congress to lay such a tax to defray public expenditures, including those for the general welfare, but because the use to which its proceeds are put is disapproved."

Few things are more dangerous than for a court to invalidate legislative acts on the ground of improper underlying purpose, with the judges the censors of congressional motives. The *Butler* approach may, indeed, render ineffective the federal power to further the general welfare. In Stone's apt words,

> The limitation now sanctioned must lead to absurd consequences. The government may give seeds to farmers, but may not condition the gift upon their being planted in places where they are most needed or even planted at all. The government may give money to the unemployed, but may not ask that those who get it shall give labor in return, or even use it to support their families. It may give money to sufferers from earthquake, fire, tornado, pestilence, or flood, but may not impose conditions, health precautions, designed to prevent the spread of disease. . . . All that, because it is purchased regulation infringing state powers, must be left for the states, who are unable or unwilling to supply the necessary relief.

It is not, however, because of its mere rebuttal of the majority decision that the *Butler* dissent has become a classic. The Stone opinion marks the culmination of the pre-1937 judicial restraint theme originally sounded by

Justices Holmes and Brandeis. In a letter on *Butler,* Stone commented, "We see it frequently enough in the common untrained mind, which is accustomed to think that legislation which it regards as bad or unwise must necessarily be unconstitutional." To Stone, the *Butler* majority had followed the same approach. The Court, asserted Stone's dissent, had ignored the "guiding principle . . . which ought never to be absent from judicial consciousness. . . . that courts are concerned only with the power to enact statutes, not with their wisdom."

Here, Stone urged, the Court had stricken congressional power specifically granted "by judicial fiat" and "a tortured construction of the Constitution." The majority had acted on the assumption "that it is the business of courts to sit in judgment on the wisdom of legislative action." It should, however, be remembered, the dissent declared, that "Courts are not the only agency of government that must be assumed to have capacity to govern." Instead, "while unconstitutional exercise of power by the executive and legislative branches of the government is subject to judicial restraint, the only check upon our own exercise of power is our own sense of self-restraint." For "unwise laws . . . appeal lies, not to the courts, but to the ballot and to the processes of democratic government."

"Never before," a *New York Times* article on *Butler* noted, "has a dissenting minority gone quite so far toward calling into question the motives of the majority and clearly implying that they have abused their judicial prerogative."

10. Black, J., in *Adamson v. California*

The most recent great dissent, by Justice Hugo L. Black in *Adamson v. California* (1947), presents a paradox: even though the Black dissent was wrong in its reasoning, it transformed the law on the question at issue. That question starts with the 1833 decision that held that the federal Bill of Rights (the first eight amendments to the constitution) limited only the federal government, not the states. However, the Fourteenth Amendment, adopted in 1868, prohibits the states from denying due process to any person. To what extent does this due process clause protect against state interference with individual rights? More specifically, does the Fourteenth Amendment's due process clause incorporate the Bill of Rights so as to make its protections binding on the states as well as the federal government?

Since 1884, the Court had rejected the view that the Fourteenth Amendment absorbed all the provisions of the Bill of Rights and hence placed on the states the specific limitations that the first eight amendments had theretofore placed on the federal government. In *Adamson v. California*, Justice Black refused to follow this more than half-century of uniform precedents. Defendant in *Adamson* had been convicted under a California procedure permitting the failure of the accused to testify to be commented on by court and counsel and to be considered by the jury. The Supreme Court assumed that such a procedure would violate the Fifth Amendment privilege against self-incrimination if this were a federal trial. However, repeating the holding that the due process clause of the Fourteenth Amendment did not draw the Bill of Rights as such within its scope, the Court decided that the California procedure did not violate the Constitution.

This decision called forth the vigorous dissent by Justice Black. Rather than accept the view of the majority, he declared, "I would follow what I believe was the original purpose of the Fourteenth Amendment—to extend to all the people of the nation the complete protection of the Bill of Rights."

To support his interpretation, Black added a lengthy appendix to his dissent "which contains a resume of the [Fourteenth] Amendment's history." It is, however, fair to say that all historians who have examined the matter (including myself) have concluded that the legislative history of the amendment does not substantiate the Black conclusion that it was intended to make the Bill of Rights binding on the states. And, as indicated, all the case law on the question was the other way.

Justice Black was thus wrong on both the history and the law. Despite this (and here we have the paradox), Black's opinion turned out to be one of the most influential dissents ever delivered. Not that the Court has overruled *Adamson* and held that the Fourteenth Amendment incorporates the Bill of Rights as such into its Due Process Clause. To the contrary, Black's *Adamson* position has never been able to command a Court majority. Black's prodding, nevertheless, led the Justices increasingly to expand the scope of the Fourteenth Amendment's due process clause. Since *Adamson*, the meaning of due process has become flexible enough to accomplish virtually the result Black had urged in his *Adamson* dissent, absorbing one by one almost all the individual guarantees of the Bill of Rights into the due process clause. By the end of Black's judicial tenure, the rights that had been held binding on the states under the Fourteenth Amendment included all the rights guaranteed by the Bill of Rights except the right to a grand jury indictment and that to a jury trial in civil cases involving more than $20.

Moreover, the Black dissent has served as a catalyst for the new emphasis, starting with the Warren Court, on protection of personal rights against the states. To the claim that that would unduly expand the Court's power, the *Adamson* dissent replied, "The Federal Government has not been harmfully burdened by the requirement that enforcement of federal laws affecting civil liberty conform literally to the Bill of Rights. Who would advocate its repeal?"

In *Adamson*, Black rejected the view that the Bill of Rights is "an outworn 18th Century 'strait jacket.'" To some, "its provisions may be thought outdated abstractions. . . . And it is true that they were designed to meet ancient evils." But, Black eloquently declared, "they are the same kind of human evils that have emerged from century to century wherever excessive power is sought by the few at the expense of the many. In my judgment the people of no nation can lose their liberty so long as a Bill of Rights like ours survives and its basic purposes are conscientiously interpreted, enforced and respected so as to afford continuous protection against old, as well as new, devices and practices which might thwart those purposes."

By opinions such as his *Adamson* dissent, Justice Black as much as anyone changed the very way Americans think about law. If the focus of juristic inquiry has shifted from duties to rights, if personal rights have been elevated to the preferred plane—that has in large part been the result of the Black jurisprudence. The Black legacy is to be found in the totality of today's judicial awareness of the Bill of Rights and the law's newfound sensitivity to liberty and equality. Black as much as any Justice has helped make the Bill of Rights the vital center of our law.

Dissents and Great Cases

Justice Holmes is, of course, still known as the "great dissenter"; his reputation rests, in large part, on his dissents. It is, however, erroneous to assume that Holmes delivered more dissents than other Justices. In fact, on a list of those who have written the most dissenting opinions, Holmes is down in eleventh place. His total was only 72 (compared with the 486 dissents of Justice William O. Douglas, the author of the greatest number of dissents).

The greatness of Justice Holmes as a dissenter lay in the fact that he did not dissent merely for dissent's sake. This was acutely seen by Sir Frederick Pollock, the Justice's English correspondent. "Some people seem to think that Mr. Justice Holmes is always dissenting," his comment reads. "Does he really dissent much oftener than his learned brethren, or is the impression due to the weight rather than the number of the dissents?"

In reality, as students of Holmes's life and character have concluded, he himself hated to dissent; he by no means desired to be known as fighter, reformer, or dissenter. This is clear from his very first dissent on the Supreme Court. After stating, at the beginning of that opinion, that he was unable to agree with the majority judgment, he went on to assert, "I think it useless and undesirable, as a rule, to express dissent."

Why, then, did Holmes express dissent and give his reasons for it? The answer is to be found in the very next sentence of his opinion: "Great cases like hard cases make bad law." A judge is, in other words, justified in expressing his own views in dissent, when the particular decision disposes of a "great case" or a "hard case." But if the case is an ordinary one, that does not shape the law, a separate statement is not justified merely because the judge may happen to disagree with his colleagues.

With the possible exception of the *Adamson* dissent, all the dissents on my list were delivered in great cases—and the issue in *Adamson* was a "great" one. More than that, in these cases, the dissents pointed the way to the law of the future. In all of them, not only the court of history, but the law itself, has adopted the view stated by the dissenters. Perhaps this was not technically true of the *Adamson* dissent; yet there too, we saw, the Court has followed the substance, if not the exact form, of the Black dissenting approach.

The best of our dissents, we saw, were masterpieces of the English language—examples of literary, as well as legal, craftsmanship. All of them contributed more to the law—albeit the law of the future—than the decisions with which they disagreed. All produced a positive effect upon jurisprudence. These were cases where the creative element in the dissenting process found its opportunity and power.

6

TEN

GREATEST

SUPREME COURT

"MIGHT HAVE BEENS"

For of all sad words of tongue or pen,
The saddest are these: "It might have been."
John Greenleaf Whittier, "Maud Muller"

One interested in the "might have been" can find ample store for reflection in the history of the Supreme Court. Throughout its history, cases decided by the Court were close to having been decided differently. This has been true of both leading cases and lesser-known ones—some of them now of interest only to Supreme Court specialists. In many, the vote the other way had already been taken, a draft opinion of the Court in accordance therewith prepared, and the decision ready to be announced. Then a switch in votes, a change in the grounds for decision, the illness or resignation of a Justice, or some other last-minute factor resulted in a changed decision and a new opinion explaining it.

There is also a broader type of "might have been" in Supreme Court history that is even more consequential than its effect on particular decisions, however significant they may be. The most important of them has to do with the personnel of the Court itself. Had vacancies not occurred and been filled as they were, the history of the Court would have been entirely different. It may, indeed, be said that, but for fortuitous circumstances, the two greatest Chief Justices would never have been appointed. Instead of the Marshall and Warren Courts, we would have had Courts headed by two entirely different men. Think what that would have meant not only to our law, but to the history of the nation itself.

— ★ — ★ — ★ —

Ten Greatest Supreme Court "Might Have Beens"

1. John Marshall as Chief Justice

2. Earl Warren as Chief Justice

3. *Marbury v. Madison*

4. *Brown v. Board of Education*

5. *Dred Scott v. Sandford*

6. *Lochner v. New York*

7. *Baker v. Carr*

8. *Roe v. Wade*, 410 U.S. 113 (1973)

9. *Webster v. Reproductive Health Services*, 492 U.S. 90 (1989)

10. *Mapp v. Ohio*, 367 U.S. 643 (1961)

1. John Marshall as Chief Justice

The first Chief Justices accepted extrajudicial duties that seriously interfered with their Court work. Thus, a 1989 opinion tells us, "the first Chief Justice, John Jay, served simultaneously as Chief Justice and as Ambassador to England, where he negotiated the treaty that bears his name. [His successor] Oliver Ellsworth served simultaneously as Chief Justice and as Minister to France." His extrajudicial service had a serious effect on Chief Justice Ellsworth's health. Not in the best of condition when he was appointed, Ellsworth's health completely broke down on his journey to France. The result was that, on October 16, 1800, Ellsworth sent a letter resigning as Chief Justice to President John Adams.

By the time the resignation letter reached him, Adams had lost the 1800 election to Thomas Jefferson. In the interim before the new president took office, Adams was able to appoint John Marshall as Chief Justice. Marshall's appointment was one of the happy accidents that changed the course of history. To appreciate its fortuitous nature, we have to go back to even before Ellsworth's resignation. When the first Chief Justice, John Jay, resigned in 1795, President Washington nominated William Cushing, a member of the first Court, in his place. Then, as summarized by John Adams in a letter to his wife, "Judge Cushing declines the place of Chief-Justice on Account of his Age and declining Health." Had Justice Cushing not declined the appointment or had Chief Justice Ellsworth not made the arduous journey to France, there would have been no vacancy in the Chief Justiceship until after President Adams's term had expired. But, even with them, Marshall's appointment was not ensured. After Ellsworth's resignation, the president offered his place to John Jay. The Senate confirmed the appointment, and had Jay accepted, there would, of course, still have been no place for Marshall. Jay, however, also refused the position because he wanted to retire to his farm in Bedford, New York.

After Jay declined the Chief Justiceship, it was widely expected that the President would nominate Justice William Paterson. Marshall himself recommended Paterson. Adams, however, refused to select him because he belonged to the Hamiltonian faction of his party.

Marshall tells us what happened next in an autobiographical sketch: "When I waited on the President with Mr. Jays letter declining the appointment, he said thoughtfully, 'Who shall I nominate now'? I replied that I could not tell, as I supposed that his objection to Judge Paterson remained. He said in a decided tone 'I shall not nominate him.' After a moments hesitation he said 'I believe I must nominate you.' . . . Next day I was nominated."

The Ellsworth breakdown not only gave Adams the opportunity to appoint Marshall, but also deprived Jefferson of the opportunity to appoint the Chief Justice. Had Ellsworth sent in his resignation a little later, the new president would have been able to choose the Court head. It is well known that Jefferson had planned to appoint Spencer Roane, head of the highest Virginia court, as Chief Justice. Marshall and Roane differed drastically in their constitutional approaches. In particular, the two asserted opposing views on what Woodrow Wilson was to call "the cardinal question of our time"—"the question of the relation of the States to the federal government." Marshall was, of course, the great exponent of the national conception of governmental power, elevating that view to the supreme law of the land. Roane had a diametrically opposed view of the legitimate sphere of federal authority. He has been called "the most energetic states' right ideologue of all."

Roane's appointment would have meant the defeat of Marshall's constitutional principles. Unlike Marshall, Roane shared the Jeffersonian vision of national development—emphasizing an idealistic agrarianism instead of the emerging centralizing capitalism. Jefferson had urged the danger of a consolidated government, which invariably tended toward self-aggrandizement—with the inevitable result a political Leviathan. The danger could be avoided by circumscribing central power and emphasizing states' rights.

Marshall's vision was entirely different. For him, what was required was a truly national government that would meet the needs of an expanding people and promote the physical and economic conquest of the continent. The sovereignty of the nation was the fixed conception that dominated Marshall's judicial tenure. His constitutional jurisprudence was consistently molded to give effect to this overriding conception.

The landmark decisions of the Marshall Court would have been decided far differently under Chief Justice Roane. As Marshall's leading biographer summarized it, "Had [Roane] become Chief Justice those cases in which Marshall delivered opinions that vitalized the Constitution would have been decided in direct opposition to Marshall's views."

If President Adams had not been given the opportunity to appoint Marshall, not only our law but the very development of the nation might have been entirely different.

2. Earl Warren as Chief Justice

Soon after the 1952 election, President-elect Dwight D. Eisenhower told California Governor Earl Warren, "I intend to offer you the first vacancy on the Supreme Court." A half year later, the governor accepted an offer by President Eisenhower to appoint him as solicitor general. It had been some time since Warren had actively practiced law, and service as solicitor general—the officer who handled government cases in the Supreme Court—would be valuable prior to membership on the Court.

Warren did not, however, become solicitor general. His prospects dramatically changed when Chief Justice Fred M. Vinson died unexpectedly of a heart attack in September 1953. Vinson's death was a complete surprise. No one expected, or had grounds to expect, the vacancy in the Court's central chair. Vinson was only sixty-three, in apparent good health, and came from a notably long-lived family.

Had Vinson not died when he did, Warren could not have been named Chief Justice. Yet even Vinson's sudden death did not necessarily mean that Warren would be appointed. True, President Eisenhower had promised to appoint Warren to the first Supreme Court opening. But did Eisenhower's commitment apply to the Chief Justiceship? The president himself doubted that it did. In fact, Eisenhower wrote in his memoirs, "I gave serious thought to the possibility of appointing John Foster Dulles." The president spoke to the secretary of state, but the latter said that he was not interested in any other position. If Dulles had given a different answer, Warren could not, of course, have been appointed.

Eisenhower then discussed with Attorney General Herbert Brownell whether any member of the Court should be appointed Chief Justice. Justice Robert H. Jackson was mentioned, but the president felt that his Republican administration could hardly appoint a Democrat to head the Court. The only Republican then on the Court was Justice Harold H. Burton. However, he scarcely had the leadership ability to make the president consider him seriously. Had there been another Republican Justice who did have that ability, he might have been chosen and Warren again would have been barred.

The lack of a candidate among the Justices meant that the appointment would have to go to someone not on the Court. But would that someone be Warren? The president was still reluctant to appoint him to head the Court. Eisenhower asked Brownell to fly to California to sound out Warren. The attorney general told the governor that his commitment applied only to an ordinary Court vacancy. Warren, says Brownell in his memoirs, "made it plain that he regarded the present vacancy as the 'next vacancy.'" The next day, the president chose Warren.

It took a concatenation of fortuitous circumstances for Warren to be appointed. If Chief Justice Vinson had not unexpectedly died when he did, if John Foster Dulles had desired his place, if there had been a Republican Justice who deserved the promotion, if Warren had not insisted and the president had chosen some other nominee—Warren would never have become Chief Justice.

If that had happened, there never would have been a Warren Court. Instead, either Chief Justice Vinson would have continued in his position or someone else would have been chosen to fill his place. What, then, would have happened to Warren?

Warren as solicitor general would still have had Eisenhower's commitment on the next Supreme Court vacancy. Would he then have been appointed Chief Justice if a vacancy in that office occurred? That is most unlikely. Although Warren was a resounding success as Chief Justice, he would scarcely have been the same as a mere Associate Justice. But for Chief Justice Vinson's death, Warren might have served out his career as only a mediocre member of the Court. And that, in Robert Frost's phrase, would have "made all the difference." Without Warren, there would have been no Warren Court, any more than there would have been a Marshall Court had President Adams not been able to name John Marshall when he did.

3. *Marbury v. Madison*

If the fortuitous events that enabled John Marshall to become Chief Justice had not occurred, the decision in *Marbury v. Madison* (1803) would never have been made. But there is another *Marbury* "might have been" that does not depend on Marshall's appointment.

Marbury is now rightly considered the very keystone of the constitutional arch, for, in it, the Supreme Court first ruled that it possessed the authority to review the constitutionality of laws. Yet when the case came before the Court, it seemed to present anything but the question of judicial review. William Marbury, who had been appointed to be a District of Columbia judge by President Adams at the very end of his administration, had been confirmed by the Senate; his commission had been signed and sealed, but had not yet been delivered when Jefferson took office. The new president ordered James Madison, just designated secretary of state, to withhold the commission. Marbury then applied directly to the

Supreme Court for a writ of mandamus ordering the secretary to deliver the commission. He did so under section 13 of the Judiciary Act of 1789, which vested the highest Court with jurisdiction to issue mandamus against federal officials.

In form, all that *Marbury v. Madison* appeared to present was the question of whether mandamus could issue in such a case against the secretary of state. In answering it, the Supreme Court could apparently either disavow its power over the executive branch and dismiss the application or assert such a power and order the commission to be delivered. To choose the first course would have been to abdicate the essentials of "The judicial Power" conferred by the Constitution. But the second was no more satisfactory. For while it would declare the vindication of authority to hold the executive to the law, the declaration would, without a doubt, remain a mere paper one. There was no way for the Court to enforce its mandate against the administration. In fact, bearing in mind the low esteem in which the Court was then still held, it is doubtful that it could have emerged other than fatally wounded from a direct clash with the executive. Hence, as Marshall's leading biographer puts it, no matter which horn of the dilemma Marshall selected, it was hard to see how his views could escape impalement.

That Marshall was able to choose neither is perhaps the best tribute to his judicial statesmanship. He escaped from the dilemma by convincing his Brethren of the unconstitutionality of section 13 of the Judiciary Act on the ground that, since the original jurisdiction conferred on the Supreme Court by the Constitution was exclusive, it could not validly be enlarged by statute. Thus the Court could deny Marbury's application, not because the executive branch was above the law (Marshall's opinion, on the contrary, contains a strong repudiation of that claim), but because the Court itself did not possess the original jurisdiction to issue the writ requested.

The holding that section 13 was unconstitutional had been raised neither by the parties nor by any of the Justices during the argument of the case. But Marshall was able to assert the judicial power to review constitutionality in a manner that could not be directly challenged. From a strategic point of view, a better case could not have been chosen for declaration of the power. Since the Court's decision denied relief, there was nothing to execute—nothing that would give rise to direct conflict with the Jefferson administration. More than that, the assertion of the greatest of all judicial powers was made in a case that ostensibly denied authority to the Court. The Jeffersonians themselves found it hard to attack a decision that declined, even from the hands of Congress, jurisdiction to which the Court was not entitled by the Constitution.

If *Marbury v. Madison* had been decided only on the issues presented to the Court, our constitutional system might have been very different. Had Marshall not confirmed the review power at the outset, it might never have been established. For it was not until the *Dred Scott* case in 1857 that the authority to invalidate a federal statute was next exercised by the Supreme Court. Had Marshall not taken his stand in *Marbury v. Madison*, nearly sixty years would have passed without any question arising as to the omnipotence of Congress. After so long a period of judicial acquiescence in congressional supremacy, opposition to it might well have been futile.

4. *Brown v. Board of Education*

Of course, the Warren Court's outstanding "might have been" was the decision in *Brown v. Board of Education* (1954). Had Chief Justice Vinson not died when he did, he would have presided over the Court that decided *Brown*. We saw, in our discussion of Vinson, that he would have led the Court to uphold segregation. As he put it at the *Brown* conference that he headed, he "can't say that schools shouldn't be separate." To the contrary, Vinson indicated that he favored following the *Plessy v. Ferguson* (1896) decision, refusing to strike down segregation. Indeed, Justice William O. Douglas wrote in a contemporary memorandum, "Vinson was of the opinion that the *Plessy* case was right and that segregation was constitutional." Hence, Douglas wrote, with Vinson as Chief Justice, "it is apparent that . . . there would probably have been many opinions and a wide divergence of views and a result that would have sustained, so far as the States were concerned, segregation of students."

The same would probably have been true if President Eisenhower had appointed one of the men whom he was considering, in preference to Earl Warren, as Vinson's successor. John Foster Dulles, who, Eisenhower said, had turned down the appointment, was a conservative Republican lawyer who was not likely to take the activist role needed to turn the *Brown* Court around. The same was true of the Republican judges who, Attorney General Brownell wrote in his memoirs, were turned down because of age or poor health. If Dulles or one of those judges had been selected, it is most improbable that *Brown* would have been decided as it was.

Great men do make a difference even in the law. It took Chief Justice Warren to make *Brown* turn out the way it did. Just before the *Brown* decision was announced, Justice Harold H. Burton wrote in his diary, "It looks like a unanimous opinion—a major accomplishment for his [Warren's] leadership." This was no more than a statement of fact. More than most commentators have realized, the unanimous decision outlawing segregation was the direct result of Warren's leadership. He was responsible not only for the *Brown* opinion, but for the unanimous decision.

Had Chief Justice Vinson not died when he did, had Dulles not turned down the nomination, or had President Eisenhower appointed one of the others he considered, there would not only have been no Warren Court. Without Chief Justice Warren's leadership, there would have been no ringing invalidation of segregation by a unanimous bench. Certainly, had Chief Justice Vinson still headed the Court, *Brown* would have been decided differently than it was, with segregation probably upheld by a fragmented 5 to 4 decision—a result well characterized in a Frankfurter letter as "catastrophic." Without the unanimous *Brown* decision, both our law and our society might be very different. The transformation that has occurred in both, catalyzed by *Brown* itself, might never have gotten off the ground.

5. *Dred Scott v. Sandford*

Dred Scott v. Sandford (1857) is a prime example of a Supreme Court "might have been" that almost *was*. Scott had originally brought suit in a Missouri court for his freedom, arguing that his prior service in Illinois and in the Wisconsin Territory, from which slavery had been excluded by the Missouri Compromise enacted by Congress, made him a free man. The Missouri Supreme Court held that Missouri law governed the case, and under it Scott was still a slave. Scott then sued in a federal court in Missouri as a citizen of that state. The case came to the Supreme Court on appeal from a judgment against Scott.

After the first *Dred Scott* conference, Justice Benjamin R. Curtis wrote to his uncle, "The court will not decide the question of the Missouri Compromise line—a majority of the judges being of the opinion that it is not necessary to do so." At the conference, a majority were of the opinion that the case should be decided without consideration of the two crucial issues presented: blacks' citizenship and congressional power to prohibit slavery in the territories specified by the Missouri Compromise. The conference felt that the issue of citizenship was not properly before them and also took the position that they need not consider the Missouri Compromise because Scott's status was a matter for Missouri law and had already been determined against him by the state's highest court. Justice Samuel Nelson was selected to write an opinion disposing of the case in this manner, and he did write such an opinion.

Had the Nelson opinion (limiting itself to Scott's status under Missouri law after his return to that state) prevailed as the opinion of the Court, the *Dred Scott* case would scarcely be known today except to the curious student of Supreme Court miscellany. The Justices, however, were to abandon their initial resolve to decide the case without considering the issues of citizenship or slavery in the territories. The change was brought about by Justice James M. Wayne, a Georgian who, while serving as a judge in Savannah, had sentenced an offender for "keeping a school for Negroes." Two years before *Dred Scott*, he had declared that there was no possibility that even free blacks "can be made partakers of the political and civil institutions of the states, or those of the United States." As Justice Curtis later recalled it, "it was urged upon the court, by Judge Wayne, how very important it was to get rid of the question of slavery in the Territories, by a decision of the Supreme Court, and that this was a good opportunity of doing so."

Justice Wayne moved in conference that the decision deal with the two vital issues that Justice Nelson was omitting. "My own and decided opinion," he said, "is that the Chief Justice should prepare the opinion on behalf of the court upon all of the questions in the record." The five who voted in favor of Wayne's motion were from slave states. Wayne himself told a southern senator that he had "gained a triumph for the southern section of the country, by persuading the chief-justice that the court could put an end to all further agitation on the subject of slavery in the territories."

Justice Curtis, on the contrary, according to a book by his brother, "in the conferences of the court, explained in the strongest terms that such a result, instead of putting an end to the agitation in the North, would only increase it." In addition, Curtis stressed that it was "most unadvisable to have it understood that the decision of these very grave and serious constitutional questions had been influenced by considerations of expediency." The fact that the votes for the new decision were by Southerners would lead to anything but Wayne's conference prediction that "the settlement . . . by judicial decision" would result in "the peace and harmony of the country." Instead, as Horace Greeley wrote in the *New York Tribune*, settlement of the slavery issue by the Court meant submitting it to five slaveholders, and "I would rather trust a dog with my dinner."

As it turned out, of course, Justice Curtis proved correct. "The *New York Herald* remarked editorially," the leading history of the Taney Court tells us, "that although officially this was a case involving the freedom of a nigger of the name of *Dred Scott*, the people were beginning to say that the . . . Supreme Court was on trial." More than that, the *Dred Scott* decision is considered by most historians to be one of the factors that hastened the conflict that soon took place.

Might all of this have been avoided if Justice Nelson's opinion had come down as the opinion of the Court? Certainly that would have prevented the tarnishing of the Court's reputation and the judicial nadir that lasted for a generation after *Dred Scott*. But no Supreme Court decision could have made a difference to the onset of the Civil War. The *Dred Scott* Court expected too much of judicial power—too readily accepting the notion that the controversy that was tearing the nation apart could be settled in the forum. We should not make the mistake of assuming that judicial abstention alone could have helped prevent the ultimate resolution of that controversy.

6. *Lochner v. New York*

If not for a vote switch, one of the most discredited Supreme Court decisions would have been decided differently. At the first *Lochner v. New York* (1905) conference, the Justices voted by a bare majority to uphold the maximum-hours law for bakery workers. The case was assigned to the first Justice John Marshall Harlan, who wrote a draft opinion of the Court. Justice Rufus Peckham wrote a strong draft dissent. Before the decision came down, however, there was a vote switch. The Peckham dissent became the opinion of the Court, and the Harlan opinion a dissent. It is not known who changed his vote. The probability is that it was Chief Justice Melville W. Fuller. Although Fuller had voted to uphold other maximum-hour laws, his biographer tells us, "the ten-hour law for bakers seemed to him to be 'featherbedding,' paternalistic, and depriving both the worker and employer of fundamental liberties."

The other cases in which laws regulating hours of labor had been sustained were treated by the Court as health measures. In *Lochner*, it has been suggested, Justice Joseph McKenna, whose father had owned a bakery, persuaded Fuller and others in the majority that bakery work was not dangerous and that the health rationale was a sham. Justice Peckham himself needed no persuading. His *Lochner* opinion of the Court is the groundwork for this century's early jurisprudence striking down regulatory laws.

If there had been no vote switch and the Harlan opinion had come down as the Court opinion, it might have made a substantial difference.

Without *Lochner* as a foundation, the restrictive decisions that followed its approach might not have been made. Instead of the *Lochner* approach to judicial review, the cases might have followed that in what would have been the Harlan opinion of the Court—presumably the one taken in what is now Justice Harlan's dissent.

Lochner then would have stressed not liberty of contract, but the police power, under which, as the Harlan dissent puts it, "liberty of contract may . . . be subjected to regulations . . . to promote the general welfare, or to guard the public health." More than that, Harlan emphasized the "large discretion . . . vested in the legislature" to enact reasonable regulations to protect public health. "Whether or not this be wise legislation it is not the province of the court to inquire." To the contrary, Harlan wrote, "It is enough for the determination of this case, and it is enough for this court to know, that the question is one about which there is room for debate and for an honest difference of opinion." If this early statement of judicial restraint had been contained in an opinion of the Court upholding the law challenged in *Lochner*, volumes of now-discredited jurisprudence might never have been written.

It is, of course, also true that had there had been no *Lochner* vote switch, the Holmes dissent would never have been written. That would have deprived us of what most now consider one of the greatest dissenting opinions. The loss would, however, be more to literature than to law. If the Harlan opinion had been the opinion of the Court, it would—more pedestrian though it was—have contained the essentials of the Holmes restraint posture and might have established it in the law decades before the Court adopted it.

7. *Baker v. Carr*

Baker v. Carr (1962) held that actions challenging legislative apportionments could be brought in the federal courts. That holding served as the basis for the rule laid down in *Reynolds v. Sims* (1964) that the Constitution requires both houses of a state legislature to be apportioned on the basis of equality of population among districts. However, had Justice Tom C. Clark switched his *Baker* vote earlier, the Court might have decided on a different apportionment rule that would have had a less drastic effect.

Baker v. Carr presented two issues: jurisdiction, and the merits of the constitutional claim. The conference originally divided 4 to 4 on whether to reverse the lower-court decision that it had no jurisdiction over the case. After reargument, Justice Potter Stewart, who had been undecided, voted to reverse. However, Stewart went out of his way to emphasize that he would agree only to decide that the district court had jurisdiction. The other four in the majority (Warren, Black, Douglas, and Brennan) wanted to go beyond the jurisdictional issue. They also wanted to decide the merits and hold that the challenged apportionment law violated the equal protection clause. Their view was that, as Justice Frankfurter summarized in a letter at the time, "the Fourteenth Amendment . . . requires what Hugo called 'approximately fair' distribution or weight in votes."

Justice Stewart, as stated, would vote for reversal only if the decision was limited to the holding that the district court had jurisdiction. Since Stewart's vote was then necessary for the bare majority in favor of reversal, the Chief Justice and the other three agreed that Justice Brennan would limit his draft opinion to the jurisdictional issue.

At the conference (held in October 1961), Justice Clark had voted to affirm the decision that the lower court had no jurisdiction. After the Brennan draft opinion of the Court was circulated in January 1962, Clark stated that he was going to write in dissent. Then, in March, Clark switched his vote. He wrote a concurrence not only agreeing that there was jurisdiction, but also stating that he would invalidate the apportionment law on the merits. Clark tried to persuade Justice Brennan to change his opinion to also hold the law unconstitutional. Brennan refused, saying that he had given an undertaking to Justice Stewart that he would not do so. Stewart himself indicated to Brennan that he would not agree to any changes of importance. In a memorandum to Chief Justice Warren and Justices Black and Douglas, Brennan informed them that he and Stewart had discussed the changes requested by Clark. "Potter felt that if they were made it would be necessary for him to dissent from that much of the revised opinion. I therefore decided it was best not to press for the changes."

When Brennan announced the *Baker* decision, the opinion of the Court was substantially that which Stewart had joined before Clark changed his vote. If Clark had switched his vote earlier and been with the majority at the October 1961 conference, that would have made for a majority without Stewart's vote. That majority would have voted not only to exercise jurisdiction, but also to decide the constitutionality of the apportionment law.

If that had happened, it would have meant a different rule of equality in apportionments than that enunciated two years later in *Reynolds v. Sims*. At the time of *Baker v. Carr*, those who favored the requirement of what Justice Black called "approximately fair" weight in votes were willing to apply that requirement to only one house of the legislature. Chief Justice Warren, in particular, was swayed by the situation in California where only the Assembly was apportioned by population, while the Senate represented counties equally, regardless of population. He had thought that the system worked well when he was governor and was reluctant to strike it down completely at the time of *Baker*.

Thus if the merits had been decided in *Baker v. Carr*, the Court would have held that only lower-house apportionments not based on equality of population were invalid. They would have upheld unequal apportionments—based, for example, on geographical areas such as counties—for the upper houses of state legislatures. This would have made for a substantial difference in apportionment law and, through it, the distribution of political power in state legislatures. Instead of the transfer of power to urban and suburban areas that has occurred under the *Reynolds v. Sims* one-person, one-vote rule, there would still be room for rural dominance of state senates. The *Reynolds v. Sims* political death warrant for countless rural senators, whose seats have been reapportioned out of existence, would never have been issued.

8. *Roe v. Wade*

Roe v. Wade (1973) was the most controversial Supreme Court decision during the past half-century. Few decisions ever handed down were more bitterly attacked. Justice Harry A. Blackmun, the author of the opinion, has stated that *Roe* was "a landmark in the progress of the emancipation of women." But that could hardly have been said had Blackmun's original draft come down as the opinion of the Court. Although the draft did strike down the abortion statute before the Court, it did so on the ground of vagueness and not because it restricted a woman's right to have an abortion.

In his *Liberty and Sexuality*, David J. Garrow called the Blackmun *Roe* draft "an almost wholly unremarkable document." More than that, Justice Blackmun's vagueness analysis was extremely weak, because *United States v. Vuitch*, decided the year before, had upheld a similar District of Columbia abortion law against a vagueness attack. Nevertheless, the draft's disposition of the case on vagueness enabled it to avoid the basic constitutional question. As the Blackmun draft stated, "There is no need in Roe's case to pass on her contention that . . . a pregnant woman has an absolute right to an abortion." Indeed, the draft tended to support state substantive power over abortions. "Our holding today," the draft noted, "does not imply that a State has no legitimate interest in the subject of abortions or that abortion procedures may not be subjected to control by the State." On the contrary: "We do not accept the argument of the appellants and of some of the amici that a pregnant woman has an unlimited right to do with her body as she pleases. The long acceptance of statutes regulating the possession of certain drugs and other harmful substances, and making criminal indecent exposure in public, or an attempt at suicide, clearly indicate the contrary." This was, of course, completely different from the approach ultimately followed in the *Roe v. Wade* opinion of the Court.

Had the Blackmun draft come down as the final *Roe v. Wade* opinion, the last twenty years in American life and politics might have been quite different. Instead of the flat prohibition against state interferences with the right to abortion, there would have been only a weak decision that implied that the states did possess substantive authority over abortions.

Despite the weakness of the Blackmun draft, it was supported by the Justices who favored striking down the abortion law. The conference minority Justices who had voted to uphold the statute now sought to delay—and perhaps reverse—the abortion decision. *Roe* had come before a seven-Justice Court. The two vacancies were not filled until Justices Lewis F. Powell and William H. Rehnquist took their seats in January 1972. After the Blackmun draft was circulated, Chief Justice Warren E. Burger led an effort to secure a reargument in the case, arguing that the decision in such an important case should be made by a full Court. Burger's move to secure reargument was opposed by the Justices who favored striking down the abortion laws. However, Justice Blackmun himself agreed that the case should be decided by a full Court, and, with the vote of the two new Justices, reargument was ordered.

Chief Justice Burger had hoped to secure the votes of the two new Justices and then persuade Justice Blackmun himself to switch. Instead, he got a split vote from the new Justices (Powell for the abortion law, and Rehnquist against) and a vastly stronger *Roe* opinion. Justice Blackmun now wrote a new *Roe* draft that abandoned the vagueness holding and decided on the constitutional merits. The new Blackmun draft contained the essentials of the final *Roe v. Wade* opinion, with its flat ruling that the Texas abortion law violated the constitutional right of privacy. The new draft also adopted the time test followed in the final opinion, with later drafts refining it to the tripartite approach of the final *Roe* opinion, under which there is an absolute right to abortions during the first trimester of pregnancy, with the right subject to state restrictions only during the second and third trimesters.

Had the original Blackmun draft come down as the Court opinion, the case would not have dealt with the constitutional merits of abortion prohibitions, but would have been only a narrow decision striking down a state law for vagueness. The subsequent schism that has been a major factor in American life might have been postponed or avoided—or possibly mitigated by its relegation to political rather than legal resolution. *Roe* itself might have been only a constitutional footnote used by law professors to illustrate how the Court can evade important legal issues.

9. *Webster v. Reproductive Health Services*

Justice Rehnquist had been one of the two dissenters in *Roe v. Wade*. Moreover, the Rehnquist dissent had been an unusually strong one, which compared the Court's decision with that in *Lochner v. New York*. "While the Court's opinion," the Rehnquist dissent asserted, "quotes from the dissent of Mr. Justice Holmes in *Lochner v. New York* . . . , the result it reaches is more closely attuned to the majority opinion of Mr. Justice Peckham in that case." "As in *Lochner*," *Roe* requires "this Court to examine the legislative policies and pass on the wisdom of these policies."

Justice Rehnquist continued to assert his opposition to *Roe v. Wade*, as well as efforts to expand its doctrine, in the Burger Court's later abortion cases. When Rehnquist became Chief Justice, the overruling of *Roe* was high on his agenda. *Webster v. Reproductive Health Services* in 1989 appeared to give him the opportunity to accomplish that result.

At issue in *Webster* was a Missouri law regulating abortions, characterized at the time as one of the most restrictive laws on the subject. The lower courts had ruled that these provisions violated the decision in *Roe v. Wade*. At the *Webster* conference, five voted to uphold the Missouri law—Chief Justice Rehnquist and Justices Byron R. White, Sandra Day O'Connor, Antonin Scalia, and Anthony Kennedy—with the Chief Justice stating squarely that he "disagrees with *Roe v. Wade*." Justices William Brennan, Thurgood Marshall, and Blackmun voted to strike down the law.

Since he was in the conference majority, Chief Justice Rehnquist could choose the writer of the *Webster* opinion. He assigned the opinion to himself, following the tradition that the Chief Justice should prepare the opinions in important cases. In addition, Rehnquist wanted the opportunity to strike what could be a mortal blow against *Roe v. Wade*.

The first draft of the *Webster* opinion was headed, "CHIEF JUSTICE REHNQUIST delivered the opinion of the Court." After the conference vote, Rehnquist naturally assumed that he was writing for a majority of the Justices.

The Rehnquist draft virtually overruled *Roe v. Wade*. The draft recognized that although stare decisis was "a cornerstone of our legal system," it should give way in a case involving "a prior construction of the Constitution that has proved 'unsound in principle and unworkable in practice.'" That was the case here: "We think the *Roe* trimester framework falls into that category."

The Rehnquist draft called the *Roe* framework "rigid" and asserted that it "is hardly consistent" with a Constitution such as ours: "The key elements of the *Roe* framework—trimesters and viability—are not found in the text of the Constitution or in any place else one would expect to find a constitutional principle. Since the bounds of the inquiry are essentially indeterminate, the result has been a web of legal rules that have become increasingly intricate, resembling a code of regulations rather than a body of constitutional doctrine."

Instead of the *Roe* guarantee of the abortion right, the Rehnquist draft offered a new test for abortion restrictions: whether it "reasonably furthers the state's interest in protecting potential human life." This was a far less restrictive standard than the "compelling interest" test that *Roe* required abortion restrictions to pass—at least during the first trimester of pregnancy.

At the end of his draft, Chief Justice Rehnquist noted that the Court had been urged to "overrule our decision in *Roe v. Wade.*" The draft ostensibly declined the invitation, saying of *Roe* that "we leave it undisturbed." All that the draft opinion did was to state, "To the extent indicated in our opinion, we modify and narrow *Roe.*"

The disclaimer at the end of the Rehnquist draft could scarcely disguise the potentially fatal effect it would have on *Roe v. Wade.* Justice Blackmun pointed this out in an impassioned draft dissent. The Blackmun draft referred to the "feigned restraint" of the Rehnquist draft when it stated that *Roe* was not overruled. "This disclaimer," Blackmun asserted, "is totally meaningless." Instead, the draft dissent declared, "[t]he simple truth is that *Roe* no longer survives, and . . . the majority discards a landmark case of the last generation, and casts into darkness the hopes and visions of every woman in this country who had come to believe that the Constitution guaranteed her the right to exercise some control over her unique ability to bear children."

The Blackmun draft conclusion was bitter: "I rue this day. I rue the violence that has been done to the liberty and equality of women. I rue the violence that has been done to our legal fabric and to the integrity of this Court. I rue the inevitable loss of public esteem for this Court that is so essential. I dissent."

As it turned out, Justice Blackmun did not have to deliver his unusually strong draft. That was the case because, a month after she received the Rehnquist draft, Justice O'Connor circulated an opinion headed, "JUSTICE O'CONNOR, concurring in part and concurring in the judgment." The O'Connor opinion indicated that the *Webster* majority was not holding, since O'Connor categorically refused to agree with the portion of the Rehnquist draft repudiating *Roe v. Wade* and concurred only in the judgment upholding the Missouri law on other grounds. More specifically, according to the O'Connor opinion, this case "cannot provide a basis for reevaluating *Roe*." On this—the crucial aspect of the Rehnquist draft—the Chief Justice's opinion had now lost its majority.

Although the Chief Justice still fought to secure a majority—a new draft after O'Connor's circulation still was headed "the opinion of the Court"—he did not succeed. Justice O'Connor circulated a new draft that was the first opinion referring to the Rehnquist opinion as a plurality opinion, rather than that of the Court or of a majority. Justice Blackmun also abandoned his draft's alarmist tone. His final opinion stated that the plurality opinion did not make "a single, even incremental, change in the law of abortion."

The final Blackmun dissent deleted his draft language about "*Roe*'s passing" and concluded instead, "For today, at least, the law of abortion stands undisturbed. For today, the women of this Nation still retain the liberty to control their destinies. But the signs are evident and very ominous, and a chill wind blows."

By this point, even Chief Justice Rehnquist recognized that his opinion's "wind" would not blow away *Roe v. Wade*. When the Chief Justice circulated his final opinion, he headed it, "Chief Justice REHNQUIST announced the judgment of the Court . . . and an opinion with respect to" the portions that challenged *Roe* in which Justices White and Kennedy alone joined. The Rehnquist opinion was thus announced only as the opinion of a plurality. In his published opinion, the Chief Justice had to modify his earlier draft statement that "we modify and narrow *Roe*." Instead, the final plurality opinion concluded, "To the extent indicated in our opinion, we would modify and narrow *Roe*." As handed down, the Rehnquist *Webster* opinion concluded not, as the earlier drafts had done, that it narrowed *Roe* (or, as the Blackmun draft dissent had asserted, that it overruled *Roe*), but only that the plurality would do so if a later case gave it the opportunity.

Had the Chief Justice not lost Justice O'Connor's vote, the result would have been different. The Rehnquist draft would have become the *Webster* opinion of the Court. *Roe* would have been all but relegated to judicial limbo. The situation would have become that described in Justice Blackmun's draft dissent: "Let there be no misunderstanding: the two isolated dissenters in *Roe*, after all these years, now have prevailed, with the assent of the Court's newest Members, in rolling back that case and in returning the law of procreating freedom to the severe limitations that generally prevailed before January 22, 1973"—the date of *Roe v. Wade*. That "might have been" was avoided only because Justice O'Connor ultimately refused to join Chief Justice Rehnquist's *Webster* opinion.

10. *Mapp v. Ohio*

According to a *New York Times* survey of the 1960 term, the decision in *Mapp v. Ohio* (1961) was the "most far-reaching constitutional step of the term." Former Justice Abe Fortas went even further when I interviewed him. "To me," he said, "the most radical decision in recent times was Mapp against Ohio." *Mapp* deserved this characterization because it overruled the decision in *Wolf v. Colorado* (1949)—until then one of the cornerstones of our criminal law. *Wolf* held that the exclusionary rule was not required by the Constitution in state criminal cases. The result was, in the words of the *Wolf* opinion, "that in a prosecution in a State court for a State crime the Fourteenth Amendment does not forbid the admission of evidence obtained by an unreasonable search and seizure."

Dollree Mapp had been convicted of having obscene books and pictures. Mapp had refused to admit the police without a search warrant, but they forcibly opened her door, searched the house, and discovered obscene materials. Mapp maintained that her conviction was invalid because the Ohio statute prohibiting possession of obscene books and pictures violated the First Amendment.

The briefs and arguments in the Supreme Court were almost entirely devoted to the First Amendment issue of the constitutionality of the Ohio statute barring possession of obscene material. The conference discussion also focused on the constitutionality of the Ohio obscenity statute. Chief Justice Warren set the theme by declaring that the law "cuts across First Amendment rights. It's too broad a statute to accomplish its purpose, and on that basis I'd reverse." All the others agreed that the conviction should be reversed on the First Amendment ground.

The conference discussion and vote was summed up by Justice Stewart in a 1983 lecture on the *Mapp* case: "At the conference following the argument a majority of the Justices agreed that the Ohio statute violated the *first* and fourteenth amendments." In his conference discussion, Justice Douglas had agreed with the reversal on the First Amendment. But he also gave *Wolf* as an alternative ground for reversal and said that he was prepared to overrule that case. The Chief Justice and Justice Brennan indicated that they would vote with Justice Douglas on *Wolf*, but when there was no support on this from the others, the three agreed to go along with the reversal on First Amendment grounds. The opinion was assigned by the Chief Justice to Justice Clark.

Justice Stewart's lecture described what then occurred. "I have always suspected," he said, "that the members of the soon-to-be *Mapp* majority had met in what I affectionately call a 'rump caucus' to discuss a different basis for their decision." His suspicion was confirmed, he told his audience, when he learned from my biography of Chief Justice Warren "that an impromptu caucus of the *Mapp* majority took place in an elevator at the Court immediately after the conference at which the case was discussed."

What happened was that Justice Clark changed his mind just after the conference. On the elevator after leaving the conference room, Clark turned to Justices Black and Brennan and asked, "Wouldn't this be a good case to apply the exclusionary rule and do what *Wolf* didn't do?" The Clark switch to the anti-*Wolf* position made four Justices in favor of the *Wolf* overruling. The key was now Justice Black, who, if persuaded, would become the fifth vote. Black tended to a restrained approach in Fourth Amendment cases. This time, however, Black showed willingness to agree to a decision overruling the *Wolf* holding that the states were not required to apply the exclusionary rule.

That was, of course, the final *Mapp* decision, since Chief Justice Warren and Justices Douglas, Brennan, and even Black agreed without difficulty to Clark's opinion of the Court, based on his changed approach in *Mapp*. To the others, however, the opinion reversing on the *Wolf* ground came as a complete surprise. "I was shocked," said Justice Stewart in his 1983 lecture on *Mapp*, "when Justice Clark's proposed Court opinion reached my desk. I immediately wrote him a note expressing my surprise and questioning the wisdom of overruling an important doctrine in a case in which the issue was not briefed, argued, or discussed by the state courts, by the parties' counsel, or at our conference following the oral argument."

Justice Clark was the catalyst for the *Mapp* decision. Had he not told Stewart's "rump caucus" that the decision should apply the exclusionary rule, the conference consensus might well have prevailed. The Warren Court's most important criminal-law holding would have remained stillborn. *Mapp* itself would have come down as a minor First Amendment case, of interest only to specialists on the subject.

"Might Have Beens" and "Was"

All these "might have beens" might easily have happened. If they had, it might have made a significant difference not only to our law, but even to our society. Think of what the effect would have been if John Marshall and Earl Warren had not been appointed to head the Supreme Court. There would have been no Marshall Court and no Warren Court—the first the Court that laid down the foundations of American constitutional law and the second the Court that recast the constitutional corpus in its mid-twentieth-century image. The two most creative periods in our public law might never have taken place if the two great Chief Justices had not been able to serve.

Had the "might have beens" in the cases listed taken place, they would also have made a substantial difference. Certainly, if *Marbury, Dred Scott, Lochner,* and *Brown* had been decided differently, the consequences would have been tremendous. *Marbury v. Madison* decided only on the issues raised by the parties might have meant congressional supremacy similar to parliamentary supremacy in Britain, with no review at all of constitutionality. *Dred Scott v. Sandford* decided under Justice Nelson's draft opinion would scarcely have had anything like the polarizing effect of the actual decision. *Lochner v. New York* with the Harlan opinion of the Court might have been a leading precedent for judicial restraint, rather than the foundation for the cases invalidating regulatory laws. A *Brown v. Board of Education* decision upholding segregation might have prevented the racial progress made since the actual *Brown* decision. Plainly, these are "might have beens" that might have had seismic effects had they happened.

The impact of the last four "might have beens" would have been less dramatic, but they, too, would have had substantial effects. If *Baker v. Carr* had decided the merits of legislative apportionments as the Justices then would have decided that question, it would have limited the redistribution of political power from rural to urban and suburban areas that has since occurred. If *Mapp v. Ohio* had been decided on the obscenity ground originally agreed on, it would have remained an obscure First Amendment case; more important, the exclusionary rule might never have been applied to the states. The *Roe v. Wade* opinion as originally drafted would not have confirmed the right to an abortion; instead, it would have confirmed state power to restrict abortions. If the Rehnquist draft opinion in *Webster v. Reproductive Health Services* had retained its majority, *Roe v. Wade* would have been virtually overruled. That would have meant, Justice Blackmun urged in his impassioned draft dissent, "that *Roe* no longer survives."

All these "might have beens" never happened. Both their baneful and beneficial effects were avoided by the events and decisions that did take place. Both vain regrets and praises are ineffective to change the course that Supreme Court history actually took.

7

TEN

GREATEST

NON-SUPREME COURT

JUDGES

Students of law concentrate their major attention on the Marble Palace in Washington. The greater part of our law has, however, been developed in the state and lower federal courts, and their jurisprudence has played a significant role in legal development. Judge Learned Hand tells us that American law is a structure fashioned by generations of judges, each professing to be a pupil, yet each a builder who added his few bricks. During our history, most of the bricks were added by non-Supreme Court judges. Most of them are now all but unknown except to legal specialists. Yet it was these judges who ensured that the English common law would be adapted to the needs of the new nation and, more recently, that American law would be remade in the image of the evolving twentieth-century society.

Who were the greatest non-Supreme Court judges in our history?

In my opinion, the nine state judges and one federal judge in this chapter's list deserve inclusion in the non-Supreme Court elite.

I had planned to call this list "The Greatest Judges Never to Sit on the Supreme Court"; yet that would have excluded Benjamin N. Cardozo, who clearly belonged on the list. As mentioned in Chapter 1, Cardozo did sit on the U.S. Supreme Court, but his tenure was too short for him to play the part there that would have warranted his inclusion in the list of Supreme Court greats. This, then, is a list of the nine greatest judges never to sit on the Supreme Court and one who did, but who made his major contribution to our law on a state court.

— ★ — ★ — ★ —

Ten Greatest Non-Supreme Court Judges

1. Lemuel Shaw (1781-1861), Chief Justice of Massachusetts, 1830-1860

2. James Kent (1763-1847), Justice, New York Supreme Court, 1798-1804; Chief Justice, 1804-1814; Chancellor, 1814-1823

3. Benjamin Nathan Cardozo (1870-1938), Justice, New York Supreme Court, 1914-1917; Judge, New York Court of Appeals, 1917-1926; Chief Judge, 1926-1932; Justice, United States Supreme Court, 1932-1938

4. Learned Hand (1872-1961), Judge, U.S. District Court for the Southern District of New York, 1909-1924; Judge, U.S. Court of Appeals for the Second Circuit, 1924-1961.

5. Charles Doe (1830-1896), Justice, New Hampshire Supreme Court, 1861-1876; Chief Justice, 1876-1896

6. Thomas McIntyre Cooley (1824-1898), Judge, Michigan Supreme Court, 1864-1885

7. John Bannister Gibson (1780-1853), Justice, Pennsylvania Supreme Court, 1816-1827; Chief Justice, 1827-1853

8. Roger John Traynor (1900-1983), Justice, California Supreme Court, 1940-1964; Chief Justice, 1964-1970

9. John Appleton (1804-1891), Justice, Maine Supreme Judicial Court, 1852-1862; Chief Justice, 1862-1883

10. Arthur T. Vanderbilt (1888-1957), Chief Justice, New Jersey Supreme Court, 1947-1957

1. Lemuel Shaw

Although largely forgotten today, Lemuel Shaw (1781–1861) was one of the giants of American law. Indeed, according to Justice Oliver Wendell Holmes, Shaw was "the greatest magistrate which this country has produced." As Chief Justice of the most prestigious state court during the pre–Civil War period, Shaw played a primary role in recasting the common law into an American mold.

When Shaw came to the bench, our law was in the midst of its period of greatest expansion. Shaw himself noted that the age was characterized by "prodigious activity and energy in every department of life." In the thirty years that he presided over the Massachusetts Supreme Judicial Court, a new social order took over. Great manufacturing corporations came into existence; the railroads and a host of inventions revolutionized transportation and commerce. These developments precipitated new legal problems, giving Shaw a unique opportunity to adapt the law to the new society. How well he succeeded is shown by the conclusion of his most recent biographer: "Probably no state judge has so deeply influenced commercial and constitutional law throughout the nation."

Shaw's opinions ranged the whole gamut of the law. He virtually laid the foundation of American tort law. The great need was to erect a system of liability that would encourage people to venture for productive ends. The common-law rule, under which, in Holmes's phrase, "a man *acts* at his peril," had to be replaced by one that determined liability by blameworthiness. The changing law marked a natural response in a society that placed such stress on free individual action and decision. The injured person had to show why the law should shift the loss onto the one who caused the injury. Liability became a corollary of fault instead of being attached indiscriminately to all acts causing injury.

The leading case in this development was *Brown v. Kendall* (1850), where Chief Justice Shaw declared that "the plaintiff must come prepared with the evidence to show either that the intention was unlawful, or that the defendant was *in fault*; for if the injury was unavoidable, and the conduct of the defendant was free from blame, he will not be liable." Shaw and the judges who followed his lead were not, however, concerned with *fault* in the sense of personal moral shortcoming. Instead, as Holmes summarized it, there was a "general principle of our law . . . that loss from accident must lie where it falls." Judges like Shaw believed that economic development would be hindered as long as enterprisers were exposed to liability for the consequences of pure accident, unless a prudent man would have foreseen the possibility of harm—that is, unless there was fault of some sort. Risk-creating enterprise was thus made less hazardous to entrepreneurs than it had been at common law.

The shift in American tort law mirrored the difference between the closed society in Britain and the relatively open society of the new nation, where the market was the key institution and belief in maximum individual self-assertion the prime article of faith. Only within a framework fostering individual initiative were men likely to act with the boldness and energy required.

The law of railroads was also largely molded by Shaw. Shaw's decisions furnished the legal environment in which the railroads could develop from the early rudimentary conception of "an iron turnpike" to the prime catalyst of the burgeoning economy. Shaw's railroad decisions, like his tort decisions, tilted the law in favor of railroad expansion. At the same time, however, Shaw laid the groundwork for the modern law of regulation. The railroad, he stressed, "is in every respect a public grant, a franchise, which no one could enjoy but for the authority of the government. This grant . . . is subject to certain regulations, within the power of the government." Thus the Shaw court had no difficulty in upholding rate-making and other regulatory measures.

If these decisions upholding public power seem incompatible with those of an individualist cast already discussed, the inconsistency is more apparent than real. The common law, in Shaw's conception, was to be construed to erect a private-law system that encouraged people to venture for productive ends. But that did not prevent Shaw from recognizing an overriding governmental power to regulate in the public interest. Shaw was the first state judge to recognize "the police power, the power vested in the legislature by the constitution, to make, ordain and establish all manner of wholesome and reasonable laws . . . as they shall judge to be for the good and welfare of the commonwealth." This now-classic definition of the police power was rendered in *Commonwealth v. Alger* (1851), where Shaw made the first comprehensive attempt at analysis of this vital power.

There was, however, one area where Shaw failed to move the law forward. Like other judges at the time, Shaw felt compelled to follow the positive law in cases involving slavery, particularly those under the Fugitive Slave Act. The ultimate picture becomes a poignant one—with the judge refusing to adapt the law to the moral imperative in which he firmly believed. In the slavery cases, Shaw and the other judges of the day displayed all the moral blindness of Captain Vere in *Billy Budd*, which

Herman Melville probably wrote to illustrate the dilemma of judges like Shaw, who happened to be his father-in-law.

2. James Kent

James Kent (1763–1847) is known today primarily as the author of *Commentaries on America Law*, the first systematization of American law during its formative period. Before he wrote his classic work, however, Kent served as a judge for twenty-five years, until compulsory retirement.

Kent's primary judicial contribution was, like Shaw's, to help lay the common-law foundation for the developing American law. We have by now all but forgotten the hostility toward the common law that was an almost inevitable accompaniment to the Revolutionary struggle for independence. The common law was looked on as a system of *English* law—as what a critic called "this last seeming badge and mortifying memento of their dependence." At political dinners and meetings after the Revolution, a common toast proclaimed, "The Common Law of England: may wholesome statutes soon root out this engine of oppression from America."

Kent, as much as any judge, helped reverse the trend toward rejection of the common law. Kent came to see in the common law the instrument by which the law of the new nation could be fashioned. More than that, he said that the common law had "fostered the soundest and most rational principles of civil liberty." Through its principles, he wrote in an 1800 case, the English courts had "protected right to a degree never before witnessed in the history of civil society."

Kent could sum up his years on the bench by saying, "I have spent the best years of my life in administering the old common law of the land . . . with all its imperfections on its head." His tenure on the New York bench ensured the carrying of the day by the traditional English body of law. Just before his death, he wrote to his son that "the progress of jurisprudence was nothing in New York prior to 1793." When he retired as a judge thirty years later, the New York courts under his leadership had worked out a consistent corpus of common law jurisprudence, though, as Kent put it, only "established here *so far* as it was adapted to our institutions and circumstances."

However, Kent did more than lead the bench in establishing the common law as the foundation of American law. He also helped to ensure that the new jurisprudence would serve as the basis for a written case-law system. "When I came to the bench," Kent wrote, "there were no reports or State precedents. . . . I first introduced a thorough examination of cases and written opinions." Kent then urged the appointment of an able reporter, William Johnson, whose reports were soon cited as authority throughout the country.

Just as important was Kent's work as Chancellor. It was largely because of Kent's influence that equity became an essential part of American law. The volumes of *Johnson's Chancery Reports* (containing Kent's opinions) made the principles of equity jurisprudence familiar to both bench and bar. Because of Kent's opinions, the work of the great English chancellors became a part of American law.

Why was this so important? Because it gave American courts the broad remedial powers that had been developed by the English chancellors— powers that enable them to issue whatever orders may be necessary to correct violations of law and to punish refusals to carry out those orders. The civil courts in no other legal system have such sweeping authority. If our judges now actively supervise education, voting, prisons, and so many other aspects of our life, it is because they are vested with the powers traditionally exercised by courts of equity. If Kent had not laid the foundation, such judicial activism could never have gotten off the ground.

3. Benjamin Nathan Cardozo

Benjamin Nathan Cardozo (1870–1938) was probably the only famous judge who had Horatio Alger as a tutor. That is, of course, not why he is on my list of great non-Supreme Court judges. To be sure, at the end of his career Cardozo did serve on the Supreme Court. However, his inclusion in the elite does not stem from his service there, which, as stressed, was not long enough for him to make the substantial contribution to its jurisprudence that his ability warranted. Cardozo's judicial contributions were made on the New York Court of Appeals, that state's highest court, where he served for eighteen years, five as Chief Judge. During the Cardozo years, the New York court was recognized as the strongest in the country, and its judgments had a decisive influence on our law.

To Cardozo, the job of the judge was to adapt the experience of the past so that it would best serve the needs of the present. During Cardozo's years on the New York bench, the traditional common-law technique confronted the momentum of mature industrialization, which transformed economic and social relations. Cardozo recognized the essentially innovative nature of the judicial task in such a period. Few judges of the day were as aware as he of the extent to which judges must legislate. Reasoning by analogy, he showed how existing doctrines could be adapted to the new setting. His mastery of judicial technique made the emerging law appear to be the logical product of established doctrines; in his hands, the changing common law served only to underscore common law continuity.

For Cardozo, the key change that had occurred in the law was what he termed "the change from the analytical to the functional attitude." The test of legal rules is their social value. Legal rules are to be viewed instrumentally, by how they serve the welfare of society. If they do not do so, they should be modified or eliminated. Above all, Cardozo showed that the law was not a static collection of rules, but a living body of principles capable of growth and change, with law as the servant of human needs. As he put it, "The end which the law serves will dominate . . . all."

Cardozo's tort opinions, in particular, exemplified his use of the common-law method to meet the requirements of a modern legal system. They played a major part in the transformation of the negligence concept during the twentieth century. The now classic 1916 Cardozo opinion in *MacPherson v. Buick Motor Co.* (1916) has had more influence than any other on the development of tort law. Cardozo held that the manufacturer, by placing a product such as an automobile on the market, assumes a responsibility to the consumer, resting not on contract or tort in the traditional sense, but on the relation arising from the purchase and the fact that harm was foreseeable in a large proportion of cases. "Precedents drawn from the days of travel by stage coach," Cardozo declared, "do not fit the conditions of travel to-day." The principles of tort liability "are whatever the needs of life in a developing civilization require them to be."

The Cardozo opinions in *MacPherson* and other cases showed that the common law was not a static collection of rules inherited from the past, but a living body of principles still capable of growth to meet new conditions. As Cardozo once put it, "The inn that shelters for the night is not the journey's end. The law, like the traveler, must be ready for the morrow. It must have the principle of growth."

Cardozo not only stated that goal as the main thing, but he also showed how the goal could be attained by traditional common-law methods. We are told that *MacPherson* "brought the law into line with 'social considerations.'" Yet Cardozo did so not by stressing the ends served by the extension of liability, but by purporting to proceed only by the common-law technique of analogy from the decided cases. There is no better illustration of Cardozo's use of the common-law technique to make needed changes in the law.

Cardozo once noted that people assert "that a judicial opinion has no business to be literature. The idol must be ugly, or he may be taken for a common man." Cardozo's own opinions were additions to literature as well as law. With Holmes, he remains the acknowledged master of language as a legal instrument. The judge, he said, may be "expounding a science, or a body of truth which he seeks to assimilate to a science, but in the process of exposition he is practicing an art." By the lever of art, Cardozo lifted the most technical subjects to the heights.

4. Learned Hand

If there is one person on everyone's list of those who should have sat on the Supreme Court, it is Learned Hand (1872–1961). Judge Hand spent his judicial career on the lower federal courts, serving first as a district judge and then on the Court of Appeals for the Second Circuit. Hand was the outstanding lower federal court judge in our history and, during most of his career, the unanimous choice of the legal profession for the next Supreme Court vacancy.

Hand himself said that he was not sorry that he did not serve on the Supreme Court. Interestingly, however, he recognized that his disclaimer of earlier ambition was colored by the fact that the ambition had not been realized. "I will concede," Hand wrote to Justice Frankfurter, "that for years I should have said that I wanted to be on your court as much as I wanted anything that could come from the outside. But now I ask myself whether it can be a paradise? I know, I know—the fox said, 'those grapes are sour anyway.' But yet, but yet, maybe they really were."

Sour grapes or not, Hand's work on the lower federal courts made him virtually everyone's favorite non-Supreme Court judge. Indeed, according to Judge Richard A. Posner, "Learned Hand is considered by many the third-greatest judge in the history of the United States, after Holmes and John Marshall; some might even rate him higher." It is more difficult to answer the question of why this is true.

In discussing Hand's greatness, Posner emphasizes his "creativity." Posner himself, we will see in Chapter 10, has been largely responsible for adding a new dimension to jurisprudence—what he himself has called "the most important development in legal thought in the last quarter century . . . the application of economics to an ever-increasing range of legal fields."

Yet Posner tells us that it was Judge Hand who wrote the tort opinion that laid the doctrinal foundation for the Posner approach. In it, Hand articulated a balancing approach to the question of whether negligence had occurred: the burden of the necessary precautions were to be weighed against the magnitude of the loss and the probability of the accident if the precautions were not taken. Instead of the traditional tort test, which determined negligence in the light of the conduct of a "reasonable man" under the circumstances, Hand substituted the approach of an economist, holding that there was liability only when an accident could have been avoided at a cost less than that of the accident itself. To Hand, the "reasonable man" was one who took a cost-justified approach to precautionary care.

According to Judge Posner, it is the " 'Hand formula' of negligence which has played so seminal a role in the economic analysis of law." Hand also helped to lead the way in other important areas of the law. "More than any other lower-court judge," we are told by Charles E. Wyzanski, himself an outstanding federal judge, "[Hand] was the architect of our present structure of antitrust law." His most noted antitrust opinion was in the *Aluminum Company* case, characterized by Posner as "one of the most celebrated antitrust decisions of all time, as well as a landmark in the economic approach to antitrust law."

Alcoa is also a striking illustration of Hand's prestige. Because of disqualifications, the Supreme Court could not muster a quorum and Congress passed a special act permitting the case to be assigned for final decision to Hand's court. The case was so complicated that *Life* amused its readers by photographing the judge surrounded by the volumes of the 40,000-page record. Yet, Wyzanski tells us, "he cut through the jungle a path which has been to all his successors the clearest route for decision of cases charging monopolization."

The Hand oeuvre includes numerous other influential opinions in most important areas of the law. Of particular note are pioneer opinions protecting freedom of speech, stressing "the tolerance of all methods of political agitation which . . . is a safeguard of free government." Back in 1913, when the law of obscenity was used as a broadside censorship tool, a Hand opinion asserted that "however consonant it may be with mid-Victorian morals," it was not consistent with changing morality. "I question," he wrote, "whether men will regard that as obscene which is honestly relevant to the adequate expression of innocent ideas, and whether they will not believe that truth and beauty are too precious to society at large to be mutilated in the interests of those most likely to pervert them to base uses."

The Hand opinions are models of what he called "the joy of craftsmanship." They give painstaking attention to both the facts and the law. Indeed, it has been said, there is in Hand a polyphony between the smallest detail of fact and the law writ large. Judge Wyzanski summed it up: "A Hand opinion is comparable to a sonnet: a distillation of thought, prepared within limits strictly defined by convention, but emanating an afflatus beyond the established boundaries."

Hand, like Holmes (whom Hand referred to as the Great Master), was more than a great judge. He, too, became a part of American legend with his famous address, "The Spirit of Liberty" (1944), more a contribution to literature than to law. Hand may never have sat on the Supreme Court, but he was still one of the greatest judges in our history. Hand once described his law professors: "In the universe of truth they lived by the sword; they asked not quarter of absolutes and they gave none." This was even more a description of the author than of his subjects.

5. Charles Doe

Charles Doe (1830–1896), was one of the most eccentric judges ever to sit upon the bench. According to a Boston newspaper article about him, "The judge was a good deal of a character, and his own townsmen confessed that they did not understand him." Doe always refused to conform to accepted standards of judicial dress and wore the clothes of a country farmer. He never shined his shoes, and he wore the same Prince Albert coat for over twenty years. Once, while sitting in the lobby of Boston's leading hotel, Doe was taken for a tramp and ordered out.

Doe was eccentric enough for his day to write one of the first opinions admitting a woman to the bar. In 1873, in *Bradwell v. Illinois*, the Supreme Court had refused to order a state to make a similar decision, with Justice Bradley pontificating, "The paramount destiny and mission of woman are to fulfill the noble and benign offices of wife and mother. This is the law of the Creator." In Doe's 1890 opinion, the law of the Creator was construed differently. In deciding that "women could [not] . . . lawfully be kept out," Doe pointed to the changed "social conditions . . . in this age, and in this country." Doe further wrote, "Who will be bold enough to say now that in a hundred years hence it will not be true that . . . courts will not be as much surprised to see a lawyer appear dressed as a lady as they would now to see him appear dressed as a gentleman." At the time, this statement was apparently too visionary for Doe's colleagues, and they had the sentence deleted before the opinion was printed.

What makes Doe's jurisprudence relevant in the development of

American law, however, is not its singular character, but its accordance with the concept of law that was becoming dominant. Doe helped to further the view that the law should be interpreted to give economic enterprise a free hand. Under the Doe conception of law, as he put it in a case, the state was only "a limited agency for the purchase of common benefit, security, and protection."

The Doe jurisprudence in favor of private enterprise was not limited to decisions protecting business against state intervention. Doe also furthered the trend toward making the law an adjunct of economic expansion by rejecting doctrines that would have placed undue burdens on entrepreneurs. In an important case, Doe applied a version of caveat emptor, the doctrine that was then considered an essential prop of the burgeoning market economy. Doe refused to construe a lease of a furnished hotel as containing an implied covenant that it was suitable for occupation. The Doe opinion stressed that it was up to the lessee himself to examine the property and that it cannot be presumed that he relied on any warranty by the lessor. "The reasonableness of the doctrine expressed by the maxim, 'Caveat emptor,'" Doe wrote, "would preclude such an inference."

Doe's most famous opinion was in *Brown v. Collins* (1873), limiting tort liability to cases where there had been fault. The fact pattern, like that in so many leading cases, involved a relatively minor legal controversy. Defendant's horses were frightened by a locomotive and ran on plaintiff's land and broke a post there. Plaintiff sued to recover the value of the post. Doe's opinion held defendant not liable.

Doe used the case to deal with the rule laid down in England five years earlier in the famous case of *Rylands v. Fletcher*, where the defendant was held liable for the escape of water from a reservoir on his land, although he was not negligent.

John Reid's biography explains Doe's *Brown v. Collins* opinion: "The issue could not have been drawn more clearly: can a defendant who acted lawfully be held liable for damage resulting from an inevitable accident not his fault? The *Rylands* decision held that under special circumstances he could. Judge Doe's answer was that he could not."

Brown v. Collins is a prime example of how law is molded by changing economic conditions. As the Reid biography tells us, *Rylands* may be analyzed "in terms of England's dominant class (the landed gentry) as unsympathetic to industry, and Judge Doe's *Brown* decision in terms of New England's dependence on cotton mills." In this country, the law had become a prime instrument of economic expansion, and the businessman's idea of land as something to be used for commercial purposes led to the rejection of *Rylands*. To Americans, land had become not merely a private domain, but an asset to be utilized for economic advantages.

Basic to the reasoning in *Brown* was Doe's conviction that *Rylands* was injurious to economic enterprise. He also stressed "the rights of civilization" as controlling in the case. Whatever may have been true, his opinion stated, in "an undeveloped state of agriculture, manufacturers, and commerce," rejection of *Rylands* was now "demanded by the growth of intelligence, trade and productive enterprise."

Thus like the other great state judges of his day, Doe interpreted the law to meet what were deemed the needs of the burgeoning economy. Like many of them, Doe also showed that greatness on the bench is not necessarily determined by the greatness of the particular judicial arena. Doe is on my list of non-Supreme Court judges, though he spent his entire professional career in New Hampshire; his only opportunities were those furnished by the cases brought in the rural society of one of the smallest states. Doe gained national renown because he was able to use the legal tools at hand to fashion landmark opinions. He took run-of-the-mill matters and transformed them into leading cases. The Doe jurisprudence, too, served as the legal foundation for the developing industrial economy.

6. Thomas McIntyre Cooley

As we will see in the list of great law books, Thomas McIntyre Cooley (1824–1898) was the author of what may have been one of the most influential works ever published on American law. Cooley's *Treatise on the Constitutional Limitations. . .* , (1868), furnished the doctrinal foundation for American jurisprudence during the next half-century.

In addition, Cooley was one of the greatest state judges; his contributions to American law gained him a place, alongside Shaw and Kent, on the list of America's ten best judges published in 1938 by Roscoe Pound, this century's preeminent legal scholar.

Born in New York, Cooley moved west and studied law in Michigan, where he practiced and taught in the new law department at the University of Michigan. He became a member of the Michigan Supreme Court, where he sat for twenty-one years. From 1887 to 1891, he served as head of the newly created Interstate Commerce Commission, and capped his career in 1893 by being elected president of the American Bar Association.

Cooley's work showed judges how they could use the due process clause to review the reasonableness of laws and to strike down those that interfered with business operations. With Cooley's jurisprudence as a foundation, American law enlisted for decades in behalf of the fullest freedom for the businessman.

Underlying Cooley's opinions was a basically negative conception of law. Law was not to be used to further the juristic vision of the society, but to restrain interferences with economic freedom. Cooley carried this approach to the point of holding that government might not extend special privileges that would give certain businesses an advantage. In his most noted opinion for the Michigan court, Judge Cooley ruled invalid a law that authorized municipalities to issue bonds in aid of railroad construction.

Cooley's conception of law required it to keep hands off, as far as business was concerned—for purposes of both regulation and subsidization. The purpose of law, Cooley's opinion stated, was "to protect the industry of all, and to give all the benefit of equal laws." The law could not favor certain economic interests at the expense of others. Indeed, once the state was permitted to grant subsidies such as that at issue, the strong and powerful interests were likely to control the legislation, and "the weaker will be taxed to enhance the profits of the stronger."

Cooley was reluctant to allow government regulation involving what he termed "blind efforts to do away with the laws of supply and demand." When the Supreme Court upheld the regulation of railroads and other businesses "affected with a public interest," Cooley wrote an article to show the dangerous potential of the new doctrine.

To Cooley, the Supreme Court had opened the way to a return to the paternalism that had prevailed before the Industrial Revolution. If government could regulate all businesses that affected the public, it could fix prices, control wages, and even create monopolies. Cooley argued that price control, wage control, and state-created monopoly all belonged to the earlier "age of despotism." To allow the regulation of those who had secured advantages by "superior industry, enterprise, skill, and thrift," would, he urged, "authorize the industrious, the enterprising and the successful to be held in check whenever it was discovered that they were outstripping their fellows."

Given these views, it is not surprising that Cooley took an essentially negative view of the police power. To Cooley, that power existed only to "insure to each the uninterrupted enjoyment of his own, so far as is reasonably consistent with a like enjoyment of rights by others."

Cooley's treatment of the police power was crucial in the transformation of law from an affirmative instrument to shape the society to a negative conception that was not to interfere in the economic arena. In addition, the Cooley approach confirmed the broadside freedom of contract that would soon be considered the basic part of the liberty safeguarded by the law.

It was Cooley who originated the famous phrase usually associated with Justice Louis D. Brandeis: "the right to be let alone." In 1880, Cooley referred to "the right to be let alone" as the basic right to be protected by tort law. But it was also the foundation of both Cooley's conception of law and the jurisprudence developing under his influence. The basic theme of the merging law was that people should be left alone by the legal order—that the law should not intervene while economic interests exerted themselves freely. Law was to be conceived of negatively, a hands-off system while men did things. From this point of view, it may be said that Cooley, as much as any judge, helped to supply laissez-faire capitalism with its legal ideology.

Cooley helped to set a pattern, as to both doctrine and method, that prevailed for half a century. The pattern was not always adhered to; but it constituted the prevailing current in American public law. That the Cooley approach has been all but discarded during the twentieth century does not change its importance in its day, or the vital role that judges such as Cooley played in making it the dominant jurisprudence for so long.

7. John Bannister Gibson

John Bannister Gibson (1780–1853) must be the only judge who designed and made his own false teeth. Like other jurists of the day, however, Gibson had broad extrajudicial interests. He was a keen student of Shakespeare, read widely in French and Italian literature, and was a skilled mechanic, an expert piano tuner, and a gifted violinist. He also displayed talent as an artist; one of his best likenesses is a self-portrait.

Gibson's contribution to law is contained in his opinions—over 1500 of them during his thirty-seven years on the Pennsylvania Supreme Court. They range over the whole spectrum of legal issues and are prime examples of both their author's mastery of the common law and his ability to use it to meet American needs and conditions. To Gibson, as to Shaw, the law was essentially based on the common law. "He clung to the common law as a child to his nurse," says his biographer. However, to Gibson, the outstanding feature of the common-law method was its flexibility. Where the common-law rule was inappropriate in the new American environment, Gibson refused to follow it.

Gibson's primary contribution, like that of Shaw, was to adapt the common law to the needs of American society. Thus he refused to be bound by the paternalistic theory that then governed the law of employer–employee relations. Under the classical common-law rule, the master's relation to the apprentice stood in loco parentis. The earlier parental system was, however, being replaced by a purely monetary relationship that grew out of the emerging factory system. Gibson recognized the change when he held that the law no longer required an apprentice to live in the master's house. "In the country," he recognized, "[the apprentice] is still a part of the family." That was no longer true in the city, and "it is our duty to interpret statutes so as to fit them . . . to the business and habits of the times." Hence the courts could no longer ignore the economic reality that apprentices were being paid wages instead of board and lodging.

The overriding economic reality of the day was, of course, the expanding market economy. Like other jurists at the time, Gibson shaped the law to meet its burgeoning needs.

One of his most significant decisions confirmed the trend toward caveat emptor as an essential principle of American law. As Gibson saw it, the contrary rule that would make the seller liable would be harmful to the health of the economy. It "would put a stop to commerce itself in driving everyone out of it by the terror of endless litigation."

Just as important for the emerging capitalist economy was the spread of insurance, which enabled entrepreneurs to minimize the risks of individual losses. For the entrepreneur to feel secure in this respect, the law had to eliminate restrictive doctrines that limited the extent of coverage. An important Gibson opinion helped erode the distinction between coverage of extraordinary and ordinary risks in insurance policies. "This distinction," Gibson wrote, "has been nearly, if not altogether, obliterated by the later cases." Thus recovery should be allowed on an insurance policy for damage brought about "even by the negligence of those who had the injured vessel in charge."

Perhaps Gibson's boldest opinion was delivered in an 1850 case where the legislature had ordered a new trial to be granted in a trespass case after plaintiff had recovered judgment. To Gibson, the legislative order was patently unconstitutional. "If anything is self-evident in the structure of our government," he declared, "it is, that the Legislature has no power to order a new trial, or to direct the Court to order it, either before or after judgment. The power to order new trials is judicial."

Whatever we may think about the individualist conception on which Gibson and his confreres acted, there is no doubt that they were making law in the grand manner—or in what Karl Llewellyn called the Grand Style, a term that refers to the manner in which they made decisions, not their literary style. Gibson's place in the pantheon is based on his use of Llewellyn's Grand Style to accomplish an ongoing renovation of legal doctrine. Like Shaw, Story, and the other great jurists of the period, Gibson used the common-law method to fashion law appropriate to the changing condition of American society and the new economic era on which it was entering. Precedents were welcome and persuasive; yet they had to be tested against both principle and policy. The prospective consequences of the rule under consideration—the extent to which it would meet what Holmes was to call "the requirements of the community"—was ultimately to be the deciding factor. Selection, modification, and even invention were the tools of judges like Gibson, rather than strict adherence to received doctrine.

Gibson and his counterparts used the common-law technique, in Llewellyn's words, "not only to work toward wisdom with the materials, but, again within flexible leeways, to reword the materials themselves into wiser and better tools for tomorrow's judging." This was true throughout Gibson's judicial career. The last opinion he wrote begins in characteristic fashion: "In [prior cases] this Court infused a drop of common sense into the law of slander; and it will do no harm to infuse another. Can it be endured in the middle of the nineteenth century, that words which impute larceny of a dead man's goods are not actionable?"

8. Roger John Traynor

"It was aptly said," wrote the *New York Times* on his death, "that Roger Traynor [1900–1983] was one of the finest jurists who never sat on the United States Supreme Court." Traynor served on the California Supreme Court for thirty years—the last sixteen as Chief Justice. During the creative period through which our law passed during the middle of this century—almost a second formative era of America law—no state judge exerted a stronger influence. While Traynor sat on the bench, California became the paradigm of the mid-twentieth century. If American society became increasingly complicated, heterogeneous, diversified and anomic, California was at the crest of these trends. No state had developed so rapidly; none had undergone such massive changes in so short a time.

As one writer puts it, it was Traynor who "was to develop a theory and a technique of judging that proved responsive to the symbolic experience of California life." Under his influence, the American legal, as well as the physical, center of gravity moved westward. Before Traynor's day, the California Supreme Court had been considered a sanctuary for legal mediocrity. This all changed under Traynor's leadership. What the Massachusetts Supreme Judicial Court had been under Shaw and the New York Court of Appeals under Cardozo, the California Supreme Court became under Traynor—the most prestigious state bench in the United States. As it was put by another state judge, "There is no sounder currency in the courts across the country than a Traynor opinion."

According to the *New York Times*, "Chief Justice Traynor . . . led his court, and thus often the nation, in adapting the law to current needs and realities." The courts, he insisted, could not continue "standing by ghosts as well as living law"; they had "a creative job to do when . . . a rule has lost its touch with reality and should be abandoned or reformulated to meet new conditions and new moral values." Traynor's work emphasized the creative capabilities of the judiciary; his contributions to the changing American law can be compared with those made by earlier American masters of the judicial craft. All branches of the law felt the innovative Traynor touch.

In constitutional law, Traynor anticipated landmark decisions of the United States Supreme Court. A Traynor opinion struck down a California miscegenation law, prohibiting marriages between whites and blacks, years before the Supreme Court decision invalidating such a law. Another opinion adopted the exclusionary rule, barring evidence obtained unlawfully. The Traynor opinion directly influenced the Supreme Court to later hold that the Constitution requires the exclusionary rule in state criminal cases.

In torts, the area of his widest impact, Traynor pioneered in the development of strict liability, helped create the new tort of intentional infliction of emotional distress, and undermined the defense of immunity in tort actions—whether charitable, family, or sovereign. In most other substantive areas, too, Traynor helped set the law's ghosts at rest in the past to which they belonged. In property, family law, conflict of laws, taxation, and procedure, he discarded or reformulated older doctrines to recast the law in contemporary terms.

As much as any judge, Traynor was an exemplar of twentieth-century pragmatic jurisprudence. As he saw it, the law had "a creative job to do" in adapting itself to the burgeoning problems of contemporary life. In performing the job, Traynor may have been as activist as any jurist in our history. Yet he masked his activism beneath a layer of reasoned discourse; his mastery of legal technique covered his opinions with a tone of relentless impersonality which hid his pursuit of policy objectives in a mass of traditional reasoning.

Traynor's opinion in *Escola v. Coca Cola Bottling Co.* (1944) was an outstanding example of his technique. A waitress was injured when a Coca-Cola bottle exploded. Traynor wrote that negligence should no longer be the sole basis for recovery in such a case. Instead, he stressed the changing relationship between producer and consumer in present-day society, where the consumer could not guard adequately against defective products. The party best situated to bear the risks of defective products was the manufacturer, which, even if not negligent in manufacture of the product, is responsible for its reaching the market. The cost of injury should be borne by it: "The manufacturer's obligation to the consumer must keep pace with the changing relationship between them."

Like Cardozo's *MacPherson v. Buick Motor Co.* opinion, change was presented as though it were the inevitable result of the evolving law of defective products—an impersonal, rational solution that any objective judge would have reached. Far-reaching change was masked by the use of traditional techniques of logical analysis that made the result appear the natural outcome of the developing tort law.

Traynor's effectiveness stems from his mastery of those techniques, which enabled him to persuade the law to accept his innovations. Traynor was a greater virtuoso of the judicial art than any judge since Cardozo. The Traynor opinion is a craftsman-like working-out of the issues within the frame of reference given by the existing law. The great judge, Traynor once said, must "create some fragments of legal order out of disordered masses of new data." The quality of the "fragments of legal order" which came from Traynor's bench helped bring American law closer to his own ideal of law as a structured system of norms at once rationally ordered and responsive to contemporary needs.

9. John Appleton

The fox, goes the old saying, knows many things, but the hedgehog knows one great thing. John Appleton's (1804–1891) contribution to law consisted of one great thing: an overriding conception that the true end of a legal proceeding "is the ascertainment of the truth."

So far as Appleton is remembered today, it is for his efforts to give effect to this conception by reforming the law of evidence. According to a contemporary commentator, Appleton's conclusions on evidence "are, in a legal sense, extremely radical." The essence of Appleton's "radical" proposals is contained in the principle that was the foundation of his work: "The end, alike to be attained in civil or criminal procedure by the introduction of testimony, is the ascertainment of the truth." This led Appleton to his basic conclusion that all persons who "can perceive, and perceiving can make known their perceptions to others, should be received and examined as witnesses." Objections, he urged, "may be made to the credit, but never to the competency of witnesses."

To us today, Appleton's principle and conclusions are all but self-evident. The situation was different when he wrote. At that time, the parties to actions and criminal defendants were not permitted to give evidence. Appleton's principal attack was against this rule. His premise was that the courts should seek information from those most fully acquainted with the facts.

When Appleton began his attack on the evidentiary exclusion rules, he was the proverbial voice crying in the wilderness. Yet as time went on, most of the reforms Appleton advocated were adopted, starting with an 1857 Maine statute permitting interested persons, including parties, to testify. Appleton tells us that this change "struck with horror that class of minds whose conservatism consists in the love of abuses, and in the hatred of their reformation." Similar statutes were, however, soon enacted in the other states. Comparable laws were passed permitting criminal defendants to testify, culminating in an 1878 statute extending the reform to the federal courts.

When Appleton urged his evidence reforms, he was already a member of Maine's highest court. He was elevated to the office of Chief Justice and served in that position until his retirement. As a judge, Appleton was a state counterpart of Justice Field, who, we saw was the leader in the constitutionalization of laissez-faire during the latter part of the nineteenth century. On the bench, Appleton's laissez-faire approach went so far that he even condemned usury laws as an unjust interference with freedom of contract. What he called in an opinion "the barbarous laws in relation to interest" had to give way to "unrestricted liberty of contracting as to the rate of interest."

For Appleton, the proper legal posture was that which was becoming the prevailing one as the century went on: hands off while private interests asserted themselves freely. "Restrictions," Appleton declared, "are always considered *prima facie* inexpedient. Any infringement on liberty of action is dangerous. . . . It may be assumed as an unquestionable truth that each individual is *best* competent to manage his own concerns."

The restrictions Appleton condemned were not only those imposed by social legislation, but also those in legal rules that resulted in burdens on economic enterprise. Thus Appleton followed Shaw in helping to ensure that fault would become the basis of American tort law. As an Appleton opinion pithily put it, "The defendants have done no wrong, and why should they suffer?"

Underlying the Appleton jurisprudence was the nineteenth century's commitment to an untrammeled market economy. Individual liberty in the marketplace was his root principle—in law as in economics. Operation of the market should not be interfered with by government—whether to impede it by regulation or to favor certain participants in its operation. As an 1871 opinion declared, "the less the State interferes with industry, the less it directs and selects the channels of enterprise, the better." For Appleton, state intervention in the market "is communism incipient."

Appleton mirrored the jurisprudence of the day in his economic and legal views. But he was more than the legal theorist. His position as the head of a state high court enabled him to play a leading part in the legalization of laissez-faire. The Appleton jurisprudence contributed directly to the changing conception of law from a positive instrument of social and economic development to the more negative conception that was emerging.

Yet Appleton's jurisprudence was not a mere laissez-faire clone. To the commentator today, what sets Appleton apart from other leading jurists of the day was his emphasis on reform—reform not in substantive law, but in the rules of evidence on which the vindication of substantive rights depends. The jurists of the new nation had focused on the legal rules that could meet the needs of the emerging society and economy. Appleton saw that this was not enough: justice could scarcely be done while the law excluded so much pertinent evidence. No matter how sound the substantive law may be, Appleton wrote, "if the rules of evidence are erroneous, the wisdom of the law is no better than so much folly, the will of the legislator is unheeded, his rewards unreapt, his penalties unimposed." In Appleton's day, what has been called the "sporting theory" of justice was still dominant. Adherence to the rules of the game was just as important as, if not more important than, the search for truth. The adversary justice system was a prime example of the survival of the fittest, with truth more often the victim than the result of the law in action.

Now Appleton announced that truth, not mere observance of the rules, was what the legal process was all about. Indeed, it was the evidence rules themselves that were the main barriers to truth. Appleton's work helped to remove many of those barriers. With Appleton, too, a new dimension was added to American jurisprudence.

10. Arthur T. Vanderbilt

According to America's foremost legal scholar, Roscoe Pound, "the life of the law is in its enforcement." Much of the progress in twentieth-century law has involved giving effect to this Pound dictum. As the century went on, jurists increasingly came to see that more had to be done than simply to bring legal rules up to date. A new, pragmatic approach to both law and its effectiveness was needed. The new approach would stress not only substantive law, but also court organization and procedure; it increasingly recognized that through the latter, rules and precepts were translated into reality.

If there has been increasing stress on judicial reform, much of the credit must be given to Arthur T. Vanderbilt (1888–1957). Vanderbilt was the outstanding judicial administrator in our history. His administrative accomplishments have been emphasized so much that even lawyers have tended to forget that he was an outstanding jurist.

The challenge of law reform (the title of one of his books) became Vanderbilt's great passion. He practiced in New Jersey, a state whose court system had become a byword for judicial inefficiency. Vanderbilt devoted his professional life to the reform of the New Jersey court system. More than that, he was the rare example of a reformer who not only designed, but was given what he called the opportunity to "practice what I have been preaching." Years of effort culminated in setting up a modern, integrated New Jersey court system in 1947—a reform of which Vanderbilt was the principal architect. He was then appointed Chief Justice of the New Jersey Supreme Court, which made him the administrative head of the new court system. Under his leadership, the New Jersey courts, so long synonymous with judicial inefficiency, speedily became the model judiciary. Calendar lag was virtually eliminated, as the new chief used his powers to bring court management into the twentieth century.

To Vanderbilt, however, securing a sound court structure and effective judicial administration was only a part of law reform. Equally important was the modernization of substantive law and procedure. Like the other judges who have contributed to the growth of American law, he had, as he once put it, "always in mind the necessity of adapting the law to the needs of our rapidly changing society." According to a biographer, "A common thread woven through many of his 211 opinions was an attempt to make the substantive law of New Jersey suitable to contemporary conditions." The common law, declares a typical Vanderbilt opinion, "is a living and growing body of legal principles. It derives its life and growth from judicial decisions which alter an existing rule, or abandon an old rule and substitute in its place a new one in order to meet new conditions."

On the bench, Vanderbilt had two overriding judicial themes. The first was that, in the words of one opinion, "the courts are under as great an obligation to revise an outmoded rule of the common law as the legislatures are to abolish or modernize an archaic statute." In addition, the courts were under an obligation to maintain their position as a coordinate governmental branch against even the legislature itself. This position led to Vanderbilt's most important opinion, and also his most controversial, which held that the judicial department was vested with inherent power to prescribe its own rules of practice and procedure—power that was not subject to legislative control. A contrary view, Vanderbilt asserted, would mean that "the courts in some of their essential judicial operations, instead of being one of the coordinate branches of the state government, would have been rendered subservient to the Legislature."

The Vanderbilt position that the judiciary is endowed with autonomy over its own internal functioning appears preferable to the federal rule that recognizes congressional primacy in the matter. Analytically, there is no more warrant for permitting the legislature to impose a straitjacket of statutory procedure on the courts than there is for permitting the converse to happen.

In summing up, however, one must concede that Vanderbilt's legal contribution rests more on his work as a law reformer (particularly in judicial administration) than as a jurist. In this respect, Vanderbilt's career gave substance to one writer's assertion that, as far as law reform was concerned, "without doubt, he was the country's most effective man in one state in this century." As a leading federal judge summed it up, Vanderbilt used his constitutional position to "make the legal system of [his] state a model for the other states of the Union." The relative weight to be given to such an accomplishment is shown by the comment of Chief Justice Hughes to a denigrator of the administrative role of a chief justice: "You are quite mistaken. What I have accomplished in the Federal Courts will live for decades after my opinions are forgotten."

Federal Judges and Greatness

Perhaps the most surprising thing about this list is my failure to include more federal judges. There is no doubt that the caliber of federal judges has generally been higher than that of judges in the state courts. Almost everyone will agree that Learned Hand should be on any list of non-

Supreme Court greats. But are there no other federal judges worthy of inclusion in the elect?

Judge Richard Posner has complained that there is little interest in the operation of the lower federal courts: "[T]o so many legal academics nowadays, a Supreme Court Justice is the *typical* judge and the rest of the judiciary is invisible." The reason, however, is that, in our system, the federal lower court judges have few opportunities to mold the growth of the law. As far as constitutional law is concerned, that opportunity is virtually confined to members of the Supreme Court. "The body of constitutional law," Posner tells us, "has been created very largely by the Supreme Court rather than by . . . lower-court judges; . . . and all the great constitutional law cases are Supreme Court cases."

As far as our private law—what Immanuel Kant called the law of "meum and teum"—is concerned, the creative role has been performed almost entirely by the state courts. Indeed, in our federal system, the federal courts are normally bound on matters of private law by the decisions of the relevant state courts. Those matters present questions of state, not federal law; and it is only federal questions that the federal judges may decide independently.

Justice Holmes, we saw, once said that John Marshall's greatness consisted in his being *there*—that he led the Supreme Court when the Constitution was still plastic and malleable. The outstanding fact about the lower federal judges consists in their not being *there*—however qualified they may have been, they did not have the opportunity to mold the law that Supreme Court Justices and the great state judges have had.

This brings me back to the discussion of judicial greatness at the end of the Supreme Court list. The judges on this non-Supreme Court list are also there because of their influence on our law. Kent, Shaw, and Gibson were foremost in the movement to mold the common law to meet the conditions of the new nation. Appleton added an additional dimension in the search for legal truth. He also, with Cooley and Doe, led the adaptation of the law to the needs of the new industrial economy. Cardozo and Traynor helped to ensure that the law would deal with twentieth-century societal change, while Vanderbilt sparked the effort to obtain court reform. Learned Hand remains what Holmes once called a "uniquity." Considered by all the greatest judge never to sit on the Supreme Court, he transcended the limitations that keep lower court judges out of the pantheon and had more influence on the law than most members of the highest Court.

The judges on this list are not there because their jurisprudence accords with today's conceptions. Indeed, few at present would agree

with the extreme laissez-faire of nineteenth-century law as it was molded
by the judges on the list. Where they saw only the need to free enterprise
from restraints, we stress the cost to others in the society. They developed
tort law as they did to relieve employers of what one termed "an intolerable . . . burden upon the development of business." Instead, the cost of
industrial accidents was thrown on the injured worker. "The encouragement of 'infant industries,'" wrote Leonard W. Levy in his biography of
Chief Justice Shaw, "had no greater social cost."

But that is not the point. "Some might insist," Judge Posner tells us,
"that a judge's greatness consists in the 'rightness' of his decisions as
judged by the test of time." For Posner, "this is too demanding a standard. Most judicial decisions, even of the agreed-to-be-the-greatest
judges, like most scientific discoveries, even of the universally acknowledged greatest scientists, usually are superseded and in that sense even-
tually proved 'wrong.'" The judges on this list molded the law to meet
what they deemed the "felt necessities of [their] time," and their success
in doing so by use of the traditional techniques is what places them at the
judicial apex. After all, as Posner puts it, "the test of greatness for the substance of judicial decisions . . . should be, as in the case of science, the contribution that the decisions make to the development of legal rules and
principles rather than whether the decision is a 'classic' having the permanence and perfection of a work of art." To be sure, if Posner thinks that
permanence is a characteristic of art considered "great," he should consult the shades of painters such as Bougereau and Meissonier, who were
considered *the* greats of painting when Cooley and Doe presided over
their courts. That aside, however, Posner is surely correct. What makes
for judicial greatness is the contribution that the judge's decisions make
to the development of the law. The judges on this list meet that standard
with flying colors.

8

TEN

GREATEST

NON-SUPREME COURT

DECISIONS

Our law has been, in the main, a product of judicial lawmaking—the prime agency in its shaping the court decision. It is the judges who received the common law and adapted it to American conditions. More recently, they have developed new principles, in the process remolding and refashioning the law to meet the needs of a changing society. In private law particularly, our law is the product primarily of the great state judges, and the decisions producing it deserve inclusion in this book. In constitutional law, too, state courts have made important contributions, though they are usually overshadowed by the decisions of the highest Court. Some of the most important Supreme Court doctrines were originally formulated in state decisions on this list. Also included is a decision by a federal district court that was a landmark in First Amendment law.

— ★ — ★ — ★ —

— ★ — ★ — ★ —

Ten Greatest Non-Supreme Court Decisions

1. *Bayard v. Singleton,*
   1 Martin 42 (N.C. 1787)

2. *Wynehamer v. People,*
   13 N.Y. 378 (1856)

3. *Commonwealth v. Alger,*
   7 Cush. 53 (Mass. 1851)

4. *Brown v. Kendall,*
   6 Cush. 292 (Mass. 1850)

5. *MacPherson v. Buick Motor Co.,*
   217 N.Y. 382 (1916)

6. *Brown v. Collins,*
   53 N.H. 442 (1873)

7. *Muskopf v. Corning Hospital District,*
   359 P.2d 457 (Cal. 1961)

8. *Palsgraf v. Long Island Railroad Co.,*
   248 N.Y. 339 (1928)

9. *United States v. One Book Called "Ulysses,"*
   5 F. Supp. 182 (S.D.N.Y. 1933)

10. *Commonwealth v. Peaslee,*
    177 Mass. 267 (1901)

1. *Bayard v. Singleton*

Before the decision in *Marbury v. Madison* (1803), and even before the adoption of the Constitution, state courts exercised the power to rule on constitutionality. The clearest pre-Constitution case in which a state court exercised review power was *Bayard v. Singleton* (1787), decided just before the Constitutional Convention met in Philadelphia. The North Carolina Supreme Court held a statute invalid because it violated the guarantee of trial by jury in cases involving property contained in the state constitution. The court's language is a ringing affirmation of judicial review. According to a contemporary report of the case,

> the judges observed. . . . [t]hat by the Constitution every citizen had undoubtedly a right to a decision of his property by a trial by jury. For that if the legislature could take away this right, and require him to stand condemned in his property without a trial, it might with as much authority require his life to be taken away without a trial by jury, and that he should stand condemned to die, without the formality of any trial at all; that if the members of the General assembly could do this, they might with equal authority, not only render themselves the legislators of the State for life, without any further election of the people, from thence transmit the dignity and authority of legislation down to their heirs male forever.

In language that foreshadowed that in *Marbury v. Madison*, the North Carolina court declared "that no Act they could pass, could by any means repeal or alter the Constitution. . . . Consequently the Constitution (which the judicial power was bound to take notice of as much as of any other law whatever), standing in full force as the fundamental law of the land, notwithstanding the Act on which the present motion was grounded, the same Act must of course, in that instance, stand as abrogated and without any effect."

Even clearer was the defense of *Bayard* by James Iredell, later a Justice of the Supreme Court, who had been attorney for plaintiff in the case. While attending the Constitutional Convention, Richard Dobbs Spaight wrote to Iredell condemning the *Bayard* decision as a "usurpation," which "operated as an absolute negative on the proceedings of the Legislature, which no judiciary ought ever to possess." Iredell replied, "[I]t has ever been my opinion, that an act inconsistent with the Constitution was void; and that the judges, consistently with their duties could not carry it into effect." Far from a "usurpation," the power to declare unconstitutional laws void flowed directly from the judicial duty of applying the law; "either . . . the *fundamental unrepealable* law must be obeyed, by the rejection of an act unwarranted by and inconsistent with it, or you must obey an act founded on authority not given by the people." The exercise of review power, said Iredell, was unavoidable: "It is not that the judges are appointed arbiters . . . ; but when an act is necessarily brought in judgment before them, they must, unavoidably, determine one way or another. . . . Must not they say whether they will obey the Constitution or an act inconsistent with it?"

Bayard and Iredell's answer show that *Marbury v. Madison* was anything but a radical innovation. Even before the Constitution, Americans had come to accept judicial review. Marshall only authenticated this pre-Constitution consensus. Because of decisions like *Bayard*, he could state in *Marbury* not that the Constitution establishes, but that it "confirms" the Court's review power.

2. *Wynehamer v. People*

Taken literally, the constitutional guarantee against deprivation of life, liberty, or property without due process of law is only a guarantee of fair procedure. By now, of course, due process has developed into a substantive, as well as a procedural, limitation. The decision that laid the foundation for this development was the New York case of *Wynehamer v. People* (1856).

Wynehamer arose out of a law that prohibited the sale of liquor except for medicinal purposes and the storage of liquor not intended for sale in any place but a dwelling house. The law further provided for immediate summary destruction of all liquor held in violation of its provisions, and made any violation a misdemeanor. The New York Court of Appeals ruled that the law operated to "annihilate and destroy the rights of property which the citizens of this state possessed, at the time it took effect, in intoxicating liquors." This might not be done consistently with the due process clause. In so holding, the court was clearly giving due process a substantive connotation. Such a deprivation, providing for the destruction of property already in the possession of its owner, was beyond the power of government, "even by the forms which belong to 'due process of law.'" The statute at issue, though it contains no procedural defects, falls "certainly within the spirit of a constitutional provision intended expressly to shield private rights from the exercise of arbitrary power." In fact, according to *Wynehamer*, the very "object of [the due process clause] was . . . to interpose the judicial department of the government as a barrier against aggressions by the other departments."

The *Wynehamer* decision was recognized as epoch-making almost as soon as it was rendered. This was true even though it was soon seen that the immediate holding in *Wynehamer* went too far, because of the well-nigh complete power of the states over intoxicating liquors, which even the New York courts came to recognize. The reasoning of the *Wynehamer* court—its use of substantive due process as a check on arbitrary governmental power—was to be that ultimately adopted by American courts, including the highest bench in the land after ratification of the Fourteenth Amendment.

What the *Wynehamer* approach has meant to our law was well pointed out by the second Justice Harlan in a 1961 opinion: "Were due process merely a procedural safeguard it would fail to reach those situations where the deprivation of life, liberty or property was accomplished by legislation which . . . could, given even the fairest possible procedure . . . , nevertheless destroy the enjoyment of all three." Hence it is, Harlan explains, that "the guaranties of due process . . . have in this country also 'become bulwarks against arbitrary legislation.'"

3. *Commonwealth v. Alger*

The greatest decisions are, of course, usually produced by the greatest judges. Lemuel Shaw was the outstanding nineteenth-century state judge. As Massachusetts Chief Justice, Shaw wrote some of the seminal opinions that helped lay the foundation for our evolving law. Two deserve inclusion on this list: *Commonwealth v. Alger* (1851), the first state case to speak of the *police power*—ever since a vital part of governmental authority—and *Brown v. Kendall*, which established fault as the basis of tort liability.

At a time when the law's "be all and end all" was the sanctity of private property—"The moment," wrote John Adams, "the idea is admitted into society that property is not as sacred as the laws of God . . . anarchy and tyranny commence"—Shaw's contribution was to recognize government regulatory power. Like the other great judges during our law's formative era, Shaw helped to construct a private-law system that encouraged people to venture for productive ends. But this did not prevent him from recognizing an overriding governmental power to regulate in the public interest. Shaw was the first American judge to recognize "the police power, the power vested in the legislature by the constitution, to make, ordain and establish all manner of wholesome and reasonable laws . . . not repugnant to the constitution, as they shall judge to be for the good and welfare of the commonwealth." This now-classic definition of the police power was rendered in *Alger*, where Shaw made the first comprehensive attempt at analysis of this vital power.

Defendant in *Alger* had violated a statute that prohibited building a wharf beyond boundary lines fixed by the legislature. Defendant claimed that since he had built the wharf on his own property, the law was invalid; the state might not interfere with his property rights without compensation. In rejecting the defense, the Shaw opinion emphasized the paramountcy of public over property rights. All property rights, it declared, "are subject to some restraint for the general good." The legislature has the power "of defining and securing the rights of the public" and "to make such reasonable regulations as they judge necessary to protect public . . . rights."

Shaw's language was magisterial: "We think it is a settled principle, growing out of the nature of well ordered civil society, that every holder of property, however absolute and unqualified may be his title, holds it under the implied liability that his use of it may be so regulated, that it shall not be injurious to . . . others. Rights of property, like all other . . . rights, are subject to . . . such reasonable restraints and regulations established by law, as the legislature . . . may think necessary and expedient."

Shaw's leading biographer calls *Alger* "an opinion that is one of the most influential and frequently cited in constitutional law." Only four years after *Alger*, the Missouri court could say of the power given classic connotation by Shaw that it was "known familiarly as the police power." By the time of the Civil War, the term was in common use throughout the land. Thenceforth, a principal task of the courts was to be determination of the proper balance between individual rights and the police power.

4. *Brown v. Kendall*

Brown v. Kendall (1850), the second great Shaw decision, was largely responsible for the rule that negligence must be proved before a defendant is liable in tort. As the case was later summarized by Holmes, "the defendant while trying to separate two fighting dogs, had raised his stick over his shoulder in the act of striking, and had accidentally hit the plaintiff in the eye, inflicting upon him a severe injury. The . . . court held that, although the defendant was bound by no duty to separate the dogs, yet, if he was doing a lawful act, he was not liable unless he was wanting in the care which men of ordinary prudence would use under the circumstances." In the words of Shaw's *Brown* opinion, "unless it also appears . . . that the defendant is chargeable with some fault, negligence, carelessness, or want of prudence, the plaintiff . . . is not entitled to recover."

"In such a matter," Holmes was to comment, "no authority is more deserving of respect than that of Chief Justice Shaw." *Brown v. Kendall* was speedily followed in other states, and the Supreme Court also gave its sanction to the Shaw doctrine. Under Shaw's leadership, American law shifted from the common law's absolute liability (even without fault) to "no liability without culpability"—the basic maxim of the new tort law. Because of the Shaw decision, Holmes could state as established law "that the general notion upon which liability to an action is founded is fault or blameworthiness."

Shaw and the judges who followed his lead were not, however, concerned with *fault* "in the sense of personal moral shortcoming." Instead, there was a general principle that the law should not get involved in the accident arena, where both sides were blameless. As Holmes put it, the state's "cumbrous and expensive machinery ought not to be set in motion unless some clear benefit is to be derived from disturbing the *status quo*. State interference is an evil, where it cannot be shown to be a good."

The result was the evolution of tort law as a reflection of business needs. The common-law rule of absolute liability could not serve an expanding economy that depended upon entrepreneurs' willingness to take risks. Now businessmen knew that they would not be subjected to liability unless they themselves were negligent or otherwise at fault.

5. *MacPherson v. Buick Motor Co.*

Benjamin N. Cardozo was the preeminent state judge of the twentieth century. More than any judge, he demonstrated how the common-law technique could be adapted to contemporary needs. During Cardozo's years on the New York bench, the traditional law confronted the momentum of mature industrialization, which transformed economic and social relations. Cardozo showed how the common-law method could be used to meet the requirements of a modern legal system. The Cardozo opinion in *MacPherson v. Buick Motor Co.* (1916) played a major part in the transformation of the negligence concept during this century. The *MacPherson* issue was summarized by Cardozo himself in a lecture: "A maker of automobiles is sued by the victim of an accident. The plaintiff bought the vehicle, not from the maker, but from someone else. He asserts that there was negligence in the process of manufacture and that privity of contract is unnecessary to confer a right of action."

Before *MacPherson*, plaintiff could not recover from the manufacturer, but only from the dealer from whom he had bought the auto. Cardozo's *MacPherson* decision held that "the law . . . must be said to be in accordance with the plaintiff's claim." The manufacturer, by placing a product such as an automobile on the market, was held to assume a responsibility to the consumer, resting not on contract or tort in the traditional sense, but on the relation arising from the purchase and the fact that harm was foreseeable in a large proportion of cases. "Precedents drawn from the days of travel by stage coach," Cardozo declared, "do not fit the conditions of travel to-day." The principles of tort liability "are whatever the needs of life in a developing civilization require them to be."

In a 1931 address, Cardozo referred to the refusal of British courts to follow the *MacPherson* doctrine. From this, he said, "I see that we have come to a fork in the road; that the branch we have laid out is something more than a blind alley; that we are developing a technique of our own, and are shaping the law of today in response to a philosophy which is indigenous, which is something more than a mechanical reproduction of philosophy abroad." The Cardozo opinion in *MacPherson* showed that the common law in the United States was not a static collection of rules, but living law still capable of growth and adaptation to new conditions.

MacPherson adapted the experience of the past to serve the needs of the present. In it, Cardozo carried forward the work of reshaping the law to changing conditions, which has always been the contribution of our greatest judges. To Cardozo, the end of law was that of serving contemporary needs. But he not only saw that that goal was the main thing, but also showed how the goal could be attained by traditional common-law methods. The *MacPherson* opinion has been characterized by Judge Richard A. Posner as "Cardozo's classic manipulation of precedent." In it, Cardozo wrote in terms of the prior decisions and purported to apply them with only modifications to fit present conditions. The policy considerations that had motivated the decision were left virtually unstated. Yet, in Posner's words, "modest though it was in pretending to be restating rather than changing the law of New York, reticent as it was about the policy considerations relevant to the change it made, the opinion nevertheless managed to change [the law] profoundly."

It was, however, Posner goes on, "the very caution, modesty, and reticence of the opinion that explain its rapid adoption by other states." A commentator tells us that *MacPherson* "brought the law into line with 'social considerations.'" Yet Cardozo did so not by stressing the ends served by the extension of liability, but by purporting to proceed only by the common-law technique of analogy from the decided cases. If, in terms of tort law, *MacPherson* was revolutionary, it was, in Judge Posner's phrase, "the quietest of revolutionary manifestos, the least unsettling to conservative professional sensibilities." There is no better illustration of Cardozo's use of the common-law method to make needed changes in the law.

6. *Brown v. Collins*

The opinion of Chief Justice Charles Doe in *Brown v. Collins* (1873) is a prime example of a great judge adapting English law to American needs. The fact pattern, like that in so many leading cases, involved a minor legal controversy. As stated in one report, "Defendant's horses, while being driven by him, with due care, on a public highway, were frightened by a locomotive, became unmanageable and ran upon plaintiff's land and broke a post there." Plaintiff brought an action to recover the value of the post. Doe's opinion held that defendant was not liable.

Doe used the case to deal with the rule laid down five years earlier in the famous English case of *Rylands v. Fletcher*. As summarized by the young Oliver Wendell Holmes, *Rylands* held "a man liable for the escape of water from a reservoir which he has built upon his land, or for the escape of cattle, although he is not alleged to have been negligent, they do not proceed upon the ground that there is an element of culpability" but that "those who go into extra-hazardous employments take the risk."

"We take the case," Doe's opinion states, "as one where, without actual fault in the defendant, his horses broke from his control, ran away with him, went upon the plaintiff's land, and did damage there, against the will, intent, and desire of the defendant." Stated that way, Doe's biographer tells us, "the issue could not have been drawn more clearly: can a defendant who acted lawfully be held liable for damage resulting from an inevitable accident not his fault? The *Rylands* decision held that under special circumstances he could. Judge Doe's answer was that he could not."

Doe rejected the *Rylands* rule because he thought it unsuited to American economic needs. In this country, the law had become a prime instrument of economic expansion, and the businessman's idea of land as something to be used for commercial purposes led to Doe's rejection of *Rylands*. According to Doe's opinion, *Rylands* had adopted "an arbitrary test of responsibility" that was inappropriate in a "nation [that] had . . .

settled down to those modern, progressive, industrial pursuits which the spirit of the common law, adapted to all conditions of society, encourages and defends."

Doe's ultimate rationale was that *Rylands* "puts a clog upon natural and reasonably necessary uses of matter, and tends to embarrass and obstruct much of the work which seems to be man's duty carefully to do." To create such an exception to fault liability would, he wrote, impede "the growth of . . . trade and productive enterprise" by penalizing acts of commerce conducted in a careful manner. To follow *Rylands* would have made American manufacturers responsible for all the consequences of their operations, even those performed in a prudent manner. For Doe, "[i]t is impossible that legal principle can throw so serious an obstacle in the way of progress and improvement."

The greatness of *Brown v. Collins* is not affected by the fact that, as the individualistic law of Doe's day gave way to that of the welfare state, *Rylands v. Fletcher* made a comeback. With this century's emphasis on compensation for those injured, the situation has changed. In its time, *Brown v. Collins* was a leading case adapting the law to the demands of business expansion. In a developed economy, changing social needs as now perceived by the judges have led the pendulum to swing toward acceptance of *Rylands*.

7. *Muskopf v. Corning Hospital District*

We now look on the early judges who made our law as mythical figures who have become legends to generations of lesser men. After all, as a Supreme Court Justice stated just before the Civil War, "There were giants in those days." Yet even in our own day, as the lists of greatest Justices and judges show, there have been giants who belong in the judicial pantheon.

The most recent of them was Roger J. Traynor, Chief Justice of the California Supreme Court. He did more than any judge since Cardozo to help adapt our law to present-day needs. When Traynor felt that the law needed changes, he was as bold as any judge in accomplishing them. Like Chief Justice Earl Warren himself, he was not deterred by a mass of precedents the other way, however august and ancient they might be. Few legal doctrines were of greater vintage than that of sovereign immunity, which had completely barred tort suits against government. The doctrine is one of the oldest in Anglo-American law. Almost from the dawn of English legal history, the principle barring suits against the king has been followed.

Why the English doctrine came to be applied to the United States is, as Traynor himself pointed out, one of the mysteries of legal evolution. Sovereign immunity in American law was, in Justice Frankfurter's phrase, "an anachronistic survival of monarchical privilege"—and that in a country whose very independence was based on successful resistance to the demands of monarchical privilege. But however anachronistic it may be, it was plain that, when Traynor became a judge, even in the American democracy, a basic principle of public law was that the king could do no wrong.

Before Traynor, sovereign immunity remained firmly entrenched in American law. Indeed, in a survey of the subject in a 1958 book just before Traynor's landmark opinion in *Muskopf v. Corning Hospital District* (1961), I concluded that "the doctrine of sovereign immunity has never been expressly repudiated by an American court."

Traynor's *Muskopf* opinion changed all that. It held flatly that "the rule of governmental immunity from tort liability . . . must be discarded as mistaken and unjust." If the reasons for the immunity rule "ever had any substance they have none today"; none of them "can withstand analysis." Sovereign immunity in tort "is an anachronism, without rational basis, and has existed only by the force of inertia." That was not enough, regardless of the plethora of cases over the centuries following the doctrine, to stop Traynor from pronouncing its requiem. The Traynor decision was that "the doctrine of governmental immunity for torts . . . has no place in our law." *Muskopf* "concluded that it must be discarded as mistaken and unjust" and held that suits against government might be brought.

Traynor's *Muskopf* opinion has had a seminal effect. The courts in a majority of states have followed the Traynor lead in disavowing sovereign immunity and thus, in the words of one court, resolved "a great problem which has festered in the courts for many years."

8. *Palsgraf v. Long Island Railroad Co.*

The facts in *Palsgraf v. Long Island Railroad Co.* (1928) presented what has been called "a law professor's dream of an examination question." A passenger was running to catch defendant's train. Defendant's guards, trying to assist the passenger, pushed him onto the train. In doing so, they dislodged a package from the passenger's arms. It contained fireworks, which exploded. The explosion overturned some scales at the other end of the platform, and they fell on plaintiff and injured her. The jury found that the guards had been negligent in the way they pushed the passenger.

The Cardozo opinion held that there was no liability, because there was no negligence toward plaintiff. Negligence, Cardozo said, was a matter of relation between the parties: "The risk reasonably to be perceived defines the duty to be obeyed, and risk imports relation; it is risk to another or to others within the range of apprehension." The key was the foreseeability of harm to the person injured.

Defendant's conduct was not a wrong toward plaintiff merely because it was negligence toward someone else. Instead, "wrong is defined in terms of the natural or probable." A plaintiff "must show that the act as to him had possibilities of danger so many and apparent as to entitle him to be protected against the doing of it though the harm was unintended." Hence, Cardozo concluded, "[t]he law of causation, remote or proximate is thus foreign to the case before us." If the court held otherwise, the opinion asserted, "[l]ife will have to be made over, and human nature transformed, before provision so extravagant can be accepted as the norm of conduct, the customary standard to which behavior must conform."

According to a leading text, *Palsgraf* "has become the most discussed and debated of all tort cases." To law students, it is perhaps the most famous non-Supreme Court decision; untold thousands of them have been weaned on it, and it is still a principal case in current tort casebooks.

9. *United States v.* *One Book Called "Ulysses"*

This celebrated First Amendment decision was made not by the Supreme Court or another appellate court, but by an otherwise obscure federal district judge: John M. Woolsey. Aside from his decision in *United States v. One Book called* "Ulysses," (1933), Woolsey was a pedestrian judge, who could be characterized by Gerald Gunther as one whose "personal idiosyncracies soon overshadowed his professional abilities." The law is, however, made not only by the Holmeses and Cardozos. Throughout legal history, average judges have risen to the occasion presented by great cases.

Such an occasion was presented to Judge Woolsey when customs officials seized a copy of James Joyce's *Ulysses* and brought an action to condemn it that came before Woolsey for decision. The law on obscenity at that time was restrictive. As summarized by Woolsey, "The meaning of the word 'obscene' as legally defined by the courts is: Tending to stir the sex impulses or to lead to sexually impure and lustful thoughts." This test had been criticized by Judge Learned Hand, who questioned whether "truth and beauty are [not] too precious to society at large to be mutilated in the interests of those most likely to pervert them to base uses." Woolsey's opinion narrowed the test to the effect on "the normal person": "Whether a particular book would tend to excite such impulses and thoughts must be tested by the court's opinion as to its effect on a person with average sex instincts—what the French would call *l'homme moyen sensuel*."

In addition, Woolsey rejected the prevailing rule that obscenity was to be judged by isolated passages; the practice was to mark offending passages in red and rest the decision solely on them. According to Woolsey, the obscenity decision must be based on "reading 'Ulysses' in its entirety, as a book must be read on such a test."

Applying his approach to *Ulysses*, Woolsey found that the work was not obscene. First of all, Woolsey stated, "in 'Ulysses,' in spite of its unusual frankness, I do not detect anywhere the leer of the sensualist. I hold, therefore, that it is not pornographic." Instead, "Joyce sought to make a serious experiment in a new, if not wholly novel, literary genre. . . . Joyce has attempted—it seems to me, with astonishing success—to show how the screen of consciousness with its ever-shifting kaleidoscopic impressions carries, as it were on a plastic palimpsest, not only what is in the focus of each man's observation of the actual things about him, but also in a penumbral zone residua of past impressions, some recent and some drawn up by association from the domain of the subconscious. He shows how each of these impressions affects the life and behavior of the character which he is describing."

What Joyce was trying to do was "to tell fully what his characters think about." This attempt, wrote Woolsey, required "the passages of which the government particularly complains": "For his attempt sincerely and honestly to realize his objective has required him incidentally to use certain words which are generally considered dirty words and has led at times to what many think is a too poignant preoccupation with sex in the thoughts of his characters." Despite this, "I hold that 'Ulysses' is a sincere and honest book," and even "an amazing tour de force." It does not contain "anything that I consider to be dirt for dirt's sake."

In addition, "[i]f one does not wish to associate with such folk as Joyce describes, that is one's own choice." No one has to read the book, and it is understandable if many do not. "But when such a great artist in words, as Joyce undoubtedly is, seeks to draw a true picture of the lower middle class in a European city, ought it to be impossible for the American public legally to see that picture?"

"I am quite aware," the Woolsey opinion concluded, "that owing to some of its scenes 'Ulysses' is a rather strong draught. . . . But my considered opinion, after long reflection, is that, whilst in many places the effect of 'Ulysses' on the reader undoubtedly is somewhat emetic, nowhere does it tend to be an aphrodisiac. 'Ulysses' may, therefore, be admitted into the United States."

A columnist wrote that Judge Woolsey's opinion "read like an exceptionally intelligent and enthusiastic book review." According to Morris L. Ernst, the famous civil-rights lawyer who argued the case, "[I]t would be difficult to overestimate the importance of Judge Woolsey's decision. . . . [It] marks a turning point. It is a body blow for the censors." And so it turned out. The decision proved a First Amendment landmark. Affirmed on appeal, it made for a quantum change in the law governing obscenity and censorship that was ultimately recognized by the Supreme Court itself.

10. *Commonwealth v. Peaslee*

Before his appointment to the Supreme Court, Oliver Wendell Holmes served on the highest Massachusetts court, the Supreme Judicial Court, for twenty years, three of them as Chief Justice. After Shaw and Cardozo, Holmes was the greatest state judge in our history.

A case may be great because it may cast shadows beyond its particular facts that will influence cases yet unborn. That was true of the Holmes decision in *Commonwealth v. Peaslee* (1901), for it was an essential step in the development of the "clear and present danger" test—the great Holmes contribution to First Amendment law.

Defendant in *Peaslee* arranged combustibles in a building so that if lighted they would have set fire to the building. He then offered to pay a young man to go to the building and light it. Defendant and the other drove toward the building, but defendant then said that he had changed his mind, and drove away. "This," the Holmes opinion tells us, "is as near as he ever came to accomplishing what he had in contemplation."

For Holmes, the case must have seemed an author's dream, for he had given a similar example two decades earlier in his seminal book *The Common Law* (1881). Discussing the law of criminal attempts then, Holmes had given the case of "lighting a match with intent to set fire to a haystack." Holmes wrote that that "amount[ed] to a criminal attempt to burn it, although the defendant blew out the match on seeing that he was watched." Holmes explained that, "the otherwise innocent act [was rendered] harmful, because it raises a probability that it will be followed by such other acts and events as will altogether result in harm."

Peaslee gave Holmes the opportunity to apply this reasoning in an actual case. According to the Holmes opinion, "The question on the evidence, more precisely stated, is whether the defendant's acts come near enough to the accomplishment of the substantive offense to be punishable." In *Peaslee*, unlike the example in his book, a criminal attempt had not been shown because defendant had not gone beyond preparing the combustibles, intending someone else to light them. Defendant might have been prosecuted for soliciting another to commit a crime, but not for criminal attempt to burn the building.

As Holmes saw it, this was a case "when further acts on the part of the person who has taken the first steps are necessary before the substantive crime can come to pass. . . . [S]uch first steps cannot be described as an attempt, because that word suggests an act seemingly sufficient to accomplish the end." This was "preparation . . . not an attempt."

It is true that, as Holmes's opinion states, "some preparations may amount to an attempt. It is a question of degree. If the preparation comes very near to the accomplishment of the act, the intent to complete it renders the crime so probable that the act will be a misdemeanor." In *Peaslee*, the degree of proximity was held not sufficient.

The *Peaslee* opinion was vintage Holmes. Pithy and to the point, it deserves comparison with the best common-law opinions. More than that, as stated, it was a crucial stage in development of the "clear and present danger" test. When asked for the origin of that test, Holmes wrote, "I did think hard on this matter of attempts in my *Common Law* and a Mass. case"—that is, *Peaslee*. The "clear and present danger" test was *Peaslee* carried over into First Amendment law.

Law Outside the Marble Palace

Greatness is not confined to the highest Court. American law has been molded at least as much by the great decisions made by judges who do not sit in the Marble Palace in Washington. This has been particularly true of our private law, which has been almost entirely the handiwork of the state courts. The private-law decisions on this list led the way, first in reshaping the common law to American conditions and then in making the changes needed for the twentieth-century society.

Brown v. Kendall laid the foundation for modern tort law based on fault in place of the common-law liability even without fault; *Brown v. Collins* similarly rejected absolute liability for injuries caused by things escaping from property. Both decisions helped to encourage entrepreneurs to take the risks needed by the burgeoning economy. *MacPherson v. Buick Motor Co.* adapted tort law to the product-liability cases endemic in the industrial society. *Palsgraf v. Long Island Railroad Co.* showed how the judicial process could deal with a problem not encountered in earlier cases—that of the unforeseeable plaintiff.

Commonwealth v. Peaslee exemplifies the transition from private to public law; it showed the common-law technique at its best in laying the foundation for a fundamental First Amendment test. The other decisions on the list were landmarks in public law. They emphasize that not even the great decisions in constitutional law are all made in Washington. Indeed, the remaining decisions on this list pointed the path for the constitutional jurisprudence later followed by the Supreme Court. *Bayard v. Singleton* was the first clear case striking down an unconstitutional statute, laying the foundation for *Marbury v. Madison. Commonwealth v. Alger* was the first case to recognize the police power as the basis for power to regulate in the public interest. *Wynehamer v. People* invalidated a statute as arbitrary, giving a substantive content to due process that has made the courts the virtual censors of legislation. *United States v. One Book called "Ulysses"* drastically restricted censorship in its more usual meaning, paving the way for today's broad First Amendment conception. *Muskopf v. Corning Hospital District* overthrew governmental immunity from suit, which no court had dared to do previously, even though the sovereign immunity doctrine had been criticized for years as inconsistent with modern democratic notions.

All these decisions made significant contributions comparable to those made by the great Supreme Court decisions already listed. If most of them remain unknown except to specialists, that only gives added emphasis to Judge Posner's complaint that "to so many . . . a Supreme Court Justice is the *typical* judge and the rest of the judiciary is invisible."

9

TEN

WORST

NON-SUPREME COURT

DECISIONS

Characterizing appellate courts, an 1891 Georgia opinion states, "Some courts live by correcting the errors of others and adhering to their own." The decisions on this list bear out this remark. They are, in my opinion, the nadir of decision-making outside the Marble Palace in Washington. Of course, such a list is a matter of personal choice, and not all will agree with my selections. To me, however, these cases stand at the very bottom of the non-Supreme Court barrel.

— ★ — ★ — ★ —

— ★ — ★ — ★ —

Ten Worst Non-Supreme Court Decisions

1. *Mitchell v. Wells,*
   37 Miss. 235 (1859)

2. *Jaffree v. Board of School Commissioners,*
   554 F.Supp. 1104 (S.D. Ala. 1983)

3. *Samras v. United States,*
   125 F.2d 789 (9th Cir. 1942)

4. *In the Matter of the Motion to
   Admit Miss Lavinia Goodell to the
   Bar of This Court,*
   39 Wis. 232 (1875)

5. *Hickey v. Taaffe,*
   105 N.Y. 26 (1887)

6. *State v. Haun,*
   59 Pac. 340 (Kan. 1899)

7. *People v. Gillson,*
   109 N.Y. 389 (1888)

8. *Baehr v. Lewin,*
   852 P.2d 44 (Hawaii 1993)

9. *Williams v. Fort Worth,*
   782 S.W.2d 290 (Tex. App. 1989)

10. *Sims's Case,*
    7 Cush. 285 (Mass. 1851)

1. *Mitchell v. Wells*

It was to be expected that southern courts would enforce slavery law to the letter. After all, their view was that asserted in 1857 by Chief Justice Joseph Henry Lumpkin, who was to Georgia law what Shaw was to that of Massachusetts: "To inculcate care and industry upon the descendants of Ham is to preach to the idle winds. To be the 'servants of servants' is the judicial curse pronounced upon their race. And this Divine decree is unreversible. It will run on parallel with time itself. And heaven and earth shall sooner pass away, than one jot or tittle of it shall abate."

This language may appear extreme, but it pales beside that used by the Mississippi Supreme Court in *Mitchell v. Wells* (1859). Plaintiff in *Mitchell* was a former slave who had become a free black under the laws of Ohio by living in that state. She sued in Mississippi for a legacy left to her under her father's will. Mississippi law did not recognize her emancipation, and under it, a slave could not inherit property. She claimed, however, that interstate comity required recognition of the freedom she had secured under Ohio law.

The Mississippi court refused to allow plaintiff to bring suit. The opinion criticized Ohio for taking "as citizens, the neglected race . . . occupying, in the order of nature, an intermediate place between the irrational animal and the white man." Nor, according to the court, was Mississippi required to recognize Ohio law in the matter. "But," declared the opinion, "when I am told that Ohio has not only the right thus to degrade and disgrace herself, and wrong us, but also, that she has the right to force her new associates into the Mississippi branch of the American family, to claim and exercise rights here, which our laws have always denied to this inferior race, and that Mississippi is bound to yield obedience to such demand, I am at a loss to understand upon what principle of law or reason, of courtesy or justice, such a claim can be founded."

Then, in the court's view, came the clincher in its reasoning: "Suppose that Ohio, still further afflicted with her peculiar philanthropy, should be determined to descend another grade in the scale of her peculiar humanity, and claim to confer citizenship on the chimpanzee or the ourang-outang (the most respectable of the monkey tribe), are we to be told that 'comity' will require of the States not thus demented, to . . . meet the necessities of the mongrel race thus attempted to be introduced into the family of sisters in this confederacy?"

It is hard to believe that such a statement was made by an American court, even in the pre–Civil War South. Even in a jurisprudence where positive law normally trumped moral considerations, *Mitchell v. Wells* may be considered the worst decision by an American court.

2. *Jaffree v. Board of School Commissioners*

What should be said about the decision of a federal district judge that "overruled" settled Supreme Court jurisprudence? That is exactly what Chief Judge W. Brevard Hand purported to do when a complaint was filed in his district court for a judgment that an Alabama law permitting teacher-led prayers in public schools was unconstitutional. The Supreme Court had ruled in 1962 that such prayers violated the establishment clause of the First Amendment. Although that clause, on its face, provides only that "Congress shall make no law respecting an establishment of religion," the Court had held in many cases that that prohibition is binding on the states as well through the due process clause of the Fourteenth Amendment.

In *Jaffree v. Board of School Commissioners* (1983), Judge Hand found that the statute had been enacted "to encourage a religious activity." That made the law unconstitutional under the Supreme Court decisions invalidating school prayers and other religious exercises. But the judge refused to follow the precedents because he had concluded that the original intention of the framers of both the First and Fourteenth Amendments was contrary to the Supreme Court's interpretation of the establishment clause.

Judge Hand's conclusion on the matter was: "This Court's review of the relevant legislative history surrounding the adoption of both the first amendment and of the fourteenth amendment, together with the plain language of those amendments, leaves no doubt that those amendments were not intended to forbid religious prayers in the schools which the states and their political subdivisions mandate."

This was true, Judge Hand wrote, because the First Amendment was intended "to prohibit the federal government only from establishing a national religion." Nor was this changed, according to Hand, by the Fourteenth Amendment: "The historical record clearly establishes that when the fourteenth amendment was ratified in 1868 that its ratification did not incorporate the first amendment against the states." The states remained "free to define the meaning of religious establishment under their own constitutions and laws." Since "the establishment clause of the first amendment to the United States Constitution does not prohibit the state from establishing a religion, the prayers offered by the teachers in this case are not unconstitutional."

What about the mass of Supreme Court precedents the other way? Judge Hand stated, "This Court's independent review of the relevant historical documents and its reading of the scholarly analysis convinces it that the United States Supreme Court has erred in its reading of history."

Not surprisingly, the court of appeals rejected "the District Court's remarkable conclusion that the Federal Constitution imposes no obstacle to Alabama's establishment of a state religion." The Supreme Court's *Jaffree* opinion conceded that before the Fourteenth Amendment, "the First Amendment's restraints on the exercise of federal power simply did not apply to the States." But this situation was changed by the Fourteenth Amendment. According to the Supreme Court in *Jaffree*, that amendment "imposed the same substantive limitations on the States' power to legislate that the First Amendment had always imposed on the Congress' power. This Court has confirmed and endorsed this elementary proposition of law time and time again."

What still stands, however, is Judge Hand's attempt to "overrule" half a century of uniform Supreme Court precedents. Talk of chutzpah by a lower-court judge! No wonder wags sought to distinguish Brevard Hand from his famous namesake by dubbing him "Judge Unlearned Hand."

3. *Samras v. United States*

Before a 1952 statute prohibited it, the naturalization laws passed by Congress conditioned admission to naturalization on racial grounds. The first naturalization statute, in 1790, authorized the naturalization only of "free white persons." In 1870, a law extended the naturalization privilege to those of "African nativity and . . . descent." Aside from that extension, it was only white persons who could be naturalized. And as the Supreme Court explained it in 1934, "'White persons' within the meaning of the statute are members of the Caucasian race, as Caucasian is defined in the understanding of the mass of men." The words of the statutory exclusion of non-Caucasians (other than blacks) from the privilege of naturalization "import a racial and not an individual test."

This racial provision was challenged in only one case—*Samras v. United States* (1942) by the Court of Appeals for the Ninth Circuit. Samras, born in India, appealed to that court from a decision denying his petition for naturalization "on the ground of racial ineligibility." His principal constitutional claim was a denial of due process. But the court, in an opinion by Circuit Judge Bert E. Haney, dismissed the challenge without much difficulty, ruling that Congress possessed virtual plenary power over naturalization. As far as the due process claim was concerned, the court stated that the individual was not being deprived of "life," "liberty," or "property" by being denied naturalization. "Life" and "liberty" were not applicable here. As far as "property" was concerned, the question was did appellant "have a right to citizenship"? The court answered in the negative, finding that there was no such right under the Constitution.

If such scholastic reasoning had been applied generally, the Constitution could never have been construed as the barrier against racial discrimination that it has so emphatically become. Certainly, an alien resident is a "person" entitled to the protection of the due process and equal protection clauses. Federal action based on racial classification (which, if carried out by a state, would be violative of the Fourteenth Amendment's guarantee of equal protection of the laws) will today be ruled contrary to the Fifth Amendment's demand of due process. It is difficult to see why this would not be true of a denial of naturalization on racial grounds. Of course, as *Samras* put it, no alien has a "property right" to citizenship. Yet neither does a black have such a "right" to public employment, accommodation, or education. But all "persons" in this country do (under all the cases) have the constitutional right not to be discriminated against by government on racial grounds.

Samras, all the same, confirmed the constitutionality of the racial exclusion from citizenship. The Supreme Court denied certiorari in *Samras* and never ruled on the constitutionality of the exclusion, though all the federal courts applied the exclusion without question.

Application of the racial test in naturalization required the courts to introduce into the law all the pseudoscientific distinctions that are the inevitable concomitants of a social order based on race. The Supreme Court's conclusion that the phrase "white persons" and the word "Caucasian" were synonymous hardly ended the matter. "Caucasian" itself is a conventional word of much flexibility—particularly if we take it (as the Supreme Court indicated) in accordance with the understanding of the common man. Supreme Court cases ruled that the term excludes Chinese, Japanese, Filipinos, American Indians, and Hindus. In the decision last referred to, the opinion goes into the question of whether racial intermingling in India involved a "destroying to a greater or less degree the purity of the 'Aryan' blood" in a manner that is chillingly reminiscent of racist analysis in Nazi Germany.

But the cases under the statutes excluding non-Caucasians (other than Africans) from naturalization could not rest with determining which races came within the congressional bar. The courts also had to deal with the problem of racial interbreeding and to decide how much of the "tainted" blood would bar an individual from access to American citizenship. In the Supreme Court's words in 1934, "Nor is the range of the exclusion limited to persons of the full blood. The privilege of naturalization is denied to all who are not white . . . ; and men are not white if the strain of colored blood in them is a half or a quarter, or, not improbably, even less."

Although the decisions on racial purity for purposes of naturalization bear a melancholy resemblance to those interpreting the Nuremberg laws, the constitutionality of the statutes excluding non-Caucasians and non-Africans from naturalization was never challenged except in *Samras*. The decision there remains as a chilling reminder of a day when the federal courts considered the problem in naturalization cases to be to determine whether particular races and individuals came within the statutory pale of purity.

4. *In the Matter of the Motion to Admit Miss Lavinia Goodell to the Bar of This Court*

The issue in this case was the same as that in *Bradwell v. Illinois*—whether a woman should be admitted to the bar. But the Wisconsin Supreme Court's opinion (1875) denying admission was so extreme that it makes *Bradwell* appear almost a feminist tract.

Lavinia Goodell had clerked in a law firm (the common method of studying law at the time) and had passed the court examination required for admission as an attorney. In addition, the Wisconsin court conceded, this "first application for admission of a female to the bar of this court . . . is made in favor of a lady whose character raises no personal objection: something perhaps not always to be looked for in women who forsake the ways of their sex for the ways of ours."

This characterization foreshadowed the decision that there was no authority for the admission of women to the bar. "And," the opinion stated,

> with all the respect and sympathy for this lady which all men owe to all good women, we cannot regret that we do not. We cannot but think the common law wise in excluding women from the profession of law. . . . The law of nature destines and qualifies the female sex for the bearing and nurture of the children of our race and for the custody of the homes of the world and their maintenance in love and honor. And all life-long callings of

women, inconsistent with these radical and sacred duties of
their sex, as is the profession of the law, are departures from the
order of nature; and when voluntary, treason against it. . . .
There are many employments in life not unfit for female character. The profession of the law is surely not one of these.

"The peculiar qualities of womanhood," the court went on, "its gentle
graces, its quick sensibility, its tender susceptibility, its purity, its delicacy,
its emotional impulses, its subordination of hard reason to sympathetic
feeling, are surely not qualifications for forensic strife. Nature has tem-
pered woman as little for the juridical conflicts of the court room, as for
the physical conflicts of the battle-field. Womanhood is moulded for gen-
tler and better things."

The opinion referred to "all that is selfish and malicious, knavish and
criminal, coarse and brutal, repulsive and obscene" with which the legal
profession deals. "It would," it declared,

be revolting to all female sense of the innocence and sanctity of
their sex, shocking to man's reverence for womanhood and
faith in woman, on which hinge all the better affections and
humanities of life, that woman should be permitted to mix pro-
fessionally in all the nastiness of the world which finds its way
into courts of justice; all the unclean issues, all the collateral
questions of sodomy, incest, rape, seduction, fornication, adultery, pregnancy, bastardy, legitimacy, prostitution, lascivious
cohabitation, abortion, infanticide, obscene publications, libel
and slander of sex, impotence, divorce: all the nameless cata-
logue of indecencies, la chronique scandaleuse of all the vices
and all the infirmities of all society, with which the profession
has to deal, and which go towards filling judicial reports which
must be read for accurate knowledge of the law. This is bad
enough for men. . . . Reverence for all womanhood would suffer in the public spectacle of woman so instructed and so
engaged.

Indeed, said the court, this very case "gives appropriate evidence of
this truth. No modest woman could read without pain and self abase-
ment, no woman could so overcome the instincts of sex as publicly to discuss, the case which we had occasion to cite"—that is, one in which
defendant was charged with committing sodomy on an eleven-year-old
girl. Discussions of such cases, the Wisconsin court concluded, "are habit-
ually necessary in courts of justice, which are unfit for female ears. The
habitual presence of women at these would tend to relax the public sense

of decency and propriety. If, as counsel threatened, these things are to come, we will take no voluntary part in bringing them about."

It will be objected that the Wisconsin court is being judged by today's standards. Yet even at the time, there were judges who could see beyond the common-law refusal to recognize women's rights. As early as 1820, an opinion by Chief Justice John Bannister Gibson questioned what he termed the "subordinate and dependent condition of the wife" in the law of the day. "In no country . . . ," he declared, "are the interest and estates of married women so entirely at the mercy of their husbands as in *Pennsylvania*. This exposure of those who from the defenseless state in which even the common law has placed them, are least able to protect themselves, is extenuated by no motive of policy and is by no means creditable to our jurisprudence."

It is thus erroneous to assume that *Bradwell* and *Goodell* were excusable as reflections of their society. Even bearing in mind their dates, they both were so extreme that they easily deserve inclusion among the worst American decisions. Despite this, Lavinia Goodell's pursuit, like that of Myra Bradwell, had an ultimate happy ending. In 1877, the Wisconsin legislature prohibited denial of admission as attorneys "on account of sex." Soon thereafter, the Wisconsin court admitted Lavinia Goodell to its bar.

5. *Hickey v. Taaffe*

The list of worst Justices characterized Justice Rufus Peckham as the prime exemplar of the laissez-faire jurisprudence of his day. In fact, he carried that jurisprudence to what were extremes even for the judges at that time. This was notably true of the decision in *Hickey v. Taaffe* (1887), rendered while Peckham was still a judge on the New York Court of Appeals.

We saw that, under Chief Justice Lemuel Shaw's lead, the courts in the nineteenth century transformed tort law. Shaw in *Brown v. Kendall* (1850) shifted the basis of liability to liability only for fault. In another case, he laid down the doctrine of assumption of risk, under which a worker "takes upon himself the natural and ordinary risks and perils" involved in his job. Since the individual assumed the risks of his chosen occupation, the law would not protect him from the consequences of his choice. Harsh though it seems today, the law thus fashioned fitted the needs of the nascent industrial society by making the legal burden on economic development as light as possible. As industrialism expanded, factory and railroad accidents proliferated. The law in this area was developed, wrote a leading authority on torts almost a century ago, because "commercial necessity required" that employers be relieved of "an intolerable and almost prohibitive burden upon the development of business and manufacture." Instead, the cost of industrial accidents was thrown on the injured worker: "The encouragement of 'infant industries,'" declares a Shaw biography, "had no greater social cost."

Yet even Shaw would have been dismayed by the rigid application of his doctrine in *Hickey v. Taaffe*. In that case, Judge Peckham's extreme adherence to laissez-faire led him to apply the doctrine of assumption of risk to a child of fourteen whose hand had been crushed while working on a laundry machine, and who had not been warned of its dangers. As Peckham saw it, she worked "willingly" and had learned of the danger by working on the machine for six weeks. The judge conceded that "she had not . . . received any instructions as to its dangers from the defendant or his agents." But, he went on, "she had acquired the information in fact from the best of all teachers, that of practical experience. . . . This was enough."

What of the fact that plaintiff was so young? The Peckham opinion replied that she was old enough to be "competent to perform the duty demanded from her." That being the case, her tender age "does not alter the general rule of law upon the subject of employees taking upon themselves the risks which are . . . incident to the employment."

Peckham recognized that plaintiff had "sustained a most terrible and painful and permanent injury, and her case is one that appeals most strongly to the sympathies of every one." Nevertheless, the opinion concluded, "we do not see how this judgment [by the lower courts for plaintiff] can stand without overthrowing well settled and healthful principles of law."

Perhaps the doctrine of assumption of risk was a rule suited to the economic needs of the day. But did the encouragement of industrial expansion require the cost of losing her hand to be borne solely by the injured child in *Hickey*?

6. *State v. Haun*

To us, the decisions made a century ago striking down laws that protected labor on the ground that they infringed on freedom of contract were among the worst ever handed down by American courts. Three of these have been chosen for this list: the already discussed decision in *Hickey v. Taaffe*, that to be discussed in *People v. Gillson*, and that in *State v. Haun* (1899), where the Kansas Supreme Court adopted a view of freedom of contract even more extreme than that followed by the Supreme Court in cases such as *Lochner v. New York* (1905). One of the employer abuses that developed during the post–Civil War period was the practice of not paying workers in cash. Instead, many employers would pay with scrip or orders that could be redeemed from the employer for food, clothing, and other goods. This made the worker altogether dependent on the employer, and legislatures sought to correct the situation by laws that required workers to be paid with money or a check drawn on a bank. The cases toward the end of the century invalidated these laws as violative of the freedom of contract guaranteed by due process.

State v. Haun was the case in which a decision to that effect was explained most fully. The court had no difficulty in striking down the Kansas law requiring cash payments. Quoting an earlier case, the opinion stated that such statutes "are utterly unconstitutional and void, inasmuch as by them an attempt has been made by the legislature to do what, in this country, cannot be done; that is, prevent persons who are sui juris from making their own contracts. The act is an infringement alike of the right of the employer and the employee." The worker, said the court, "may sell his labor for what he thinks best, whether money or goods, just as his employer may sell his iron or coal; and any and every law that proposes to prevent him from so doing is an infringement of his constitutional privileges, and consequently vicious and void."

The cash-payment law, according to *Haun*, prevents the worker from bargaining to receive any other kind of payment. As such, it "places the laborer under guardianship; classifying him, in respect to freedom of contract, with the idiot, the lunatic, or the felon in the penitentiary." The court's conclusion was, "Laws which infringe upon the free exercise of the right of a workingman to trade his labor for any commodity or species of property which he may see fit, and which he may consider to be the most advantageous, is an encroachment upon his constitutional rights, and an obstruction to his pursuit of happiness. Such laws . . . classify him among the incompetents, and degrade his calling."

A century later, such language about a law protecting labor seems ludicrous. Yet the *Haun* court was not alone in its extreme characterization of the law. Other courts of the day portrayed such statutes as making workers wards of the state, as stamping them as imbeciles, and as "insulting attempt[s] to put the laborer under a legislative tutelage . . . degrading to his manhood."

More important, as *Haun* itself pointed out, the decision's implications were far-reaching. It applied not only to laws like that at issue, "but also any other law whose object is to regulate any of the terms of hiring, such as the number of hours of labor per day, which the employer may demand. There can be no constitutional interference by the state in the private relation of master and servant."

The *Haun* reasoning was applied by courts a century ago to invalidate a host of laws regulating employer–employee relations: laws forbidding employers from interfering with union membership; laws prohibiting imposition of fines on employees; laws providing for the mode of weighing coal in fixing miners' compensation; and laws prohibiting contracts by railway employees releasing their employers in advance from liability for personal injuries. The culmination was the *Lochner* decision, striking down a statute regulating hours of labor.

These decisions that so strictly employed the freedom of contract doctrine to strike down laws regulating the relations between employer and employee seem today to come from another world. We see now that the theory on which they were based was wholly out of line with reality, rendered obsolete by the modern industrial society. The helplessness of the individual employee, unaided by government or collective action with his fellows, has been a dominant fact since the industrial revolution.

Louis Brandeis once said, "Men are not free while financially dependent." Such dependence makes freedom of contract a misnomer as applied to a contract between an employer and an ordinary worker. As an English judge stated two centuries ago, "necessitous men are not, truly speaking, free men, but, to answer a present exigency, will submit to any terms that the crafty may impose upon them." This remark is particularly relevant in considering the industrial employee's position where he is compelled to bargain, alone and unaided, for whatever terms of employment he can secure. "There is grim irony," wrote Justice Stone, in dissenting from a decision striking down a minimum-wage law, "in speaking of the freedom of contract of those who, because of their economic necessities, give their services for less than is needful to keep body and soul together."

7. *People v. Gillson*

When he was elected president, Grover Cleveland told Judge Peckham, then on the New York Court of Appeals, "We'll get you down to Washington yet, Rufus." He did when he appointed Peckham to the Supreme Court, where he was considered in his day a more than competent Justice. Indeed, Melville W. Fuller wrote to the president recommending that

Peckham be appointed Chief Justice before he himself was chosen for that position.

Today, of course, we view Peckham differently. Not only is he on the list of worst Justices, but three of his decisions—*Lochner*, *Hickey*, and *People v. Gillson* (1888)—are among the worst handed down by an American court. Like that in *Hickey*, the *Gillson* opinion was delivered when Peckham sat in the highest New York court. At issue in the case was a state law prohibiting the inclusion of a gift or prize with the sale of food. In *Gillson*, an A & P store had given a cup and saucer to the purchaser of two pounds of coffee. *Gillson* is included in this list not so much because of the decision striking down the law, but because the opinion contains the fullest exposition of the Peckham approach that was to be made famous (or infamous) by *Lochner*.

The *Gillson* opinion began by listing the rights included in the "liberty" protected by the law: "the right not only of freedom from servitude, imprisonment or restraint, but the right of one to use his faculties in all lawful ways to live and work where he will, to earn his livelihood in any lawful calling and to pursue any lawful trade or avocation." The opinion then declared, "It is quite clear that some or all of these fundamental and valuable rights are invaded, weakened, limited or destroyed by the legislation under consideration."

Peckham compared the *Gillson* statute with medieval sumptuary laws, such as those prohibiting the wearing of fur by people below a certain rank: "Numberless statutes of a similar nature have been passed both in England and in this country, and it is generally admitted that some of the best legislation of both countries has been found in the repeal of laws enacted by former parliaments and legislatures." To Peckham, at any rate, under "this act a man owning articles of food which he wishes to sell or dispose of is limited in his powers of sale or disposition. A liberty to adopt or follow for a livelihood a lawful industrial pursuit, and in a manner not injurious to the community, is certainly infringed upon, limited, perhaps weakened or destroyed by such legislation."

The *Gillson* opinion specifically rejected "the argument that this kind of transaction naturally induces people to purchase more than they want of any article of food in order to get the other article with it which comes to them in the shape of a gift, and thus the poorer people are led to extravagance in outlay." That argument had, of course, led to enactment of *Gillson*-type legislation.

To Peckham, however, this was the argument behind all sumptuary legislation. "It seems to me," his opinion declared, "that to uphold the act in question upon the assumption that it tends to . . . prevent wastefulness or lack of proper thrift among the poorer classes, is a radically vicious and erroneous assumption and is to take a long step backwards and to favor that class of paternal legislation, which, when carried to this extent, interferes with the proper liberty of the citizen." Hence, *Gillson* concluded, it "violates the constitutional provision" guaranteeing due process.

Gillson marks an extreme in the pre-*Lochner* hostility to legislative attempts to interfere with the free working of the economic system. The New York court deemed them the illegal product of class warfare against the fittest by those left behind in what Joseph H. Coate, a leader of the bar at the time, termed "Darwin's great theory of survival of the fittest." To Peckham, the *Gillson* statute "is evidently of that kind which has been so frequent of late, a kind which is meant to protect some class in the community against the fair, free and full competition of some other class, the members of the former class thinking it impossible to hold their own against such competition, and therefore flying to the legislature to secure some enactment which shall operate favorably to them or unfavorably to their competitors."

8. *Baehr v. Lewin*

The great judges and great decisions have adapted the law to the needs of their day. This has enabled the traditional legal technique to serve the welfare of the constantly changing society. The masters of the judicial craft have made the emerging law appear the logical product of established doctrines; in their hands, the changing common law was made a blend of both continuity and creativeness.

Judicial creativeness should, however, go only so far. For the judge to make quantum leaps is to risk a transforming role more appropriate to the legislator. Justice Frankfurter once wrote, in a letter to Justice Black, "the problem is not whether the judges make the law, but when and how and how much. Holmes put it in his highbrow way, that 'they can do so only interstitially; they are confined from molar to molecular motions.' I used to say to my students that legislatures make law wholesale, judges retail."

In *Baehr v. Lewin* (1993), the Hawaii Supreme Court made law wholesale. The case involved men whose applications for marriage licenses were denied solely because they were of the same sex. They sued, claiming that the denials violated their right to equal protection. The Hawaii court stated that the statute providing for marriage between husband

and wife established a sex-based classification. To determine the validity of such a classification under the equal protection clause, the court ruled, the strict-scrutiny standard of review must be applied. This meant that the classification may be upheld only if it is supported by a *compelling* state interest and is narrowly drawn to avoid unnecessary abridgment of the applicant couples' constitutional rights.

All this may sound like only technical legal jargon. But it is of crucial importance. The review standard used by the court in a given case determines whether a statute violates equal protection. Most statutes meet the usual standard of being supported by a "rational basis" or even what is called the intermediate standard of support by a *significant* state interest. On the other hand, as the Supreme Court put it in 1995, "strict scrutiny is 'strict in theory but fatal in fact.'" Justice Thurgood Marshall explained the difference in result in a 1976 opinion: "If a statute is subject to strict scrutiny, the statue always, or nearly always, . . . is struck down." A less strict review standard, "too . . . leaves little doubt about the outcome; the challenged legislation is always upheld."

Technically, all the *Baehr* court did was to remand to the lower court to determine whether, "in accordance with the strict-scrutiny standard, the state could meet the burden of overcoming the presumption that [the statute] is unconstitutional by demonstrating that it furthers compelling state interests and is narrowly drawn." But the *Baehr* decision plainly indicated the decision that would have to be made on remand. In effect, then, *Baehr* held that the same-sex marriage requirement, to quote a dissent, "unconstitutionally discriminates against Appellants who seek a license to enter into a same-sex marriage."

The *Baehr* decision is so contrary to both established law and common sense that one is almost speechless before this patent reductio ad absurdum of equal-protection jurisprudence. In the first place, there is the universal meaning of "marriage"—for example, the *Oxford English Dictionary* definition: "an act, of marrying, the ceremony or procedure by which two persons are made husband and wife." If the state is to follow the method of Humpty Dumpty in *Through the Looking-Glass*—"When I use a word . . . , it means just what *I* choose it to mean"—it is surely for the legislature, not the courts, to redefine "marriage." The legislature has, however, continued to use the term in its universally accepted sense.

Aside from *Baehr*, stated a Federal court of appeals in 1995, "unanimously American courts have held that same-sex couples are not constitutionally entitled to attain the legal and civil status of marriage." The *Baehr* holding that such legislative use of the word is presumptively unconstitutional is contrary to that of every other court which has considered the matter. The legislative confirmation of the accepted definition of marriage as limited to a union between husband and wife does not discriminate on the basis of gender; it is based on the nature of marriage itself. In the words of the Washington court, in reaching the opposite result from that in *Baehr*, "appellants are not being denied entry into the marriage relationship because of their sex; rather, they are being denied entry into the marriage relationship because of the recognized definition of that relationship as one which may be entered into only by two persons who are members of the opposite sex." The *Baehr* decision the other way is an affront to both law and language that well deserves its place on the list of worst decisions.

9. *Williams v. Fort Worth*

Law and common sense are not mutually exclusive. You would, however, never know this from the Texas decision in *Williams v. Fort Worth* (1989).

The cases today hold that nudity alone does not violate obscenity laws. At the same time, it has long been established that nudity in public places may be regulated, or even prohibited, by the legislature. Such restrictions have been upheld for centuries. The Supreme Court has, however, recognized that nudity may be expressive conduct protected by the First Amendment. That does not mean that it is no longer subject to any regulation. To the contrary, a 1991 Supreme Court decision held that a law requiring "go-go dancers" to wear "pasties" and a "G-string" did not violate the First Amendment. Since the dancer involved in the case testified that she "wishes to dance nude because she believes she would make more money doing so," it is hard to see how her dancing constituted constitutionally protected expression. Yet, even conceding that expressive conduct was involved, the Supreme Court ruled that the given regulation was valid.

Williams v. Fort Worth dealt with a comparable regulation of "topless" dancing in "sexually oriented businesses." The Texas court conceded that the restriction barring "less than completely and opaquely covered . . . female breasts below a point immediately above the top of the aureola" did not violate the First Amendment. Nevertheless, the court struck down the regulation as based on an invalid gender-based classification: it "only regulates exposure of female breasts but not male breasts and, therefore, unconstitutionally discriminates against female topless dancers." The court rejected the argument that the regulation did not deal with females differently than males merely because they were female, saying, "While we do not quarrel with the general proposition that different physical characteristics may lead to different laws, the City has completely failed to prove how these different physical characteristics *alone* necessitate differing treatment of males and females in this ordinance."

The Texas court stated further that it would not recognize "the concept that the breasts of female topless dancers, unlike their male counterparts, are commonly associated with sexual arousal." As the court saw it, "there is no evidence that exposure of the breasts of male performers in bars which regularly feature such entertainment is not considered sexually oriented." Hence, the court held, the regulation "discriminates against women on its face" and thus "violates the right of female topless dancers to equal protection."

Every other court that has considered the matter has held the other way. A 1978 decision of the Washington court is most frequently cited. At the least, as that court states, "the female breasts . . . unlike male breasts, constitute an erogenous zone and are commonly associated with sexual arousal. . . . [C]ommon knowledge tells us . . . that there is a real difference between the sexes with respect to breasts, which is reasonably related to the preservation of public decorum and morals."

A similar point was made by Justice David Souter in the 1991 Supreme Court case upholding the requirement that the dancers wear pasties and a G-string: "Live nude dancing of the sort at issue here is likely to produce pernicious secondary effects. . . . In my view, the interest . . . in preventing prostitution, sexual assault, and other criminal activity . . . is sufficient . . . to justify the State's enforcement."

The Texas decision stands alone in not recognizing, in the words of a Hawaii opinion, that the exposure of the female breast "is still capable of provoking sexual desire or imagination, even in this day and age." Chief Justice William H. Taft once referred to a "blind" court that does not see what "all others can see and understand." If ever a court fitted this description, it is the Texas court that decided the *Williams* case.

10. *Sims's Case*

In Herman Melville's *Billy Budd*, Captain Vere pronounced the death sentence upon the sailor, though he was morally not guilty, because the positive law required it. The overriding principle, Vere urged, must be "[t]hat however pitilessly that law may operate in any instances, we nevertheless adhere to it and administer it." Melville had married Chief Justice Lemuel

Shaw's daughter, and his model for Captain Vere was his father-in-law. Like other judges of the period, Shaw was confronted with the Vere-type dilemma in cases involving slavery.

Slavery was the great albatross of the pre–Civil War nation. This was as true in law as in other areas of American life. Because of slavery, our law was characterized by a schizophrenia based on color that has had its effects down to the present day. It is hardly surprising, then, that some of the worst decisions by American courts concerned slavery.

Shaw, great judge though he was could not escape the moral dilemma posed by slavery cases. "To read *Billy Budd*," writes Charles Reich, "is to feel an intense and indelible sense of helplessness and agony." The reader of Shaw's opinion in the leading fugitive-slave case is left with a similar feeling.

Although Shaw personally regarded slavery as an abomination—"one continued series of tremendous crimes," he once called it—he refused to follow his personal view on the bench, because he considered it contrary to settled law. The Shaw posture may best be seen in *Sims's Case* (1851). A black in Boston had been taken into custody as a fugitive slave by a federal marshal. An application for habeas corpus was made to Shaw's court on the ground that the Fugitive Slave Act passed by Congress in 1850 was unconstitutional. A unanimous decision denied the writ.

The lengthy Shaw opinion quoted the statement of a predecessor in upholding an earlier Fugitive Slave Act: "Whether the statute is a harsh one, is not for us to determine." Shaw expanded on this theme: "It seems to be well established that however abhorrent to the dictates of humanity and the plainest principles of justice and natural right, yet each nation has a right, in this respect, to judge for itself, and to allow or prohibit slavery by its own laws, at its own will."

Shaw wrote that although the Constitution "is not responsible for the origin or continuance of slavery," its fugitive-slave provision gave Congress the power to provide for the forcible return of fugitive slaves. It was, the Shaw opinion concluded, "the duty of all judges and magistrates to expound and apply [the fugitive-law] provisions . . . ; and in this spirit it behooves all persons, bound to obey the laws of the United States, to consider and regard them."

Sims's Case was only one of many at the time enforcing the Fugitive Slave Act. It has been chosen for this list because it illustrates how even the greatest state judge of the day could go wrong in deciding that the positive law could sweep away the overwhelming moral considerations in the case. It is difficult today to understand how a great judge could return a man to slavery under a law that, to us, plainly violated due process. Under the statute, the testimony of the fugitive could not be received in evidence. In *Sims's Case*, Sims was not permitted to present his sworn statement that he was free and had not even heard of the man who claimed him before his arrest. Instead, the personal liberty of the seized black was to be decided solely on the basis of affidavit evidence against him.

How the law operated in practice was stated graphically by an abolitionist in 1855: "The simple truth is, at this moment, that if an affidavit comes from Georgia that A.B. has escaped from service there, and somebody can be found to testify that I am A.B., and an irresponsible *Commissioner* . . . chooses to say, for the fee of ten dollars, that he believes his testimony, I must go to Georgia . . . and there is no remedy for me whatever in the laws of my country."

Richard Henry Dana, Jr. (known to his contemporaries as a leading lawyer rather than as author of a sea classic), termed this ex parte procedure under the Fugitive Slave Act "infamous" and "odious." The wonder is that a judge as great as Shaw did not see this when he handed down one of the worst decisions in American law.

Encyclopedia of Legal Error

The law, we are told, is the only profession that records its mistakes carefully. All the decisions on this list are fully recorded in the law reports. Otherwise, we might not believe that an opinion such as that in *Mitchell v. Wells* could have been issued by a state high court—even in a pre–Civil War southern state. To be sure, as stated, slavery was the great distorting element in early American law, before which even well-established principles of justice had to bend. Even a great judge like Chief Justice Shaw felt powerless to make what we now consider (and what he undoubtedly personally felt as well) to be the right decision in a fugitive-slave case.

The other nineteenth-century cases on this list were based on social and legal considerations that we now consider egregiously mistaken. We find it hard to credit the language in Lavinia Goodell's case, forgetting that it was only the common-law posture toward women carried to a preposterous extreme. The decisions striking down regulatory laws and limiting employer liability also rest on conceptions completely rejected by present-day law. The same is true of the federal decision upholding a racist naturalization law, with its chilling jurisprudence that can be compared only with that under the Nuremberg laws.

All the decisions just mentioned have been overruled by legislation, later decisions, and the most important of all extra-judicial decisions—that at Appomattox Courthouse. That was also true of the attempt by Judge Brevard Hand to "overrule" the Supreme Court in what may have been the most extreme act of cheek by a lower-court judge. The United States court of appeals, we saw, speedily put the Hand attempt to rewrite First Amendment law to rest.

The Hawaii and Texas decisions on this list remain uncorrected—at least in the jurisdictions in which they were made. Both are based on misunderstanding of equal-protection law, based on the common, but incorrect, conception that it requires all persons to be treated exactly alike. Only judges unfamiliar with constitutional nuances could have decided *Williams v. Fort Worth* and *Baehr v. Lewin* as they did.

An English judge once replied to a lawyer, who had relied on the judge's mistaken earlier opinion, "I can only say that I am amazed that a man of my intelligence should have been guilty of giving such an opinion." We, too, can only be amazed that judges of intelligence should have added to what may (paraphrasing Lord Acton) only be called an Encyclopedia of Legal Error.

10

TEN
___
GREATEST
___
LAW BOOKS

A merican law has been primarily the product of judicial decision. Yet it has also been influenced far more than its English progenitor by writings outside the forum. In the law, as elsewhere, the situation is that described by John Maynard Keynes: "Practical men, who believe themselves to be quite exempt from any intellectual influences, are usually the slaves of some defunct economist. [Those] in authority . . . are distilling their frenzy from some academic scribbler of a few years back."

American law has been molded as much by its "scribblers" (many of them nonacademic) as by its courts. This list contains the law books that have had the greatest influence upon the developing law. It starts with the classic commentary on the United States Constitution—the very foundation for interpretation of the organic document—and continues with other books that influenced both our public and our private law. During the twentieth century, the seminal writings have dealt not with specific branches or subjects of the law, but with what we now call jurisprudence and judicial process. The works in the list changed the very way Americans think about law and the manner in which courts operate. Because of them, we view the law far differently than would otherwise be the case.

— ★ — ★ — ★ —

— ★ — ★ — ★ —

Ten Greatest Law Books

1. *The Federalist* (1788)

2. James Kent, *Commentaries on American Law* (1826–1830)

3. Joseph Story, *Commentaries on the Constitution of the United States* (1833)

4. Thomas M. Cooley, *A Treatise on the Constitutional Limitations which Rest upon the Legislative Power of the States of the American Union* (1868)

5. Christopher Columbus Langdell, *A Selection of Cases on the Law of Contracts* (1871)

6. Oliver Wendell Holmes, *The Common Law* (1881)

7. Benjamin N. Cardozo, *The Nature of the Judicial Process* (1921)

8. Jerome N. Frank, *Law and the Modern Mind* (1930)

9. James C. Carter, *Law: Its Origin, Growth and Function* (1907)

10. Richard A. Posner, *Economic Analysis of Law* (1973)

1. *The Federalist*

When he was asked about the legal sources for his study of the American democracy, Alexis de Tocqueville wrote, "I have consulted three most respected commentaries: the *Federalist* . . . , Kent's *Commentaries,* and those of Justice Story." As far as constitutional law is concerned, *The Federalist* is still as much *the* primary source as it was in de Tocqueville's day. In 1995, when the Supreme Court decided whether state term limits for members of Congress were constitutional, the basic source for both the majority and dissenting opinions was *The Federalist.* That work was discussed in detail in both opinions; indeed, it was cited some thirty-seven times by the Justices.

The Federalist may rank first on this list, but it is not, strictly speaking, a law book. In fact, it was not written as a book at all. *The Federalist* consists of eighty-five letters to the public written by Alexander Hamilton, James Madison, and John Jay during the debate over ratification of the Constitution. They were published in newspapers in New York in 1787 and 1788 under the pseudonym Publius in order to induce that state to ratify the proposed Constitution. They were published in book form in 1788. Hamilton was the prime mover behind *The Federalist.* He conceived of the letters in his effort to persuade state voters to support ratification and persuaded Madison and Jay to collaborate. Hamilton also wrote almost two-thirds of the total of 175,000 words—fifty-one of the eighty-five papers published.

As it turned out, *The Federalist* had only a small influence on the ratification struggle. It was not eloquent words in newspapers, but politics (in the nonpejorative sense of the word), that secured the hard-won victories for the Constitution. Yet *The Federalist* still contains the most profound discussion ever published of constitutional issues. Its vision has been increasingly confirmed both by the verdict of history and Supreme Court decisions.

The Federalist contains the best explanation of federalism and operation of the federal government established by the Constitution. It stresses the importance of a national government "equally energetic" to that proposed "[a]fter an unequivocal experience of the inefficacy of the subsisting [pre-Constitution] government." In particular, it urges the need for the broadest federal taxing power and rightly stresses the supremacy clause as the keystone of the new constitutional arch. Much of our constitutional history during the past two centuries has consisted in giving legal effect to *The Federalist*'s vision of national power.

The Federalist still stands as *the* authoritative commentary on the Constitution. As Clinton Rossiter put it, "Today, as all through the history of American constitutional development, a particular interpretation of some clause in that document can be given a special flavor of authenticity by a quotation from Publius." In the 1995 term-limits case, for example, both the majority and the dissenters used different portions of *The Federalist* as starting points for their constitutional analysis.

In his edition of *The Federalist*, Charles A. Beard wrote that "there is scarcely a problem or aspect of government which excites contemporary interest that is left untouched in this great work." Whatever the constitutional issue, *The Federalist* has more to tell us than any text. Is it a question of whether the states may impose term limits on members of Congress? As the 1995 Supreme Court decision recognized, *The Federalist*, in Nos. 52, 57, 59, and 60, deals specifically with the issue and furnished the foundation for the Court's analysis. Is it a question of whether a law prohibiting guns in a school zone comes within federal power to regulate commerce? Another 1995 decision uses *The Federalist* No. 45 as the foundation for its discussion of the division of powers between states and nation. Other opinions in the case rely on Nos. 46 and 51 in dealing with checks on federal power, as well as other numbers for the meaning of "commerce" in the Constitution.

What it comes down to is Beard's ultimate question: "Is it a question of 'the living Constitution'—the American system in operation today?" Answering it, Beard stressed that "from the time of publication of *The Federalist* to the latest moment, passages from it have been so constantly and persistently cited that it has entered deeply into the interpretation and spirit of the Constitution and remains an inseparable part of its meaning and application." Presidents, the Supreme Court, other judges, members of Congress, and innumerable others have sought and still seek guidance and support for their views in *The Federalist*, which remains *the* fundamental source on constitutional interpretation. All in all, it must be considered the most influential work on public law ever written.

2. James Kent, *Commentaries on American Law*

James Kent, as his inclusion in Chapter 7 shows, was one of the greatest American judges. He is remembered today, however, mainly because of his four-volume *Commentaries on American Law* (1826–1830), which Alexis de Tocqueville listed as one of his primary legal sources. Kent, together with Joseph Story, was the great early legal commentator; in his and Story's books, there appeared the first systematic expositions of the developing American law.

If New York had not required the compulsory retirement of judges at sixty, Kent's landmark work would never have been written. On his retirement, Columbia College appointed him to its professorship in law. His lectures were published as his *Commentaries*. The work dominated early legal thinking in this country and earned for its author the sobriquet "American Blackstone."

The reader today is put off by Kent's boring style. His stiff neoclassicism should not, however, lead us to overlook his seminal influence. Through most of the nineteenth century, Kent's *Commentaries* was *the* work to consult on American law. Five subsequent editions were published during Kent's life, and eight others after his death, with the last as late as 1896. The young Holmes first made a scholarly reputation by editing Kent's twelfth edition, in 1873. And even Holmes had to recognize the work's importance: "Kent in the Commentaries Caesar writ" was the way he once described Kent.

Kent's political views were extremely conservative, but the same was not true of his conception of law. His *Commentaries*, to be sure, purported only to be a restatement of existing law, stressing the common-law foundation. Throughout the work, however, Kent emphasized that the English system was to be followed only as far as it was suitable for American conditions. The underlying consideration was to present American law in a manner that served the new nation's economic development. This enabled Kent's work to authenticate the transition from a system still influenced by its feudal roots to the emerging entrepreneurial society.

In particular, the *Commentaries* drastically modified English land law. Thus, Kent declared categorically that "the doctrine of estates tail, and the complex and multifarious learning connected with it, have been quite obsolete in most parts of the United States." This statement led to the abolition of entails throughout the country. The same was true of the law governing the descent of land. Kent's assertion that "in these United States, the English common law of descents, in its most essential features, has been universally rejected" confirmed the repudiation of primogeniture and the other English rules that unduly restricted the transfer and descent of real property. In Kent, feudal land tenure was abolished and the freehold established as the basic land title. The autonomy of private decision-making could thus be dominant in land law, as it was coming to be in the other areas of American law.

In addition to property, the *Commentaries'* main focus was commercial law, which Kent molded to give American business the freedom of action needed for the challenge of the unexploited continent. As thus reworked, American law gave private entrepreneurs the autonomy needed to commit the necessary resources and energy. Where Blackstone devoted only a few pages to contracts, in Kent contract and related commercial subjects covered one out of four large volumes. The narrow common law of contracts was expanded into a legal instrument, dominated by the concept of free will, that became the solving idea for the law's response to the needs of the expanding society. The key social interest became the security of transactions freely entered into, the basic legal principle that promises be kept and undertakings be carried out in good faith. The interest of the promisee—his claim to be assured in the expectation created—became the interest primarily protected by the law. To Kent, the intent of the parties overrode conflicting interests and restrictive common-law rules. The purpose was to give contracting parties the assurance needed to induce them to venture into business enterprises.

The *Commentaries* may have purported only to summarize the common law as it applied in this country. But the common law stated by Kent was the law that he deemed appropriate to the developing nation. Conservative though he was, Kent did not hesitate to describe American law in terms of the modifications needed to foster the emerging market economy—particularly in favor of principles, as he put it, "well calculated to bring dormant capital into active and useful employment."

This was the major contribution of Kent's early text. In his hands, the common law became a flexible instrument that could be adapted to the needs of the new nation. Kent supplied American jurisprudence with the very instrument it most needed: a coherent legal rationality. He furnished our law with the methodology that enabled it to serve a nation engaged in conquering a continent. More than that, Kent helped ensure that the life of American law would not simply be a junior version of that on the other side of the Atlantic.

3. Joseph Story, *Commentaries on the Constitution of the United States*

Tocqueville listed Joseph Story's *Commentaries on the Constitution of the United States* (1833) as one of his primary sources of American law. Story, we saw, was one of the greatest Supreme Court Justices. But his contribution in helping to lay the American legal foundation was not limited to his work as a judge. In 1829, while he was on the Supreme Court, Story became the first Dane Professor of Law at Harvard; despite his heavy judicial duties, he taught two of the school's three yearly terms. He also found time to publish the first specialized treatises on American law. "I have now published seven volumes," he wrote in 1836, "and, in five or six more, I can accomplish all I propose." By the end of his career, he had published nine treatises (in thirteen volumes) on subjects ranging from constitutional to commercial law. They were major contributions to the different branches of law covered in them. As a judge, Story may have been overshadowed by Marshall; but as a law teacher and writer, he was in the first rank.

Most important in its influence on the nation was Story's three-volume *Commentaries on the Constitution of the United States*. Recognized as authoritative when it was published, it immediately began to appear in arguments of counsel and court opinions on issues covering the whole range of constitutional law. In his work, as on the bench, Story was a strong supporter of Marshall. The treatise itself was dedicated to the great Chief Justice and had a major role in confirming his constitutional conceptions. Above all, it ensured the triumph of the nationalistic view to which both Marshall and Story were dedicated.

The main body of Story's commentary was a clause-by-clause analysis of the Constitution, based on what the Justice considered the "correct"— that is, Marshall's—constitutional principles. In particular, the Story work was the definite legal repudiation of the states' rights view, which rested on the notion that the Constitution was only a compact between sovereign states. Story sought to rebut the concept of state sovereignty and that of the Constitution as a mere contract. Instead, he translated Marshall's nationalism into accepted law in a treatise acknowledged as definitive as soon as it appeared.

Story's *Commentaries* quickly became *the* leading text on constitutional law. It went through five American editions and was still in print at the end of the century. As such, it was the successor to *The Federalist*—like it, one of the primary sources of constitutional interpretation. Like *The Federalist*, too, Story continues to be relied on by the Supreme Court, more than a century and a half after the *Commentaries* were published. In the 1995 term-limits case, Story was discussed in both the majority and dissenting opinions, second only to *The Federalist* as a primary source. Indeed, the dissent by Justice Clarence Thomas complains that "the only true support for [the majority's] view of the Tenth Amendment comes from Joseph Story's 1833 treatise on constitutional law." Story, Thomas concedes, was "brilliant and accomplished," but, he states, Story "was not a member of the Founding generation, and his Commentaries on the Constitution were written a half century after the framing. Rather than representing the original understanding of the Constitution, they represent only his own understanding."

Two centuries have, however, confirmed that Story's understanding has been as crucial to constitutional interpretation as anything written on the subject. More important, his version of the Constitution, like that of Marshall, which it confirmed, has been validated by the nation's development. True, his constitutional conceptions were on the winning side of history. But it was his work, as much as any writing, that helped to make it the winning side.

4. Thomas M. Cooley,
A Treatise on the Constitutional Limitations . . .

The Fourteenth Amendment was ratified in 1868. That same year, Thomas M. Cooley published *A Treatise on the Constitutional Limitations Which Rest upon the Legislative Power of the States of the American Union*. Cooley's book laid the doctrinal foundation for conversion of the amendment into a virtual Magna Carta for business, furnishing the legal text for the post–Civil War economic expansion. If Mark Twain's *Gilded Age* set the general theme for the period, it was Cooley who set its legal theme. Cooley's work dominated legal thought between the formative era of American law and the modern period.

Cooley, we saw in Chapter 7, was one of the greatest state judges. However, his principal impact on American law was a result of his *Constitutional Limitations*; published in 1868, it went through seven further editions from 1871 through 1927. The book originated from the need for a constitutional law course at the University of Michigan. Cooley undertook the course reluctantly, only after the other professors had refused to give it. The text was written as a basis for his lectures, and Cooley was at first unable to find a publisher (the senior member of the firm to which it was first submitted later said that he would regret the mistake until his dying day).

Cooley's book was one of the most influential law books, for it established the mold into which constitutional jurisprudence was to be set during the next half-century. Under Cooley's influence, the Fourteenth Amendment was to become the basic charter of the new American economy. It could not, however, have fostered the rapid industrialization of the post–Civil War period if the due process guaranteed by the amendment had been confined to its literal import of *proper procedure*. It was the judicial importation of a substantive side into due process that made it so significant as a restriction on governmental power.

Substantive due process received its doctrinal foundation with Cooley's *Constitutional Limitations*. To Cooley, due process was the great substantive safeguard of property; its protective umbrella now included all the constitutional limitations, express and implied, on governmental interference with the rights of property. What Cooley was doing was what the New York Court of Appeals had done twelve years earlier in *Wynehamer v. People* (1856), where a law was invalidated as violative of substantive due process, and what Chief Justice Taney had done in *Dred Scott v. Sandford* (1857). The widespread obloquy attached to *Dred Scott* had made it impossible for any part of the Court's opinion there to have a germinal effect. Cooley's great contribution was to give widespread currency to the *Wynehamer* approach and thus rescue substantive due process from the constitutional cul-de-sac in which *Dred Scott* had left it.

The popularity of his treatise soon made Cooley the most frequently quoted constitutional-law authority. His book showed American judges how they could use the due process clause to review the reasonableness of laws and strike down as unreasonable those that interfered with business operations. With Cooley's book as a foundation, American public law enlisted for decades in behalf of the fullest freedom for the businessman.

Cooley's treatment of due process was crucial in the transformation of law from an affirmative instrument to shape the society to a negative conception that was not to interfere while economic interests asserted themselves freely. In addition, the Cooley notion of law confirmed the broadside freedom of contract that would soon be considered basic to the liberty safeguarded by the law.

Constitutional Limitations thus furnished the theme for the emerging jurisprudence. Cooley's doctrine was used to strike down laws that did not suit the dominant interests of the day. To the law that adopted the Cooley approach, the "liberty" protected by due process became synonymous with governmental hands-off in the field of private economic relations.

5. Christopher Columbus Langdell, *A Selection of Cases on the Law of Contracts*

Christopher Columbus Langdell, no less than his namesake, discovered a whole new world—this time in the case method of teaching law, a method that has become so ingrained in the American law school that it is easy to forget how innovative it was. When Langdell made his celebrated assertion, "First, that law is a science; secondly that all the available materials of that science are contained in printed books," he struck a responsive chord. The way to study a science was to go to the original sources. In the law, the "original sources" were the reports of decided cases. The law was to be learned through critical analysis of selected opinions of courts—a radical change in law teaching.

The case method made for a virtual revolution in legal education. Until then, classroom instruction had been entirely through assigned reading in texts and lectures. All this changed when Langdell became dean of the Harvard Law School. He not only used the case method as his system of instruction at the nation's most prestigious law school, but also published the first casebook *A Selection of Cases on the Law of Contracts* (1871)—and furnished the doctrinal foundation for the new method.

Langdell's basic theme was contained in his quoted assertion that "law is a science." He sought to apply the method of the natural sciences to law study—by the careful observation of specific specimens and then the derivation of general conclusions that would apply to other instances. Langdell's specimens were judicial opinions. The student of law, like the student of chemistry or botany, must learn close scrutiny and discriminating classification. To accomplish this, the law student must continually study, compare, and classify cases. Langdell furnished him with the necessary specimens by a collection of selected cases, which would serve as both the source of study and the basis of classroom discussion.

In selecting his cases, Langdell was influenced directly by his scientific conception of law. As he put it in his preface, "Law, considered as a science, consists of certain principles or doctrines" that are the growth of centuries. "This growth is to be traced in the main through a series of cases; and much the shortest and best, if not the only way of mastering the doctrine effectually is by studying the cases in which it is embodied."

What he had done, Langdell's preface stated, was "to take such a branch of the law as Contracts" and "to select, classify, and arrange all the cases which had contributed [to] its essential doctrines." "Such a work," the preface concluded, "could not fail to be of material service to all who desire to study that branch of law systematically and in its original sources."

Preparation of the casebook was, however, only the first part of the new teaching method. The student would still need help in learning to classify the cases, to distinguish one from the other, and to reject opinions that were poorly reasoned. This would require not only careful

study of the cases, but, even more, discussion in class, with thorough questioning of the student's judgment and recognition of error. The result was the Socratic dialogue between teacher and student, which leads the latter to an understanding of the legal principles to be derived from the case compendium.

Over a century later, when criticisms of the case method are heard on all sides, it is all too easy to forget what a forward step Langdell's case-book was. It rescued American legal education from the theoretical incursions into dogma that characterized law teaching in other countries. It furnished precisely the kind of training the potential lawyer needed and the older text and lecture method had neglected: training in intellectual independence, in individual thinking, in digging out principles through penetrating analysis, and reasoning from them in a legal manner.

Instead of serving only as receptacles for the rules spouted by professors, law students were now to be taught to think and, in the now time-worn cliché, to "think like lawyers." "Others," said Sir Frederick Pollock, "can give us rules; [Langdell] gives us the method and the power that can test the reason of rules."

6. Oliver Wendell Holmes, *The Common Law*

Twentieth-century American law really begins in 1880. It was in that year that Oliver Wendell Holmes began his lectures on the common law that were to change the course of jurisprudence. Published as a book the next year, Holmes's *Common Law* (1881) set the theme for modern law. Indeed, to describe Holmes's contribution is to describe the transition from nineteenth-century legal thought to that of the present day.

On its face, *The Common Law* was only a summary of the different legal subjects: criminal law, torts, property, contracts, and succession. But it was far more than a mere compendium. The work was one of the greatest law books because its was not limited to a summary of the subjects covered. Instead, as a state judge tells us, "[t]he book propounds an idea audacious and even revolutionary for the time." The Holmes idea has become so settled in our thinking that we forget how radical it was when it was announced. The very words used must have appeared strange to the contemporary reader: "experience," "expediency," "necessity," "life." Law books at the time used far different words: "rule," "precedent," "logic," "syllogism." As the best-known Holmes biography tells us, "The time-honored way was to deduce the *corpus* from *a priori* postulates, fit

part to part in beautiful, neat logical cohesion." To Holmes instead, as his book declared, "[t]he law embodies the story of a nation's development through many centuries, and it cannot be dealt with as if it contained the axioms and corollaries of a book of mathematics."

The great Holmes theme was stated at the very outset of *The Common Law*: "The life of the law has not been logic: it has been experience. The felt necessities of the time, the prevalent moral and political theories, intuitions of public policy, avowed or unconscious, even the prejudices which judges share with their fellow-men, have had a good deal more to do than the syllogism in determining the rules by which men should be governed."

When Holmes wrote these words, he was pointing the way to a new era of jurisprudence. The courts, Holmes urged, should recognize that they must perform a legislative function, in its deeper sense. The secret root from which the law draws its life is consideration of "what is expedient for the community." The "felt necessities of the time," intuitions of what best serve the public interest, "even the prejudices which judges share with their fellow-men"—all have much more to do than logic in determining legal rules.

In an 1897 lecture, Holmes asserted that "the judges themselves have failed adequately to recognize their duty of weighing considerations of social advantage." The judges of the day looked at the law as anything but the instrument of transforming innovation it has become. In law, as in nature, progress was considered an evolutionary process, which could be impeded only by outside intervention. As it was put by James C. Carter, then considered the outstanding legal thinker, "[t]he popular estimate of the possibilities for good which may be realized through the enactment of law is, in my opinion, greatly exaggerated." In law, as in the economics of the day, hands-off was the rule.

The judges then reached their restrictive conclusions deductively from preconceived notions and precedents. During the twentieth century, the judicial method has become inductive, reasoning from the changing facts of a relativist world. The system has become fluid and inconstant, dependent on the particular circumstances of time and place. As Holmes predicted in his 1897 lecture, the black-letter judge has been replaced by the man of statistics and the master of economics and other disciplines.

Years later, Holmes pointed out that, in his *Common Law* lectures, "I gathered the flax, made the thread, spun the cloth, and cut the garment—and started all the inquiries that since have gone over many matters therein." *The Common Law* purported to be only a descriptive statement of

what the law was and how, historically, it came to be that way. In fact, however, Holmes was making a prescriptive statement of what the law ought to be—a statement that was ultimately to set the theme for the law of the coming century.

7. Benjamin N. Cardozo, *The Nature of the Judicial Process*

According to Judge Richard A. Posner, Benjamin Cordozo's *Nature of the Judicial Process* (1921) was the first attempt by a judge to give a realistic description of how judges decide cases. The book was based on a conception of law that was anything but the fixed system posited by jurists early in the century. As Cardozo saw it, "jurisprudence is more plastic, more malleable, the moulds less definitively cast, the bounds of right and wrong less preordained and constant, than most of us . . . have been accustomed to believe."

Cardozo rejected the negative notion of law, with law derived from a system of immutable principles. The law, his book stated, "is not found, but made." In making the law, the jurist has a "choice [that] moves with a freedom which stamps [his] action as creative." This does not mean complete free will—that judges "are free to substitute their own ideas of reason and justice for those of the men and women whom they serve." Instead, Cardozo wrote, the judicial "standard must be an objective one."

Judge Posner explains that this means "objective in a pragmatic sense, which is not the sense of correspondence with an external reality." Instead, says Cardozo, the judge is to decide in accordance with his "conception of the end of law." As for the ultimate end: "The final cause of law is the welfare of society." When the courts "are called upon to say how far existing rules are to be extended or restricted, they must let the welfare of society fix the path, its direction and its distance." To Cardozo, law that strays from that path "cannot . . . justify its existence."

As *The Nature of the Judicial Process* saw it, the key change that had occurred in the law was "the change from the analytical to the functional attitude." The test of legal rules is their social value. Legal rules are to be viewed instrumentally; they must serve the welfare of society or else be modified or eliminated.

The Cardozo concept of law is, as he termed it, "teleological." To Cardozo, "[n]ot the origin, but the goal, is the main thing. There can be no wisdom in the choice of a path unless we know where it will lead." The principles of selection of both rules and decisions "is one of fitness to an end."

This means that, as Cardozo's book points out, "juristic philosophy . . . is at bottom the philosophy of pragmatism."

It is difficult for us today to understand the furor which Cardozo's book caused, for the ideas in its pages are by now, in Posner's phrase, legal old hat. At the time it was written, however, the situation was different. A leading judge had publicly repudiated the concept of law that prevailed early in the century. The Cardozo volume, written with a charm all but unequaled in legal literature, made clear what is now considered obvious about the judicial process, but had not been widely understood before.

The more common view at the time is exemplified by a leading jurist who asserted that "Cardozo had undermined that faith in the place of inescapable logic in the law which was fundamental to security." Cardozo himself, we are told by the professor who had arranged the Yale lectures on which *The Nature of the Judicial Process* was based, "was aware that his conception of the judicial process was not the generally accepted one. . . . With a touch of humor, he remarked, 'If I were to publish them I would be impeached.'"

What mattered, however, was that a master of the common law had shown the utter inadequacy of the conception that law consisted solely in logical deductions from established premises. The law, Cardozo showed, was not a static collection of rules, but a living body of principles capable of growth and change: "in its highest reaches [it] is not discovery, but creation." More than that, it was creation with a purpose. The "final principle . . . is one of fitness to an end."

The Cardozo conception is thus one that sees law as the servant of human needs. His basic theme was summed up in his book's short phrase: "The end which the law serves will dominate . . . all." The judge should seek the proper decision in light of "the comparative importance of the social interests that will be thereby promoted or impaired."

8. Jerome N. Frank,
Law and the Modern Mind

Jerome N. Frank's *Law and the Modern Mind* (1930) was the catalyst in the founding of the most important twentieth-century school of jurisprudence. This school, soi-disant Realist, gave voice to a new conception of law, unrelated to traditional theories. It was Holmes who pointed the way to Legal Realism. As one of the leading Realists explained it, "A suggestion first made by Holmes in 1897 . . . has today been taken up by a sufficient number of writers so that we may properly speak of a 'realist school.'"

The suggestion was made in Holmes's dictum, "The prophecies of what the courts will do in fact, and nothing more pretentious, are what I mean by the law." From this, it was a short step to Frank's assertion in his book that law was "only a guess as to what a court will decide. Law then . . . is either (a) actual law, *i.e.*, a specific past decision . . . or (b) probable law, *i.e.*, a guess as to a specific future decision." The basic Frank thesis was that law was not stated in the legal rules that had been the basis of accepted jurisprudence. Instead, Frank's book asserted, "[l]aw is made up not of rules for decision laid down by the courts but of the decisions themselves. . . . The 'law of a great nation' means the decisions of a handful of old gentlemen, and whatever they refuse to decide is not law."

Frank argued that the traditional approach to decision-making must be reversed. Judging, he urged, actually begins with a conclusion, and then the premises to substantiate it are worked out. Judges judge backward; they work not from rules and principles to conclusions, but the converse— from conclusions to principles. The conclusions themselves are based not on legal rules, but on factors far removed from the time-honored theory of judging. According to Frank, "The judge really decides by feeling and not by judgment, by hunching and not by ratiocination." Judging was an intuitive process, with the "judge's hunch" the determining element: "Whatever produces the judge's hunches makes the law." As Frank's book saw it, "legal rules, principles and the like are merely for show, materials for window dressing, implements to aid in rationalization . . . the principles of law often only remotely related to judicial conduct."

Under the Frank jurisprudence, there is much more play for the judge in deciding cases than traditional jurisprudence allowed. The law becomes what has been termed "a more or less disguised system of oriental cadi justice." In the Frank conception, law loses what had always been one of its essential elements—certainty. For Frank, however, this was not something to be deplored, since the law's vaunted certainty was largely fictitious. The reality to him was that the law was made in individual cases: only what individual judges did in fact was the law.

Frank's book brought him to the forefront of American jurists. It appeared at a time of ferment in legal thought. The dogmatic certainty with which the century began was increasingly giving way before the criticisms of Holmes, Cardozo, and other progenitors of the coming juristic era. Jurisprudence was, however, still hesitating between two worlds—the one dying, the other waiting to be born.

At this point, Frank appeared and carried criticism of the existing order to its logical extreme. Above all, he performed a valuable service in emphasizing the difference between law in the books and law in action—between what legal institutions said and what they did. Awareness of this was essential if the law was to attain the ends deemed appropriate in the mid-twentieth century.

The most recent study of Frank is titled *The Iconoclast as Reformer*. Frank's primary role was to break the icons of established jurisprudence, not to create new images in their stead. As an iconoclast, Frank had a seminal role in modern jurisprudence. His derision for the old ideal of mechanical symmetry and order was transmitted with a candor new in legal writing. After Frank and the other Realists, the juristic faith that had been dominant early in the century could be adhered to by only the few who still had confidence in the inexorable logic of law as the essential for security in the society.

On these terms, Frank's work was notably successful. Frank and the other Realists completed the work of Holmes and the other critics of turn-of-the-century thought. After them, what Thurman Arnold called the legal "world of eternal values and absolute certainties" had become a lost world.

9. James C. Carter, *Law: Its Origin, Growth and Function*

Despite Holmes's impact on future law, it was not he but James C. Carter, a leading practitioner of the day, who was *the* legal philosopher a century ago. It was Carter who formalized the concept of law that had become dominant.

Carter was the rare practitioner who devoted time to writing on jurisprudence. After his retirement from practice, he worked on a book on the subject. Carter died before the book could be delivered in lectures at Harvard Law School. It was published two years later, in 1907, as *Law: Its Origin, Growth and Function*. This book is the summa of both Carter's jurisprudence and the dominant legal thought at the turn of the century.

Carter's conception of law was very different from that of Holmes. He rejected law as the product of conscious law-making. Instead, the Carter conception was based on the approach of what has come to be called the historical school of jurisprudence—that the law is found, not made. To Carter, law is not made by the conscious act of a legislator or judge; it "is the necessary product of the life of a society, and therefore incapable of being made at all."

A commentator summed up the Carter view: "Carter preached, for he had all the fervor of a preacher, that legislation, except when declaratory, was a futile attempt to make what could not be made; that law must be found by courts and jurists discovering and applying principles expressing experience of the life of a people, taking form in customs of popular action." Carter's book stated it this way: law "is the necessary product of the life of society, and therefore incapable of being made at all."

In the Carter jurisprudence, it is not for the law "to engage in the business of finding out what conduct on the part of its members will secure the greatest amount of happiness to all, and then compelling its adoption by Force." Instead, it will "be found out that human conduct is in a very large degree self-regulating, and that the extent to which it can be affected by the conscious interference of man is much narrower than is commonly supposed." In his presidential address to the American Bar Association, Carter declared, "Wise legislation seeks to accomplish in relation to each human interest only what it seeks in the domain of business and finance." Laissez-faire in law was the natural accompaniment of laissez-faire in economics.

The Carter vision of law was thus essentially negative, his maxim "permanently and everywhere true that the sole function of government and of law is to secure to every man the largest possible freedom of individual action consistent with the preservation of the like liberty for every other man." The proper function of law was to give effect to this principle—the "guide which, when kept clear and constantly in view, sufficiently informs us what we should aim to do by legislation." The need to let nature take its course was to prevail in the legal, as in the economic, arena: "To leave each man to work out in freedom his own happiness or misery, to stand or fail by the consequences of his own conduct, is the true method of human discipline."

"As we think today," Roscoe Pound tells us, "Carter has no longer a significant place in the science of law. At most, the historian of juristic thought in America would note him in passing as a belated exponent of a body of doctrine already moribund when the book, by which he is best known, was published." Such a statement is unfair to Carter. True, his approach to law has been repudiated by twentieth-century legal thought. Yet it cannot be denied that Carter was a major figure in the jurisprudence of his day. In fact, according to a recent Canadian article, Carter represents "the culmination of a common current of thought which permeated the . . . last quarter of the nineteenth century."

10. Richard A. Posner,
Economic Analysis of Law

No law book has been more influential during the second half of the twentieth century than Judge Richard A. Posner's *Economic Analysis of Law* (1973), written while he was a professor at the University of Chicago Law School. Posner's book has largely been responsible for what later editions called "the most important development in legal thought in the last quarter century . . . the application of economics to an ever-increasing range of legal fields." Posner's *Economic Analysis of Law* remains the basic text of the law-and-economics school.

Jurisprudence too often appears a legal version of the blind men of Hindustan's reaction to the elephant. The aspect emphasized by the particular writer tends to dominate his conception of law. To Kent, it was the common law adapted to American needs; to Carter, it was the unwritten law, with its stress on laissez-faire; to the Realists, it was what they considered the reality of the judicial process. Posner also has his juristic vade mecum: economic analysis to resolve legal issues. To Posner, the law becomes only a junior branch of economics.

Yet although the Posner jurisprudence may profess to have all of economics as its bailiwick, it is almost entirely based on the present-day revival of classical economics, as exemplified in so-called Chicago School economics. That school has never accepted the fact that, in this century, the market has increasingly been replaced by the "public interest" as defined in regulatory legislation and administration. To the Chicago School, the overriding goal should be efficiency and efficiency is best promoted by free operation of the market.

For Posner, the goal of law, as of economics, is efficiency. As his book defines it, "Efficiency is a technical term: it means exploiting economic resources in such a way that human satisfaction as measured by aggregate consumer willingness to pay for goods and services is maximized." Efficiency is conceived of in terms of wealth maximization, which Posner sees as the norm in the law as in the economic system itself. For Posner, the law and its agencies, particularly the courts, should make decisions in such a way as to maximize social wealth.

The Posner concept of efficiency as wealth maximization is based on existence of the market. As his book puts it, "resources tend to gravitate toward their most valuable uses if voluntary exchange—a market—is permitted." Indeed, in the words of one critic, "the picture of American society presented by Posner . . . has created one grand system—the market, and those market-supportive aspects of law (notably 'common' judge-made law)—which is almost flawless in achieving human happiness."

It is, however, a short step from the Posner conception to that which dominated our law early in the twentieth century. If efficiency and wealth maximization are to be the legal lodestar and if their attainment depends on the market, then interference with free operation of the market is to be condemned. When Posner's book concludes that when judges make law, the rules of law laid down by them should be consistent with the dictates of efficiency, he is really positing judge-made jurisprudence consistent with free operation of the market and hostile to action that hampers its untrammeled operation.

It thus turns out that Posner's economic analysis of law furnishes support to those who would undermine the legal foundation of the twentieth-century welfare state. We can see this in the specific results reached under the Posner jurisprudence. Thus *Economic Analysis of the Law* states that the law was "on solid economic ground when it refused to enforce agreements to join unions, enjoined picketing . . . and enforced yellow dog contracts." The book also asserts that a statute like the Occupational Safety and Health Act is not necessary, since, without the law, "[t]he employer has a selfish interest in providing the optimal . . . level of worker health and safety." Indeed, the book concludes, "[l]egislation prescribing the health and safety conditions of employment may raise the level of health and safety beyond the level desired by the employees and the employers and then both groups will be harmed."

Posnerian law, grounded as it is on the efficiency furthered by the market, inevitably looks with a hostile eye on governmental acts that interfere with the market. As Posner's book puts it, "the idea that voluntary transactions almost always promote welfare, and regulations that inhibit such transactions almost always reduce it," is the "staple of classic [economic] theory"—as well as the foundation of Posnerian economic analysis of law.

Yet if influence on the law is what makes a law book great, Posner's book deserves inclusion on this list. It provided an entirely new method of legal analysis. In particular, Posner's approach pioneered the use of cost-benefit analysis in dealing with legal problems. Without Posner's writing, it is most unlikely that the law today would be as aware of the cost-benefit approach, much less have elevated it to accepted legal method. This is the case in private, as well as public law. Tort law has been transformed by the Posner approach and the same has been true, in varying degrees, in other areas of law. Perhaps Posner's efficiency norm has not been applied by the judges to the extent that he desires, but there is no doubt that it has had increasing impact on the forum and, even more so, the academy. All in all, the *Almanac of the Federal Judiciary* concluded a few years ago, "Posner is the most influential legal thinker in America today." Posner's *Economic Analysis of Law* has been the engine that has fueled the law-and-economics approach and made it so prominent a part of the legal agenda.

"Scribblers" and Law Development

This list illustrates the truth of the Keynes comment about the influence of "scribblers" on practical affairs. The "scribblers" who wrote the works on this list have helped to mold the law as much as anyone in the forum or the assembly. It is true that seven of those on the list were judges, including three who served on the Supreme Court. Four of them, however—Cooley, Holmes, Frank, and Posner—wrote their books before they were appointed to the bench, and Kent wrote his after he had retired to academe. Only Story and Cardozo published their works while they were judges, and Story noted that he wrote his constitutional commentary "in execution of the duties" of his Harvard Law School professorship.

It is significant that most of these works were connected with law schools. Kent, Story, Cooley, Langdell, Holmes, and Posner were on law-school faculties when they wrote their books. Cardozo wrote his *Nature of the Judicial Process* for lectures at Yale; Carter's book was prepared for lectures at Harvard. Most of the important works on American law have, in fact, been written by what Keynes called "academic scribblers"—underlining the increasing significance of the law school in the development of our law.

The books were not chosen because of their literary qualities. Indeed, most of them may be hard going for the reader. But they are *the* great American law books, not because of their style, but because of their contributions to the law's development.

All the books contributed significantly to American law. *The Federalist* remains the primary source for constitutional interpretation; it is the classic exposition of our federalism, and its use by the courts confirmed the effectiveness of national power. Kent published the first systematic exposition of the developing law, providing doctrinal guides to ensure that it would be adapted to the new nation's needs. Story gave authoritative support to the nationalist construction of the Constitution, cementing legal acceptance of the Marshall Court's jurisprudence. Cooley furnished the doctrinal foundation for substantive due process and its position for over half a century as the constitutional charter of the expanding economy. Langdell pioneered the case method, which transformed legal education. Carter summarized the jurisprudence of his day, emphasizing the negative conception of law then deemed necessary to enable economic interests to operate freely. Holmes sounded the theme of the coming law, with his stress on law that served the "felt necessities of the time" and judges who consciously relied on social needs, rather than formal logic. Cardozo built upon the Holmes approach and showed how judges should decide cases, pointing up both law's Heraclitean nature and its ultimate end—"the welfare of society." Frank pioneered the new approach to law that came to be called Legal Realism; it shifted the emphasis from what legal institutions said to what they did in practice. Posner was the prime mover in applying economics to legal analysis; his law-and-economics school has given a new dimension to both law and legal education.

The books chosen have thus had seminal influence on either the law of their day or the coming law. Each has made a contribution comparable to that of outstanding judges in molding our law. Without them, our legal history would have been different. Once again, influence is the criterion for inclusion in the legal pantheon.

11

TEN

GREATEST

LAWYERS

"Tradition has it," Justice William Brennan tells us, "that law is not made by judge alone but by Judge and Company"—meaning that counsel, by their arguments, play a large part in the shaping of law. Despite this, the bar has largely remained anonymous in history. Practicing lawyers' work tends to be noticed only by their professional contemporaries; their contributions to jurisprudence are overshadowed by those of judges and legal writers. This is true even of the leading practitioners of our formative era, when the bar attained a standard of advocacy that has become legendary. Who now remembers what the God-like Daniel—no one was as great as Webster looked!—and his fellow advocates contributed to the development of American law? John Marshall's jurisprudence has become an essential part of the nation's history. All but forgotten is the role of the Supreme Court bar in setting forth the doctrines that the great Chief Justice elevated to the constitutional plane. Yet Webster himself said of Marshall's landmark opinion in *Gibbons v. Ogden* (1824) that "the opinion . . . was little else than a recital of my argument," which Marshall did "take . . . in as a baby takes in its mother's milk."

My list of the ten greatest American lawyers: Some of them are leading figures in our history; three became presidents; two, Supreme Court Justices. They appear not because of these high attainments, but because of their skill as members of the legal profession. All appear not because of their mastery of courtroom histrionics (though all were outstanding advocates), but because they strikingly illustrate Justice Brennan's point. As practitioners they were eminently part of the "Company" that helped to make American law. Each made major contributions that compare with those of the great judges and writers on my earlier lists.

— ★ — ★ — ★ —

Ten Greatest Lawyers

1. Alexander Hamilton, 1755–1804

2. Louis Dembitz Brandeis, 1856–1941

3. Clarence Darrow, 1857–1938

4. John Adams, 1735–1826

5. Abraham Lincoln, 1809–1865

6. Daniel Webster, 1782–1852

7. David Dudley Field, 1805–1894

8. Thurgood Marshall, 1908–1994

9. John W. Davis, 1873–1955

10. Thomas Jefferson, 1743–1826

1. Alexander Hamilton: Lawyer Nationalist

When he looks at the negligible legal education of early lawyers such as John Adams, Thomas Jefferson, and above all Alexander Hamilton (1755–1804), it makes one who has devoted his life to law teaching wonder whether law-school education marks the advance that most believe it does. This is particularly true so far as Hamilton is concerned. In law, as in other respects, Hamilton was the Horatio Alger of his day.

When Hamilton left Washington's army toward the end of 1781, he decided to become a lawyer. The usual clerkship requirement was waived for him because of his war service. All Hamilton had to do was pass an examination in open court, which he did some months later, and he was admitted as an attorney.

Instead of learning law in a law office as would-be lawyers did at the time, Hamilton read on his own for about six months to prepare for his examination. We can obtain some idea of the effort he made from the practice manual he wrote while studying for the bar. This manual was the first New York procedure treatise. It was copied and widely used to prepare for the bar. The first printed book on New York practice made extensive use of the Hamilton work.

Hamilton's practice manual has been called "the first work in the field of private law by one of the great lawyers of the early Republic." Hamilton deserved the encomium, for he soon became the undisputed leader of the New York bar. James Kent wrote that Hamilton was "the leading counsel at the Bar. . . . His pre-eminence was at once and universally conceded."

Hamilton's principal legal contributions were in public law. It was Hamilton who helped lay the groundwork for essential public-law principles—notably the doctrines of judicial review and implied powers. The foundation of Hamilton's public-law principles was a strong national government. In this respect, it was Hamilton who laid the groundwork for John Marshall's greatest doctrines. *Marbury v. Madison* (1803) and *McCulloch v. Maryland* (1819) were glosses on Hamilton's essays in favor of judicial review in *The Federalist* No. 78 and of implied powers in Hamilton's opinion on the Bank of the United States.

Hamilton also enunciated the interpretation of the general welfare clause that the Supreme Court has come to accept, as well as the broad concept of presidential power that has prevailed. Indeed, the current interpretation of the Constitution is essentially Hamiltonian. The important issues of public law, on which Hamilton differed with those who favored strict construction, have been resolved in Hamilton's favor.

What made Hamilton a great lawyer, however, is not only the fact that his public-law principles have prevailed. To Hamilton, the law was a means, not an end. He interpreted the Constitution to provide for strong national government because its power could be used to foster the productive economy that he foresaw.

The Hamilton conception of law as a nationalistic tool made him more ready to approve changes in the law than most of his lawyer contemporaries. This was apparent as early as his writing of his practice manual. Even at that early stage, Hamilton was ready to deprecate useless legal procedures. His manual placed them "among the Absurdities with which the Law abounds." His basic theme was stated in a sardonic passage: "the Court . . . lately acquired . . . some faint Idea that the end of Suits at Law is to Investigate the Merits of the Cause, and not to entangle in the Nets of technical Terms."

Hamilton followed the same approach in his legal work. An example is an 1802 case. A contract provided that defendant was to buy Bank of the United States stock, but he refused to accept delivery. The court refused to admit oral evidence of an accidentally destroyed letter proving tender by plaintiff. On appeal, Hamilton argued that a copy of a document might be received where the original was "destroyed without his default" and that "[w]henever a copy may be given in evidence parole evidence of its contents may be offered." Admitting that older authority was against him, Hamilton claimed that the strict rule had been mitigated by recent English decisions and that the court should follow this liberalizing trend and allow the evidence.

Hamilton's argument was accepted. Not only did he win the case, but his argument helped fix the more liberal rule on the introduction of such evidence that has since been followed. The Hamilton view was consistent with his conception of law as a tool to further economic relations. The evidence rule should be interpreted liberally, to permit the broadest range of evidence to support an otherwise valid contract claim.

We know from Kent and others that Hamilton was the outstanding lawyer of his day. A judge who was his political enemy, before whom Hamilton had often appeared, said that in power of reasoning, Hamilton was the equal of any lawyer and, in creative power, superior to all.

Most of Hamilton's arguments at the bar are lost. An exception was his passionate defense of freedom of the press in *Crosswell v. People* (1803). Kent, one of the judges, called it Hamilton's "greatest forensic effort," and a 1971 book characterized it as one of "his finest hours." Hamilton's defense in *Crosswell* was as significant for freedom of the press as the defense of John Peter Zenger by Andrew Hamilton (no relation) three quarters of a century earlier.

Crosswell was a newspaper editor prosecuted for libel (libel could be a crime in those days). The judge refused to allow testimony of the libel's truth to be presented. He also ruled that the jury were judges of only the facts, not the law. The truth or falsity of the libel was a matter "to be decided *exclusively* by the court." A guilty verdict was returned.

The rulings of the trial judge had been consistent with English law. Hamilton's research had, however, convinced him that the English rule had been fashioned by Star Chamber, which had perverted an older, contrary, common-law rule. As Hamilton summed it up, "the doctrine of excluding the truth as immaterial originates in a tyrannical and polluted source, the Court of Star Chamber." The court should not, Hamilton asserted, "be shackled by" the current English precedents: "rather shall they not say that we will trace the law up to its source. We consider, they might say, these precedents as only some extraneous bodies engrafted on the old trunk; and as such I believe they ought to be considered."

The report we have of Hamilton's argument must be but a pale shadow of the original. But it still gives us an idea of Hamilton's forensic skill (Kent, in his judge's notes, wrote, "Mr. Hamilton . . . was sublimely eloquent.") Hamilton argued that the principle he was asserting was essential to freedom of the press: "The Liberty of the Press consists, in my idea, in publishing the truth, . . . though it reflect on government, on magistrates, or individuals." If the truth could not be published, a vital safeguard against governmental abuses would be lacking. "But, if under the qualifications I have mentioned, the power be allowed, the liberty for which I contend will operate as a salutary check."

Nor should truth be determined by the judges: "let me ask whether it is right that a permanent body of men, appointed by the executive, and, in some degree, always connected with it, should exclusively have the power of deciding on what shall constitute a libel on our rulers." To the contrary, "[i]t must be with the jury to decide . . . and pronounce on the combined matter of law and of fact." Indeed, "[a]s far as the safety of the citizen is concerned, it is necessary that the Jury shall be permitted to speak to both."

Hamilton's eloquence did not win the case; the court was equally divided. But Hamilton's argument was soon vindicated in a higher forum. The rule advocated by him was enacted into New York law in 1805 and was later made a part of the state constitution.

Hamilton has, of course, been considered an extreme conservative. Yet it was his nationalistic approach to law that laid the legal foundation for the twentieth-century welfare state. It was also Hamilton the lawyer who made the argument that led, in Kent's phrase, to "the vindication and establishment of those rights of the jury and of the press for which he contended." As another counsel in the case put it, the statute and constitutional provision adopting Hamilton's argument "was a maxim taken from" Hamilton's argument in *Crosswell*.

2. Louis D. Brandeis: People's Attorney

Louis D. Brandeis (1856–1941) was one of the greatest Supreme Court Justices. He had previously been one of the greatest practitioners and the rare one who added a new dimension to law, one that emphasized the facts to which the law applied. In trying cases, Brandeis stressed the inductive method—arguing from the facts to the appropriate doctrines and decisions. His efforts culminated in the so-called Brandeis Brief— now the generic term for a new type of legal argument that emphasizes the facts leading to enactment of laws even more than the legal principles involved in the case.

Before then, Brandeis had attended Harvard Law School (where he compiled an academic record still unequaled) and gone into practice in Boston. He prospered, and success gave Brandeis the financial independence to devote an increasing amount of time to work, often without pay, on behalf of unions, consumers, and small stockholders. He came to be known as the "People's Attorney" for his dedication with, in Max Lerner's phrase, "a monastic fervor to what he conceived to be the service of the public."

Brandeis was not, however, the typical turn-of-the-century liberal— content only to expose and deplore. While the muckrakers of the day dealt in invective and generalities, he sought remedies through social legislation. He devised a "sliding scale" system that gave Boston cheaper gas rates. An exposure of insurance companies was accompanied by a plan for reorganizing the industry and by a new system of savings-bank insurance. An attack on the railroads gave him the opportunity to vitalize the principle of scientific management.

Above all, Brandeis the lawyer attacked what he termed the "evils of bigness," puncturing the prevalent delusion that efficiency must result from ever-larger economic combinations. Instead, he asserted, "[b]oth liberty and democracy are seriously threatened by the growth of big business." When he clerked for Brandeis, Dean Acheson tells us, one of the themes that "dominated the Justice's talk [was] the Curse of Bigness."

The culmination of the Brandeis practice was the Brandeis Brief— named after the brief submitted by him in *Muller v. Oregon* (1908), where a law prohibiting women from working more than ten hours a day was challenged. The problem was that only three years earlier, *Lochner v. New York*, (1905) had stricken down a maximum-hours law for bakers. Brandeis saw that the Justices had invalidated the *Lochner* law because they had not seen a relationship between the law and public health. That, he wrote, could be shown by "an investigation into the facts" to produce data showing the correlation between hours worked by women and the health of women and their families—what Brandeis termed "a great mass of data bearing upon the need [for the] legislation."

This is precisely what Brandeis did in his *Muller* brief. Almost all of it was devoted not to the law, but to what it termed "facts of common knowledge" from "[t]he world's experience upon which the legislation limiting the hours of labor for women is based." In ninety-five pages, the brief catalogued the harmful effect of long work on women. As summarized by the *Muller* opinion, this part of the brief contained "extracts from over ninety reports of committees, bureaus of statistics, commissioners of hygiene, inspectors of factories, both in this country and in Europe, to the effect that long hours of labor are dangerous for women, primarily because of their special physical organization."

In *Muller*, Brandeis let the "facts" speak for themselves to mold the law in the desired direction. As the leading Supreme Court historian characterized it, the Brandeis technique was "novel"—and it worked. The Court upheld the Oregon law, and it did so by relying on the Brandeis approach.

The Brandeis Brief became the model for constitutional cases; what Cardozo calls its "new technique" was widely followed—not least by Brandeis himself. He submitted briefs patterned on the *Muller* model in other cases. His last effort applied the technique in a lengthy brief demonstrating that "there is no sharp difference in kind as to the effect of labor on men and women"; hence a maximum-hours law for both men and women should be upheld. Before the brief was submitted, Brandeis was appointed to the Supreme Court and the case was taken over by Felix Frankfurter, who won it largely on the brief that Brandeis had prepared.

3. Clarence Darrow: Attorney for the Damned

Clarence Darrow (1857–1938) is the most famous trial lawyer in American history. Yet he was anything but representative of the practitioner of his day. He is known for his defense of those condemned by public opinion.

Lincoln Steffens called Darrow "the attorney for the damned"—a characterization that became his popular sobriquet.

Darrow began his career in Chicago as a railroad attorney. But he soon became dissatisfied with working for a corporation when that meant using the law to deprive workers of compensation for the pain and mutilation incident to industrial enterprise. When, during the Pullman strike of 1894, an injunction was secured against Eugene V. Debs and other union officials, Darrow resigned his railroad position to defend them.

For the rest of his career, Darrow's efforts were largely devoted to the defense of criminal defendants. Many of his cases were causes célèbres at the time: his securing of pardons for three of the Haymarket rioters in 1893; his defense of the dynamiters of the *Los Angeles Times* in 1911; and that of the "thrill" murderers in the Loeb–Leopold trial in 1924. His clients were often labor organizers, Socialists, Communists, and others on the leftist fringe. This gave him the undeserved reputation of a dangerous radical. Yet Darrow was far from sharing the extremist views of many of those whom he defended.

What attracted Darrow to his clients was not their political views, but the fact that they needed a defense. "Everybody," he once said, "is entitled to a defense; it is not only the right, but the duty, of every lawyer to defend." Darrow was the twentieth-century exemplar of the tradition that had led John Adams to represent the Boston Massacre defendants. Justice Hugo L. Black listed Darrow among those lawyers "who have dared to speak in defense of causes and clients without regard to personal danger to themselves."

Justice William O. Douglas wrote, "Darrow used the law to promote social justice as he saw it." Darrow employed the law to oppose prevailing legal concepts in labor law and criminal law. Darrow used his cases to tilt a continual lance against the rules that bore so heavily on the industrial worker. Throughout his life, Douglas says, "Darrow pleaded for the men and women—the flesh and blood—that made the wheels of industry move."

To the public, Darrow was the prototype of the criminal lawyer, and he constantly used his practice to further criminal-law reform. Never had an eminent practitioner urged such far-reaching changes. Steffens once described Darrow: "The powerful orator hulking his way slowly, thoughtfully, extemporizing . . . hands in pocket, head down and eyes up, wondering what it is all about, to the inevitable conclusion which he throws off with a toss of his shrugging shoulders: 'I don't know . . . We don't know . . . Not enough to kill or even to judge one another.'" The

Darrow remark contains the gist of his attitude toward criminal law. "I may hate the sin," went a famous Darrow statement, "but never the sinner." Nor did he or anyone else know enough about either the sin or the sinner to sit as judge over others. Instead, the concept of punishment that was still the criminal-law foundation was a remnant of the barbarism that had characterized the common law of crimes.

Darrow was considered particularly radical because of his opposition to the death penalty. He almost never turned down capital cases; he used them as forums against capital punishment. Darrow undertook his most controversial defense—that in *People v. Richard Loeb and Nathan Leopold*—because it would present him with a courtroom platform that could serve as the culmination of his lifelong crusade against the death penalty, so that, in the words of his final plea in the case, "I have done something . . . to temper justice with mercy, to overcome hate with love."

Although never fully accepted by the elite of the profession, to the public Darrow became a folk hero in his own time—in Irving Stone's phrase, "the Tom Paine of the twentieth century, fighting for the rights of the man, the voice that spoke when other voices were hushed and still." His Lincolnesque appearance, with his "poor man's suit" and "baggy pants," his famous galluses, and his ability to communicate in what he called "bad English"—that is, the vernacular that all could understand—all these added to the legend.

Darrow was one of those who also helped point the way to the coming legal era. His views on social legislation played their part in breaking down the negative conception of law, with its predominant hands-off theme as far as economic affairs were concerned. "Do you doubt," asked Darrow in 1903, when the courts were routinely striking down maximum-hours laws, "that the eight-hour day is coming? Does anybody doubt that it is coming?" Darrow never doubted that the law should be used as a positive instrument to meet the "demand for the individual to have a better life, a fuller life, a completer life." To promote that demand "is the purpose of every law-making power."

4. John Adams:
Lawyer for the Revolution

John Adams (1735–1826), of course, occupies a leading place in American history. He was, however, preeminently a lawyer who passed his life in the practice of the law—or at least he did until his commitment to the Revolutionary struggle and then to the needs of the new nation led him to give up his practice for his political career. But his devotion to practice and success at the bar did not result in the narrow technical outlook so frequently associated with practicing lawyers. Instead, the more successful Adams became as an attorney, the broader his conception of law became. That enabled Adams to be a legal leader in the nation's founding—the lawyer for the Revolution, as it were.

Like most lawyers in his day, Adams was trained by studying in a lawyer's office. The young apprentice spent two years following court sessions, doing rudimentary jobs for his mentor, studying law books, and generally learning law practice.

In 1758, Adams was sworn as an attorney. Two months later, he lost his first case. The initial setback did not prevent Adams from securing other clients. Drawing up deeds and wills, riding circuit, and defending persons charged with smuggling, bastardy, theft, assault, and other offenses, he steadily built up a practice, to the point where he was the busiest lawyer in Massachusetts, handling cases concerned with almost every kind of activity. His practice was typical, for every lawyer was still a general practitioner. Adams's clients came from all segments of society and included the leading citizens of the day.

As a lawyer, Adams made two particular contributions. The first was to demonstrate that even those most unpopular are entitled to legal representation. By the time of the Revolution, Adams had become a leader in the colonists' struggle. Nevertheless, in 1770, he confounded his countrymen by agreeing to defend the British soldiers prosecuted for the Boston Massacre killings and, in his own words, "hazarding a popularity very general and very hardly earned; and for incurring a clamor, popular suspicions and prejudices." When he was told that even the Crown lawyers would not touch the case, he said, "I had no hesitation in answering, that counsel ought to be the very last thing that an accused person should want in a free country."

Adams's successful defense (winning acquittal for all but two of the soldiers, who were branded on their thumbs, lectured from Scripture, and dismissed) was a high point in our legal history. To the end of his days, Adams had to deal with charges that he had turned against the patriot cause in the Boston Massacre case. But he had vindicated the right of even the most unpopular to counsel, and in old age wrote that "it has been a great Consolation to me through Life, that I acted in this Business with steady impartiality."

Adams the lawyer also helped to ensure that the Revolution was a legal, as well as a military, struggle. Adams was the principal American legal advocate, in the struggle for both independence and establishment of the new polity. Adams's writings were the legal briefs that supported the American position during the period.

And they were, too often, examples of the worst style of legal writing. But the lack of grace did not prevent Adams's from being among the most influential dull writings ever published. What was wanted were not so much popular tracts as learned essays that would confirm the American legal position. This the Adams writings supplied admirably. "By their sheer weight," writes a biographer, "they swept down the Tory argument. The grand historic names, the strings of learned quotations, the long involved paragraphs said what the Province needed to hear. The very sight of those close printed pages was convincing."

Adams also played a significant legal role in the making of what he called "the Constitutions of Government." Here his legal training and experience enabled him to propose practical solutions to deal with the legal vacuum caused by the elimination of royal governments. "The blessings of society," Adams declared, "depend entirely on the constitutions of government." Hence it was necessary to set up new governments. "Each colony," Adams wrote in March 1776, "should establish its own government and then a league should be formed between them all."

Adams outlined the solution to the problem facing Americans in his *Thoughts on Government* (1776). The plan outlined there laid the framework for the new constitutions: a two-house representative legislature, frequent elections, an executive with a veto power, and an independent judiciary with life tenure. In particular, the plan stressed a separation of powers between the different branches.

To Adams the lawyer, his plan was more than academic theory. It served as the basis for action in May 1776 when Adams became the moving force behind the resolution of the Second Continental Congress urging the colonies to set up their own governments. In response, the colonies (now become states) adopted constitutions that established new governments. The framers in the states were directly influenced by the Adams plan. Most important was that Adams demonstrated that government could be established in a form Americans were used to even though independence was to be declared.

The Revolutionary lawyers, led by Adams, ensured that our Revolution did not degenerate into the extremes so common to revolutions. Instead, the colonial lawyers managed the Revolution; by framing the conflict in legal terms, they kept it one for liberty under law. Adams the lawyer found it easy to make the transition from law to politics. He looked on law as establishing principles that were binding on both governors and governed. Adams had emphasized this aspect of law as early as his Boston Massacre defense. It was, of course, the aspect that dominated the great age of constitution-making that began our history as a nation.

5. Abraham Lincoln: Legend in Law and History

Abraham Lincoln (1809–1865) occupies almost as prominent a position in legal legend as in American history. Lincoln the lawyer has become part of the profession's folklore—the self-taught country lawyer who had almost no legal education. When Lincoln was admitted to the bar in 1836, the only admission requirement under Illinois law was "good character"—which, according to wags at the time, was the one thing most lawyers lacked. Lincoln summarized his own self-education in his advice to a would-be lawyer: "Get books and read and study them carefully. Begin with Blackstone's 'Commentaries,' say twice, take Chitty's 'Pleadings,' Greenleaf's 'Evidence,' and Story's 'Equity,' in succession. Work, work, work is the main thing."

Lincoln certainly worked at becoming an outstanding lawyer. As a biographer sums it, "He was immersed in [his] country practice like a fish in a lake. The cases in which he was engaged run not to the hundreds but to the thousands." And they run the gamut of law practice—from cases over a pig to a railroad case where his fee was $5000 (a tremendous amount then for legal work; in fact, Carl Sandburg tells us, high officers of the railroad spoke of "the payment of so large a fee to a western lawyer").

The Lincoln of legal legend is primarily a country lawyer—the gaunt backwoods figure riding circuit along trails on horseback, with saddlebags containing a spare coat, a clean shirt, a lawbook or two, and some paper. William Herndon, Lincoln's last law partner, later said, "No human being would now endure what we used to do on the circuit. I have slept with 20 men in the same room . . . and oh—such victuals."

As is often the case, however, the legend does not present a complete picture. Far from being a country bumpkin in court, the mature Lincoln was a leader at the bar, whom David Donald, author of the most recent full-scale Lincoln biography, calls "a very great lawyer." Donald's principal chapter on Lincoln as a lawyer is titled "At the Head of His Profession in This State." By the 1850s, the firm of Lincoln and Herndon had a third of all the cases in the Sangamon County Circuit Court and ranked as a leading law firm in the area. Before his election to the presidency, Lincoln had participated in 243 cases before the Illinois Supreme Court and two before the United States Supreme Court.

Still, it is Lincoln, the country lawyer, who is remembered in legal lore. And he was a trial lawyer as good as the profession has seen. The legendary "almanac trial"—at which Lincoln demolished a witness, who testified that he had seen the murder clearly because of the bright moon, with an almanac showing there was no moon at the time—did take place. But it gives us an incomplete picture of Lincoln's courtroom abilities, which included the main attributes of the great practitioner: the ability to penetrate to the heart of a matter and express it simply enough for lay understanding and consummate skill as a jury lawyer. His great antagonist, Stephen A. Douglas, stated that Lincoln had no equal before a jury.

Despite what has been said, it remains true that if Lincoln had died before 1860, no one would have heard of him again, and certainly not as a great lawyer. But he did not die in 1860. Instead, the gaunt figure, with the stovepipe hat and old shawl around his shoulders, who walked brooding through a cold February rain to the Springfield depot for his journey to Washington, was still the lawyer that he had been in his quarter-century of practice. The quondam prairie lawyer brought to the White House the knowledge of law and men that he had acquired in practice. They were continually used by him in dealing with the Civil War crisis.

In the highest office, Lincoln never lost the habit of thinking and expressing himself as a lawyer. According to the *New York Times* review of the Donald biography, "It was lessons learned in country courtrooms . . . that finally made the difference." In particular, as president, Lincoln added a new dimension to our conception of law—one called forth by his actions in dealing with the war emergency. It should not be forgotten that the crucible through which the nation passed during Lincoln's presidency was also a continuing constitutional crisis. It presented constant legal problems to the lawyer in the Oval Office. How President Lincoln dealt with these constitutional problems indicates that he must be given high marks as a constitutional lawyer.

In the law, Lincoln the prairie lawyer remains a legend. But if that was all there was to his legal life, he would not be remembered—much less on a list of great lawyers. To the legal legend, however, we must add Lincoln's crucial place in the nation's history. In fulfilling his historical role, Lincoln always thought and acted as a lawyer. From that perspective, he contributed more to our constitutional law and practice than anyone since John Marshall.

6. Daniel Webster: "God-Like Daniel" at the Bar

Daniel Webster (1782–1852) was the most famous lawyer of his day, with an ability for courtroom oratory that became legendary. The "God-Like Daniel, the Defender of the Constitution," as admirers called him, stood at the head of the most eminent Supreme Court bar in our history. William Wirt, himself an outstanding advocate, wrote of that bar, "I believe to a man, they yield the palm to Webster."

Webster graduated from Dartmouth College, and after clerking in law offices, opened practice in New Hampshire, his home state. By 1816, when he moved to Boston, his outstanding abilities were already carrying him to the pinnacle of the American bar, both as the leading Supreme Court advocate and in the fees he received. His income from practice was soon ranging from $15,000 to $21,000 a year, far more than that of other lawyers. (The amounts would have to be multiplied by at least 500 to obtain the equivalent in present-day dollars.) Despite his income, Webster's extravagance kept him in constant financial difficulties. He was the best example of his own observation: "I can give it as the condensed history of most, if not all, good lawyers that they lived well and died poor."

Webster first appeared before the Supreme Court in 1814 and until his death in 1852 rarely missed a term of the Court, frequently arguing a dozen or more cases a year. He was the Court's biggest draw during his practice there. "It was amusing," the British writer Harriet Martineau wrote in 1835, "to see how the Court would fill after the entrance of Webster, and empty when he had gone."

Webster argued the most important Marshall and Taney Court cases. He appeared in both *McCulloch v. Maryland*, (1819) and *Gibbons v. Ogden*, (1824). In the latter case, particularly, the Marshall opinion, in Webster's words, "follows closely the track of the argument"—notably, "the idea which I remember struck him at the time that by the Constitution, the commerce of the several states has become a unit." Webster's arguments led the Court to adopt essential constitutional doctrines: liberal construction, implied powers, federal tax immunity, and broad commerce power. In this respect, it was Webster who, with Hamilton and Marshall, laid the foundation of our constitutional law.

Perhaps the most famous argument ever made before the Supreme Court was that delivered by Webster for his alma mater, Dartmouth, in 1819. Under its founding charter, the college was to be governed by a board of trustees with power to fill vacancies in their number and to choose and remove college officers. Factionalism, first personal and then political, arose within the college, and a newly elected governor and legislature in New Hampshire took sides against the trustees. A state law was passed increasing the number of trustees and empowering the governor to appoint new trustees and to inspect Dartmouth and report to the legislature concerning it. In effect, the law annulled Dartmouth's original charter and brought the college under the state's control. The old trustees resisted the change, and when William H. Woodward, secretary and treasurer of the college, sided with the state government and new appointees against them, they sued Woodward.

Woodward won in the New Hampshire courts, and the case went to the Supreme Court, with Webster pleading for the original trustees. His words, "It is, Sir, as I have said, a small College. And yet, there are those who love it!" made him known throughout the country and caused Chief Justice Marshall to be filled with emotion, his eyes "suffused with tears."

Marshall's decision, ruling for Webster and the old trustees, held that the New Hampshire law violated the contract clause of the Constitution, which prohibited the states from passing any "law impairing the obligation of contracts." Finding that Dartmouth's original charter was a contract, he established, with his decision, an assurance for all investors in corporate enterprises that the terms on which they had committed their capital could not be unilaterally altered by a state. Before *Dartmouth College v. Woodward*, there were still relatively few manufacturing corporations in the country. Under the confidence created by Marshall's decision, such corporations proliferated to such an extent that they soon transformed the face of the nation.

Webster's role in all this was graphically put by his co-counsel: "I would have an inscription over the door of [Dartmouth], 'Founded by Eleazar Wheelock; Refounded by Daniel Webster.'"

7. David Dudley Field: Lawyer as Reformer

A lawyer law reformer? The very term seems an oxymoron. Yet that is what David Dudley Field (1805–1894) was—a preeminent practitioner who was the greatest law reformer in our history.

Field himself was a "man of genius in a family of geniuses." One brother, Cyrus W., laid the Atlantic cable; another, Stephen J., became one of the most influential Justices in Supreme Court history; a third, Henry M., was a well-known author of the day. After admission to practice in New York, David rose to become one of the commanding figures at the bar, arguing many important Supreme Court cases and serving as counsel to leading men of the time. According to a biographer, the number of cases in which he was retained was "beyond counting."

Although Field's practice was the largest in New York City, he still devoted untold hours to his lifelong reform effort. In doing so, he also added a new dimension to American law—codification. Proposals to codify the common law go back centuries. But it was Field who drafted the so-called Field Codes, which codified both substantive law and procedure.

In his practice, Field soon became aware of the imperfections of a common-law-based system. In particular, he was repelled by the overtechnicality of common-law procedure. Field publicly attacked the "vicious system of procedure" that then existed. "It is," he asserted, "an artificial, complex, technical system, inherited from our forefathers, and now grown so obsolete and so burdensome as no longer to command the respect or answer the wants of society."

"The remedy for this," Field wrote, "is as simple as the evil itself": substitute a code containing "a plain and rational system of procedure." Field's opportunity came when New York appointed commissioners "to reduce into a written and systematic code the whole body of the law of this State." Field was the most important member of the commissions appointed and the principal draftsman of the codes reported by them.

To Field, codification was "that greatest reform of all." Indeed, Field, whose writing is usually so flat that the reader longs for the flowery neoclassicism of Joseph Story, could soar to poetic heights when he described his goal: "a CODE AMERICAN, . . . as simple as so vast a work can be made, free in its spirit, catholic in its principles! And that work will go with our ships, our travelers, and our armies; it will march with the language, it will move with every emigration, and make itself a home in the farthest portion of our own continent, in the vast Australian lands, and in the islands of the southern and western seas." Is it coincidence that this Whitmanesque passage was written in 1855, the year that saw the publication of *Leaves of Grass*?

As Field saw it, "If every branch of the law were codified, it would naturally be arranged in five different parts or codes: that is to say, a political code, embracing all the law relating to government and official relations;

a code of civil procedure, or remedies in civil cases; a code of criminal procedure, or remedies in criminal cases; a code of private rights and obligations; and a code of crimes and punishments."

The first of the Field Codes was the Code of Civil Procedure, enacted in New York in 1848. That code marks a landmark law reform, since it substituted the modern system of code pleading for the pleadings run riot, which had made common-law procedure one (in the characterization of an English judge) "so carefully framed to exclude falsehood, that very often truth was quite unable to force its way through the barriers." The Code of Civil Procedure substituted one simplified form of action, based on fact pleading instead of the technical pleading of the common law. At one stroke, this eliminated the common-law forms of action and the distinction between actions at law and actions in equity. The dualized system of justice that had become the incubus of English law was replaced by one unified system administered by one court of general jurisdiction. A similar reform was not to occur in England until 1873.

To Field, procedure codification was only a part of his task. The major job was still ahead—codifying substantive law. "What we wanted," Field asserted, "was a codification of the Common Law," so that "we shall have a book of our own laws." He drafted three new codes: a penal code, a political code, and a civil code. The last constituted Field's attempt to codify the common law: it contained 2,034 sections and was separated into four divisions, dealing with persons, property, obligations, and general provisions.

Field's efforts to codify the law occupied a major portion of his time for eighteen years. With the final text of the codes submitted in 1865, he spent twenty years more in the struggle to have the codes enacted into law. Although only his penal code was enacted in New York, Field's procedure code was borrowed by many states ,and four other states, led by California, adopted the civil and political codes.

The Field codification concept was not one of mere compilation. Instead, it was a creative one that fitted in with the instrumentalist approach being developed by American law. One need only refer to Field's procedure code with its quantum change in procedure. Discarding entirely the common-law system, it swept aside fictions, technicalities, and foreign verbiage and completely changed the law's adjective side. None of Field's other codes had similar transforming content, but each made important changes in existing law.

The law that Field was making sought to meet the requirements of the developing society. Americans needed settled rules fixed in advance, not case by case after the facts. They wanted nontechnical, predictable decisions based on the facts, not on the accidents of writs and pleading. To Field, this meant law made by codes that swept away the common-law archaisms, with what he termed their "old abuses" and "excrescences." It was Field who, above all, furnished our law with (in James Fenimore Cooper's phrase) the "great innovation" in "the new and much-talked-of code."

8. Thurgood Marshall: Making Civil Rights Law

Thurgood Marshall (1908–1994) added a racial dimension to the Horatio Alger story. Great-grandson of a slave and son of a Pullman car steward, Marshall became an outstanding lawyer and the first African-American appointed to the Supreme Court. Throughout his career, he personally felt the prejudice against which he fought at the bar and on the bench. Justice Harold A. Blackmun tells how, "[w]hen we went up to Justice Marshall's native Baltimore for the ceremony in connection with the dedication of his statue up there in front of the Federal Building, he and I were sitting next to each other and he said, 'Why do you think that fellow asked me what high school here in Baltimore I went to? Hell, there was only one I could go to!'"

Later, as an attorney in a Virginia civil-rights case, Marshall recalled that he knew he was in trouble when he pointed out that the case had been scheduled for Lincoln's Birthday, a federal holiday, and the judge said, "Well, you follow Lincoln's Birthday up your way. Down here, we follow Jeff Davis day." Or in a case in Oklahoma where, Marshall remembered, "It was 'nigger' this and 'nigger' that."

Making Civil Rights Law is the title of a recent biography of Marshall the lawyer, by Mark V. Tushnet. The civil-rights explosion would never have taken place if Thurgood Marshall had not headed the staff of the NAACP Legal Defense Fund for over twenty years. During that time, he worked out the legal strategy and argued the cases which led to the quantum change in civil-rights law.

After a short time in private practice following his graduation from Howard Law School, Marshall began to work for the NAACP in New York. Within two years, in 1938, he took charge of its legal activities. His work consisted at first in acting as counsel in racial discrimination cases throughout the South. This involved trial work that was difficult and even dangerous. As a trial lawyer, Marshall excelled at examination and especially cross-examination. But his most important work soon began to be appellate—particularly in the Supreme Court. He helped persuade the Court to strike down the "white primary," bus segregation, and restrictive covenants.

Marshall soon saw, however, that it was in education that the crucial blow against racial discrimination could be struck. He not only developed and coordinated the NAACP strategy in attacking educational segregation, but also was the lead attorney in them, from the trial level up to the Supreme Court. Accounts of Marshall as a Justice emphasize his passive approach to his judicial role. By contrast, NAACP files, contemporary accounts, and recollections all stress his personal leadership in the NAACP segregation litigation.

Plessy v. Ferguson (1896) had held segregation constitutional, provided that equal facilities were provided for both races. Marshall designed and implemented the strategy of not confronting *Plessy* head on, but instead proving inequality of the facilities provided for blacks. In 1950, Marshall began to chip away at *Plessy* in a case where Texas had established a new law school for African-Americans, arguing that it now did not have to admit them to the University of Texas Law School.

When asked why he selected the Texas case for the first attack on segregation in higher education, Marshall replied, "It is easier to prove that a law school is unequal than it is to prove that a primary school is unequal." At the trial, particularly, Marshall was at his best in showing that the new black law school could not possibly be the equal of the prestigious University of Texas school. Joe Greenhill, then a young attorney for the state and, later Texas Chief Justice, stated that Marshall was "a real pro in examining and cross-examining witnesses"—all the more so "a credit to him" because of his personal situation, since "there was no hotel, restaurant, or restroom open to him on the main street in Austin."

After he had won the law-school case, as well as one involving a black graduate student in Oklahoma, Marshall was ready to challenge educational segregation itself. Now, as he wrote, the NAACP lawyers had to "take stock of the present situation and plan for future legal strategy." The result was *Brown v. Board of Education* (1954), the culmination of Marshall's career as a lawyer. A number of cases were brought in different states and the District of Columbia. Marshall took charge of the trial in the South Carolina case. The evidence he presented stressed segregation's psychological effects: it "sets up a roadblock in [a pupil's] mind which prevents his ever feeling he is equal." This was, of course, to be a key point in Chief Justice Warren's *Brown* opinion.

In the Supreme Court, the principal argument was a battle between John W. Davis for, and Thurgood Marshall against, segregation. Most observers agreed that Marshall had the better of the argument. He was particularly effective in the reargument. In the first place, it was Marshall who assembled the team of historians to deal with the questions on legislative history posed by the reargument order. More than that, Marshall encapsulated the strategy on that issue—to show that the legislative history of the Fourteenth Amendment was inconclusive, a principal point in the *Brown* opinion. As Marshall colloquially put it to the historians, a "nothin' to nothin' score means we win the ball game."

Before the Court, Davis had been eloquent for South Carolina, but Marshall more than held his own in what Carl Rowan called "the quintessential Thurgood in action." Davis had said that the plaintiffs were giving up their equal education for "some fancied question of racial prestige." Marshall replied, "As Mr. Davis said yesterday, the only thing the Negroes are trying to get is prestige. Exactly correct. Ever since the Emancipation Proclamation, the Negro has been trying to get . . . the same status as anybody else regardless of race."

Marshall ended his argument with what Mark Tushnet terms "his own brand of eloquence, more effective than Davis's." The only way to defend segregation, Marshall declared, "is to find that for some reason Negroes are inferior to all other human beings." True, "[n]obody will stand in the Court and urge that." Yet "[t]he only thing can be . . . an inherent determination that the people who were formerly kept in slavery, regardless of anything else, shall be kept as near that stage as is possible; and now is the time, we submit, that this Court should make it clear that that is not what our Constitution stands for."

Fittingly, the main arguments in this century's landmark case were made by two of the greatest lawyers in our history.

9. John W. Davis: The Compleat Advocate

Roger B. Taney's greatness as Chief Justice is overshadowed by his disastrous *Dred Scott v. Sandford* opinion. John W. Davis (1873–1955) was this century's greatest Supreme Court advocate. But that has largely been forgotten because he led the argument for the wrong side in the *Brown* segregation case. Yet even though we may disagree with (indeed, are repelled by) the merits of Davis's *Brown* argument, we can still recognize that he made the case for his side as well as it could be stated. Davis argued in favor of both the southern school system, which should be left "to those most immediately affected by it"—after all, he urged, "the very strength and fiber of our federal system is local self-government"—and stare decisis: "somewhere, sometime, to every principle comes a moment of repose when it has been so often announced, so confidently relief upon, so long continued, that it passes the limits of judicial discretion and disturbance."

The Davis *Brown* argument may have appeared "almost . . . irresistible" to one observer, but he plainly argued for a system whose time had passed. That should not, however, lead us to overlook Davis's preeminence at the Supreme Court bar. "Of all the persons who appeared before the Court in my time," said Justice Holmes, "there was never anybody more elegant, more clear, more concise or more logical than John W. Davis." The quality of his arguments were legend. "Come on Stone," Justice Harlan F. Stone once muttered while listening to Davis, "nothing can be this clear."

Davis first argued before the Supreme Court when he became solicitor general in 1913. During his five years in that position, he argued sixty-seven cases, winning forty-eight. These included the most important cases of the day. He won suits on federal authority over public lands, private oil company pipelines, and railroad workers' hours, as well as the constitutionality of conscription. He also successfully argued that Oklahoma had deprived African-Americans of voting rights and that Alabama's convict lease program involved peonage. He lost the Child Labor Case (1918), but his argument was for what we now consider the right side. His forensic ability as chief government counsel was shown by Chief Justice Edward D. White's half-facetious comment: "Of course, no one has due process of law when Mr. Davis is on the other side."

After serving as Ambassador to the Court of St. James's and as unsuccessful Democratic presidential nominee in 1924, Davis returned to practice and soon became leader of the Supreme Court bar. He argued another ninety-three cases in the Court; his total of 141 was the most since the days of Webster. His greatest victory was in the Steel Seizure Case (1952) where his argument led to the decision striking down President Truman's order taking over the steel industry. During his eighty-seven-minute argument, wrote the *Washington Post*, rarely "has a courtroom sat in such silent admiration for a lawyer at the bar."

Davis was a noted conservative—"a Democrat in exile," he termed himself—and he argued cases against the New Deal legislation. But he also took part in important civil-liberties cases. He argued for a pacifist minister who was denied naturalization because he refused to swear that he would bear arms in the country's defense. The Supreme Court upheld the denial despite Davis's plea for "the rights of conscience"; he sarcastically told the Justices that "the idea that a priest in his cassock, a nurse in her gown, a woman with her children hanging to her skirts, and a paralytic in his chair must all swear to bear arms before they become citizens reduces the process of naturalization to an absurdity."

Davis was also of counsel to J. Robert Oppenheimer in the battle over his security clearance. Davis took these and similar cases without fee. "There was no difficulty," Morris L. Ernst, the famed civil-rights lawyer once said, "in getting John W. Davis to take unpopular cases. This was his greatest contribution."

Above all, Davis was this century's Supreme Court virtuoso. Holmes summed it all when he wrote to Harold J. Laski, "Davis . . . makes beautiful arguments." Another time, Learned Hand confided, "I do not like to have John W. Davis come into my courtroom. . . . I am so fascinated by his eloquence and charm that I always fear that I am going to decide in his favor."

Davis's composure even in the Marble Palace was shown when, toward the end of an argument, he asked Chief Justice Hughes, "how much time I have left?" Hughes (noted for calling time on counsel) replied, "A minute and a half." Davis, with a low bow, in his most gracious voice, "I present the Court with the minute and a half."

10. Thomas Jefferson: Lawyer for Democracy

Thomas Jefferson (1743–1826) a leading lawyer? We all know that Jefferson was a Renaissance man. In an oft-quoted comment, John F. Kennedy told a dinner for Nobel laureates, "I think this is the most extraordinary collection of talent, of human knowledge, that has ever been gathered together at the White House, with the possible exception of when Thomas Jefferson dined alone." But a great practitioner?

Jefferson's protean activities make us overlook the fact that he received what was then the best legal education and devoted eight years to law practice. Jefferson's practice began with his first case in 1767; it continued until he gave up his practice in 1774. Until the end of his presidency, Jefferson then devoted himself to the public stage. During his entire career, however, he continued to take an interest in legal matters and approached issues with a law-trained mind. Long after Jefferson had given up his practice, Aaron Burr (certainly no admirer) was heard to say of him, "Our president is a lawyer and a great one, too."

John W. Davis wrote that Jefferson's "success [in practice] was striking and immediate." To Jefferson, as to Adams, law practice meant working as a general practitioner; his practice ran the gamut—with most cases involving land or slaves. Jefferson's *Case Book* does not enable us to judge the quality of his legal work, though the number of clients does indicate that his reputation at the bar stood high.

There are, in addition, several case reports that give us an idea of his work. Two are of particular interest. In a 1770 action for release from servitude, Jefferson's argument was an early version of the theme he was to immortalize in the Declaration of Independence. "Under the law of nature," Jefferson argued, "all men are born free. . . . This is what is called personal liberty, and is given him by the author of nature."

There is also a 236-page manuscript, half of it in Jefferson's hand, that contains the most complete account of the arguments made in a pre-Revolutionary case. *Bolling v. Bolling*, argued in 1771, was a complicated one involving technical issues of property and succession law. Jefferson argued for the defendant, while his law teacher, George Wythe, argued for plaintiff. Jefferson's argument strikingly illustrates his ability as a lawyer. One is almost awed by Jefferson's professional proficiency. The twenty-eight-year-old lawyer completely outshone his mentor, despite the skill with which Wythe's argument was presented.

Jefferson the lawyer is seen at his best in his revision of the laws of Virginia. In 1776, Jefferson moved a motion that the Virginia Assembly passed for a committee "to revise the laws." Jefferson was selected as chairman; he did most of the work, and the revision was largely his product.

Alexis de Tocqueville called Jefferson "the greatest democrat whom the democracy of America has as yet produced." It was natural for him to use the revision as an instrument to help create the democratic society that he favored. In particular, the revision presented the opportunity to destroy the economic base of the planter aristocracy that dominated Virginia life. The existing land law fostered the concentration of land ownership that Jefferson deplored. In addition, primogeniture, entailed estates, and the other common-law fundamentals were the worst possible foundations for American property law, for they destroyed the incentive that would induce men to settle and develop the expanding frontier.

For Jefferson, the solution was a simple one: a "repeal of the law" authorizing entailed estates and primogeniture. This, Jefferson said, was essential for "forming a system by which every fibre would be eradicated of antient or future aristocracy; and a foundation laid for a government truly republican."

Jefferson's bills reformed land tenure. Under his lead, the English law gave way to a system in which land became readily transferable. Feudal land tenure was abolished, and the freehold established as the basic land title. Freedom of contract and the autonomy of private decision-making could capture the land, as it was soon to capture other areas of American law.

Perhaps the most celebrated of Jefferson's bills was his "Bill for Establishing Religious Freedom." It was also a product of Jefferson's conception of government and law. As the Declaration of Independence asserted the right of people to choose any form of government, so the bill for religious freedom asserted the right of a person to choose his beliefs free of compulsion. If government and law rest ultimately on consent, the same must be true of religious belief.

By now, freedom of belief has become so deeply ingrained that we tend to forget how far-reaching Jefferson's bill was in its day. When he sought "[t]o establish religious freedom on the broadest bottom," heresy was still a capital crime at common law and a statute imposed imprisonment as a penalty "for not comprehending the mysteries of the trinity." Jefferson's bill swept away both state support and state coercion from the field of religion. Instead, it affirmed the right to have beliefs reign in the private kingdom of the mind.

Jefferson's revision also demonstrates his humanitarian legal approach—particularly to criminal law. As Jefferson explained it, his principal bill on the subject "proposes to proportion crimes and punishments." Jefferson sought to mitigate the harshness of the common law, which made all felonies punishable by death. He got the revisers to agree "that the punishment of death should be abolished except for treason and murder." For other felonies, Jefferson's bill substituted "hard labor in the public works."

Jefferson's humanitarian approach also extended to his day's greatest human violation—the law of slavery. As part of his revision, Jefferson prepared a bill "[t]o emancipate all slaves born after passing the act." It was not, however, included among the bills presented by the revisers because, Jefferson wrote, "it was found that the public mind would not yet bear the proposition." In writing about his aborted slavery bill, Jefferson did, however, declare, "Nothing is more certainly written in the book of fate than that these people are to be free."

In history, of course, it is not Jefferson the lawyer or Jefferson the law reformer who is of significance, but the Jefferson who made his indelible mark on the new nation. For Jefferson, the step from law to politics was a short one. The knowledge he had acquired as a lawyer enabled him to play his part in history.

Jefferson's entry on the broader stage begins, of course, with the Declaration of Independence. That famous document was essentially a lawyer's brief to justify the separation from Britain, though written with unusual nonlawyer-like elegance. To one interested in Jefferson as a jurist, the most interesting part of the Declaration is the statement that among men's "unalienable Rights" are "Life, Liberty and the pursuit of Happiness." This was a distinctly American version of John Locke's trilogy of "life, liberty and property," with which the Founders were familiar.

Locke was listed by Jefferson in "my trinity of the three greatest men." When he wrote the Declaration, however, Jefferson departed from the Locke trilogy. Vernon Parrington characterized this as "a revolutionary shift," which "marks a complete break with the Whiggish doctrine of property rights . . . and the substitution of a broader sociological conception." Jefferson's language meant that the end of American law could be broader than protection of property. The pursuit of happiness required a legal order that would emphasize the right to acquire property as much as that to secure existing property. But it could also include more, since personal rights might contribute to what James Wilson called at the time "the happiness of the society [that] is the *first* law of every government." Jefferson's support was crucial in securing the addition of the Bill of Rights to the Constitution.

In our constitutional history, Jefferson stands for the narrow view of federal power. His opinion opposing the Bank of the United States is the classic lawyer's brief for strict constitutional construction. History has, of course, confirmed the opposing Hamilton–Marshall position. In addition, Jefferson himself was too good a lawyer to allow his theory of limited federal power to override the public welfare. He was willing to overlook constitutional limitations where it was for what he termed "evidently for the good of" the nation.

The outstanding example was Jefferson's action in securing the Louisiana Purchase. There was serious constitutional doubt, since no clause in the Constitution authorized the acquisition of territory. But Jefferson acted in accordance with Hamilton's views on implied power, rather than his own more restricted conception. The key factors, Jefferson wrote, were that the government had to act promptly "in seizing the fugitive occurrence" and that the Louisiana acquisition "so much advances the good of their country." These outweighed the claim that "[t]he Executive . . . have done an act beyond the Constitution." Indeed, Jefferson asserted that, in such a case, "[t]o lose our country by a scrupulous adherence to written law, would be to lose the law itself, with life, liberty, property and all those who are enjoying them with us; thus absurdly sacrificing the end to the means."

Alexander Hamilton himself could not have said it better!

"And Company"

This list of great lawyers illustrates the truth of William J. Brennan's remark about "Judge and Company"—the Company being the attorneys in the case who help to shape the decision and hence the law made by it. That was certainly true of the lawyers on this list, all of whom made major contributions not only to the development of our law, but also to that of the nation itself.

Adams the lawyer helped establish the principle that even the most unpopular are entitled to counsel for their defense; he also used his legal skills as lawyer for the Revolution and the establishment of new American governments. Jefferson prepared the first law revision, which adapted Virginia law to the needs of the emerging republican society; he also used his legal background to write the classic justification for separation from the mother country. Hamilton employed his conception of law to ensure that our public law would have what we now term a Hamiltonian cast. Webster was the leading Supreme Court advocate whose arguments pointed the way to basic constitutional doctrines. Field led the way for the great legislative revisions of the law, through codifications that replaced the common law with procedure and substantive law adapted to American conditions. Lincoln remains the classic example of the early practitioner; what gave him greatness, however, was his use of legal experience to meet our greatest national emergency. Darrow, our most famous trial lawyer, showed how the law could be used to protect even "the damned" and was a leading advocate for criminal-law reform. Brandeis initiated a new method of factual argument that helped lay the legal foundation for the welfare state. Davis was this century's premier Supreme Court advocate, who helped the Justices to some of their most important decisions. Marshall was the attorney who, more than any other, helped the courts to make present-day civil-rights law with all the impact that it has had on the society.

The reader may be surprised that the list does not include any of the celebrated trial lawyers (except for Clarence Darrow)—the Edward Bennett Williamses, F. Lee Baileys, and their earlier counterparts, who were the masters of courtroom theatrics in their day. Yet however much these lawyers were the center of public cynosure, they contributed little to the law's development, at least compared with the lawyers on the list. Once again, it is influence on the law that has been the governing criterion. Here, too, it is not the fact that they may have had even more than Andy Warhol's fifteen minutes of fame, but that they have been the leading members of "and Company" that has led to inclusion on the greatest lawyers list.

12

TEN

GREATEST

TRIALS

Every few years, a legal proceeding is dubbed "the trial of the century." Almost all of them have their brief moment in the media spotlight and then fade from public consciousness. Yet there are trials that have more than Warhol's fifteen minutes of fame, and this chapter discusses my choices. They are the outstanding trials in our history—great because of the issues decided, the lessons learned, the interest aroused (which may still exist years or even centuries later), the ability of counsel, or even the doubt still felt about the outcome.

— ★ — ★ — ★ —

— ★ — ★ — ★ —

Ten Greatest Trials

1. Andrew Johnson Impeachment, 1868

2. *Rex v. William Wemms*, 1770

3. *Attorney General v. John Peter Zenger*, 1735

4. Samuel Chase Impeachment, 1805

5. *United States v. Aaron Burr*, 1807

6. *State v. John T. Scopes*, 1927

7. *Commonwealth v. Nicola Sacco and Bartolomeo Vanzetti*, 1921

8. *People v. Richard Loeb and Nathan Leopold*, 1924

9. *Bolling v. Bolling*, 1771

10. *People v. O. J. Simpson*, 1995

1. Andrew Johnson Impeachment

The greatest trial in our history was the impeachment trial of President Andrew Johnson in 1868. In fact, two impeachment trials rank among our greatest trials. The first was the Samuel Chase impeachment, which helped to secure the independence of the judiciary. The second was the Andrew Johnson impeachment. If Johnson had been convicted, writes Chief Justice William H. Rehnquist, "the future independence of the President could have been jeopardized."

"Here," former Justice Benjamin R. Curtis began the opening statement for Johnson's defense, "party spirit, political schemes, . . . biases can have no fit operation." Yet there is no doubt that the Johnson impeachment was motivated mainly by political considerations. In Rehnquist's words, the proceeding to impeach the president was less like one "to see if a criminal charge is warranted than like that of [a] campaign looking into what charges might be made against a political opponent."

The Johnson impeachment resulted from the effort of the congressional leaders to make over the presidency in their own image. Johnson was to be shorn of the substance of authority and, if that unfortunate still remained contumacious, was to be removed by impeachment.

To curb the president, laws were passed limiting his pardoning power and restricting his authority over the armed forces. Then came the Tenure of Office Act, which provided that senatorial consent should be necessary for the removal, as well as the appointment, of all civil officers. Johnson had vetoed the law as an encroachment on his constitutional prerogative (a view that the Supreme Court was to uphold in the leading *Myers v. United States* [1926] case); but, as in most other instances, his veto was overridden.

The Tenure of Office Act was a virtual sword at the throat of presidential power. Without removal power, the president could not hope to retain his position as effective administrative chief. Johnson was, therefore, bound to resist enforcement of the new law. Despite the Tenure of Office Act, Johnson removed his secretary of war from office, though the Senate had refused its consent. This, in turn, furnished the occasion for the president's impeachment.

The Johnson impeachment trial in the Senate, wrote John F. Kennedy, "was a trial to rank with all the great trials in history. . . . [E]very element of the highest courtroom drama was present." The Senate trial was presided over by Chief Justice Salmon P. Chase; the chief prosecutors were Benjamin F. Butler, notorious during the Civil War as the "butcher of New Orleans," and John A. Bingham, principal draftsman of the Fourteenth Amendment; leading the defense were Curtis, author of the famous *Dred Scott* dissent, and Henry Stanbery, who had resigned as attorney general to participate in the trial.

Evidence was presented during several weeks and there were elaborate closing arguments (including a three-day argument for Johnson by William Evarts, popularly known as the "Prince of the American Bar"). The proceedings took over two months, culminating in the dramatic vote. In his *Profiles of Courage*, Kennedy celebrates Edmund G. Ross, the key senator who voted for Johnson, as the man who "may well have preserved . . . constitutional government in the United States," even though he knew it meant the end of his political career.

Certainly, the failure of the Senate to vote Johnson guilty was vital for the development of executive independence. Had the impeachment of the president on political grounds succeeded, it would have ruptured the separation intended by the Framers between the executive and legislative departments. "Once set the example," declared Senator Lyman Trumbull, in explaining his vote for Johnson, "of impeaching a President for what, when the excitement of the hour shall have subsided, will be regarded as insufficient cause. . . . and no future President will be safe who happens to differ with a majority of the House and two-thirds of the Senate on any measure deemed by them important, particularly if of a political character." Had the Senate voted differently, it might well have established something like the executive dependence on the legislature that prevails in a parliamentary system.

In addition to this vital impact, the Johnson impeachment settled the important question of the reach of the relevant constitutional provision. The Constitution provides for impeachment for "Treason, Bribery, or other high Crimes and Misdemeanors." On its face, this language seems limited to criminal offenses. Johnson's impeachment was, however, based on a different theory.

The articles of impeachment charged Johnson not with any indictable offense, but with his failure to carry out certain laws and for public utterances, especially those attacking Congress. This, in the argument of the prosecution, was enough. An impeachable offense, they urged, "may consist of a violation of the Constitution, of law, of an official oath, or of duty, by an act committed or omitted, or, without violating a positive law, by the abuse of discretionary powers from improper motives or for an improper purpose."

Johnson's acquittal represents the definitive rejection of this view. Former Justice Curtis, in his argument in Johnson's defense, stated what may be taken as the prevailing law: "when the Constitution speaks of 'treason, bribery, and other high crimes and misdemeanors,' it refers to, and includes only, high criminal offenses against the United States, made so by some law of the United States existing when the acts complained of were done."

The Johnson precedent was followed in 1974, when the House Judiciary Committee's articles of impeachment against President Richard M. Nixon charged specific indictable offenses. The Nixon impeachment, of course, proceeded no further; it was terminated before any House vote as a result of Nixon's resignation. The resignation itself was a direct consequence of the revelation of a tape recording that indicated personal action by the president to obstruct investigation of criminal conduct, itself an indictable offense. Had the Nixon impeachment proceeding continued, it would have had direct evidence of criminal conduct on which to base removal of the president.

2. *Rex v. William Wemms*

"May it please your Honours and you Gentlemen of the Jury," John Adams began his argument for the British soldiers in *Rex v. Wiliam Wemms* (1770), "I am for the prisoners at the bar, and shall apologize for it only in the words of the Marquis Beccaria: 'If I can but be the instrument of preserving one life, his blessing and tears of transport, shall be a sufficient consolation to me, for the contempt of all mankind.'"

Years later, Adams's son John Quincy was to write that he had "often heard, from individuals, who had been present among the crowd of spectators at the trial, the electrical effect produced upon the immense and excited auditory, by the first sentence with which he opened his defense."

The setting of the Boston Massacre trial was as dramatic as any in legal history. In the Superior Court chamber in Boston, the case was presided over by four judges, headed by the Chief Justice of the Province—all, as Adams described them, "arrayed in their . . . rich robes of scarlet English broadcloth . . . and immense judicial wigs." The case arose out of the murder prosecution of the British captain and soldiers who fired into the mob that was taunting and pelting them with anything that came to hand. Five citizens had been killed, but the defense, led by Adams, pleaded justifiable homicide. There were separate trials for Captain Preston and the eight soldiers. It was the trial of the soldiers that was the most spectacular. Indeed, it was the greatest show ever staged in Boston, with a courtroom so packed that the shorthand reporter complained that he scarcely had room to move his right elbow.

The Boston Massacre trial began with the defendants' plea of "Not Guilty" and the selection of a jury. Adams ensured that, of the twelve chosen, not one was a Boston man; he feared that the feeling in the town made it impossible for its inhabitants to be impartial—as one Bostonian on the panel put it, "innocent blood had been shed and someone should be hanged for it."

The trial was a long one for its day: five days of testimony and two and a half for argument and charges. The evidence showed both the mob violence and the soldiers' response, though only two were precisely identified as having fired fatal shots. The high point came at the trial's end when Adams, in his barrister's wig and gown, closed the case for the defense. The Adams presentation was a classic jury argument and ensured the case its place in the trial pantheon.

The principal Adams theme was the law's benevolence; that it was more important "that innocence should be protected, than it is, that guilt should be punished." Hence, "it is always safer to err in acquitting, than punishing." Adams stressed the right of self-defense: "We talk of liberty and property, but if we cut up the law of self-defence, we cut up the foundation of both." Next came a graphic description of the mob confronting the soldiers: "You must place yourselves in the situation of Wemms or Killroy," two of the soldiers, with "the people crying Kill them! Kill them! Knock them over! heaving snow-balls, oyster shells, clubs, white birch sticks three inches and a half diameter, consider yourselves, in this situation, and then judge, whether a reasonable man in the soldiers situation, would not have concluded they were going to kill him."

Adams urged that the soldiers had, indeed, been confronted by a mob: "We have been entertained with a great variety of phrases, to avoid calling this sort of people a mob." But "[t]he plain English is gentlemen, most probably a motley rabble of saucy boys, negroes, and molattoes, Irish teagues and out landish jack tarrs. —And why we should scruple to call such a set of people a mob, I can't conceive, unless the name is too respectable for them:— The sun is not about to stand still or go out, nor the rivers to dry up because there was a mob in Boston on the 5th of March that attacked a party of soldiers."

According to the reporter, "Mr. Adams proceeded to a minute consideration of every witness produced on the crown side; and endeavoured to shew, from the evidence on that side, which could not be contested by the council for the crown, that the assault upon the party, was sufficiently dangerous to justify the prisoners; at least, that it was sufficiently provoking, to reduce to manslaughter the crime, even of the two who were supposed to be proved to have killed."

Adams concluded by declaring, "Facts are stubborn things; and whatever may be our wishes, our inclinations, or the dictates of our passions, they cannot alter the state of facts and evidence." Above all, he stated his conception of law as the dispenser of impartial justice, unswayed by the temporal desires of the moment: "The law, in all vicissitudes of government, fluctuations of the passions, or flights of enthusiasm, will preserve a steady undeviating course; it will not bend to the uncertain wishes, imaginations, and wanton tempers of men. . . . On the one hand it is inexorable to the cries and lamentations of the prisoners; on the other it is deaf, deaf as an adder to the clamours of the populace."

The jury returned verdicts of acquittal for six of the soldiers and guilty of manslaughter for the two who had been specifically identified as having fired fatal shots. The two were branded on the thumb as punishment.

Adams had braved what he later called "the abuse heaped upon . . . myself" for his defense of the British soldiers in order to vindicate the right of even the despised to counsel and to ensure the rule of law in the face of popular feeling. Our Revolution would not be dominated, as so many have been, by mob violence, but would instead be one for liberty under law. Adams summed it up in 1787: "I had good Policy, as well as sound Law on my side, when I ventured to lay open before our People the Laws against Riots, Routs, and unlawful assemblies. Mobs will never do—to govern States or command armies. I was as sensible of it in 70 as I am in 87. To talk of Liberty in such a state of things—!"

3. *Attorney General v. John Peter Zenger*

Attorney General v. John Peter Zenger (1735) was our first legal landmark. Gouverneur Morris may have overstated it when he later hailed the case as "the morning star of that liberty which subsequently revolutionized America." All the same, Zenger's trial was plainly a milestone in the development of American liberty.

Zenger was the publisher of a New York newspaper that savagely attacked the colonial governor. He was prosecuted by the attorney general for publishing seditious libels declaring that the liberties and property of the people of New York were in jeopardy, "men's deeds destroyed," judges arbitrarily displaced, new courts erected without consent of the legislature, trial by jury "taken away when a governor pleases," and men of property "denied the vote."

Soon after the trial's opening, Andrew Hamilton, the leader of the Philadelphia Bar and then the foremost advocate in the colonies, rose from the audience and said that he had been retained for Zenger. Hamilton admitted the printing, but urged that such publication "is the right of every free-born subject to make, when the matters so published can be supported with truth." Hence, "in so doing he has committed no crime."

The attorney general countered that truth was no defense; indeed, "the law says their being true is an aggravation of the crime." Hamilton disagreed, claiming that "the words themselves must be libellous, that is, *false*, scandalous, and seditious, or else we are not guilty." The attorney general countered with English cases rejecting truth as a defense. Hamilton, however, stressed that those cases were decided by Star Chamber, "the most dangerous court to the liberties of the people of England that ever was known."

Although the court expressly ruled that truth was no defense, Hamilton continued to urge that the facts printed "are notoriously known to be true." He stressed that Star Chamber law was "bad precedent," inconsistent with liberty. Hence Hamilton's famous peroration concluded that

> the question before the court and you, gentlemen of the jury, is not of small nor private concern. It is not the cause of a poor printer, nor of New York alone, which you are now trying. No! It may in its consequences affect every freeman that lives under a British government on the main of America. It is the best cause. It is the cause of liberty; and I make no doubt but your upright conduct this day will not only entitle you to the love and esteem of your fellow citizens; but every man who prefers freedom to a life of slavery will bless and honor you, as men who have baffled the attempt of tyranny; and by an impartial and uncorrupt verdict have laid a noble foundation for securing to ourselves, our posterity, and our neighbors, that to which nature and the laws of our country have given us a right—the liberty both of exposing and opposing arbitrary power . . . by speaking and writing truth.

Despite instructions that repeated that truth was no defense, the jury gave force to the Chief Justice's assertion that Hamilton had shown "how little regard juries are to pay to the opinion of the judges." The verdict of not guilty returned by the jury "in a short time" not only led to "three huzzas in the hall," but confirmed the right of the jury, established in

Britain in the seventeenth century, to vote its conscience regardless of the court's charge. It was also an important step in the establishment of truth as a defense to a criminal libel charge, which was fully confirmed in New York after the defense by Alexander Hamilton (no relation) in *Crosswell v. People* (1803). Well can the *Encyclopaedia Britannica* characterize the *Zenger* case as "the first victory for freedom of the press" in this country. Fittingly, it was Andrew Hamilton who later donated the ground for and planned the main architectural features of what we know as Independence Hall in Philadelphia.

4. Samuel Chase Impeachment

Samuel Chase is included on my list of worst Supreme Court Justices. His place in history, however, rests primarily on the fact that he was the only Justice ever impeached. The Chase impeachment trial in 1805 was one of the greatest trials not only because of its forensic drama, but even more so because, as a result of the Senate acquittal, as Justice William J. Brennan tells us, "the independence of the judiciary was secured."

In Chase's day, Supreme Court Justices also served on circuit as trial judges. In the trials over which he presided, Justice Chase was all that a judge should not be, particularly in trials under the Sedition Act of 1798. But his bench conduct was far removed from the "high Crimes and Misdemeanors" required by the Constitution. Instead, President Jefferson and his administration sought to use the weapon of impeachment to bend the judicial department to their will. Even at the time, it was generally recognized that the Chase impeachment was political in purpose. As the Jeffersonian leader in the Senate candidly expressed it to John Quincy Adams while the Chase trial was pending, "We want your offices, for the purpose of giving them to men who will fill them better." It was widely believed that the Chase impeachment was only the first step in the Jeffersonian plan. "The assault upon Judge Chase," wrote John Quincy Adams to his father, "was unquestionably intended to pave the way for another prosecution, which would have swept the Supreme Judicial Bench clean at a stroke." In his book on the impeachment, Chief Justice William H. Rehnquist writes that "contemporary observers viewed the proceedings against Chase as but one step in an assault on the entire judicial branch."

The arrangements for the Senate trial of Chase were as theatrical as the event itself. The pomp of the Warren Hastings impeachment, when, says Macaulay, "The grey old walls were hung with scarlet," was still vivid in the minds of all, and, in imitation, the Senate Chamber was, in the words of one senator, "fitted up in a stile beyond anything which has ever appeared, in the Country." The Senate Chamber, too, was "aglow with theatrical color . . . [the] benches . . . covered with crimson cloth." Henry Adams later characterized it: "The arrangement was a mimic reproduction of the famous scene in Westminster Hall; and the little society of Washington went to the spectacle with the same interest and passion which had brought the larger society of London to hear the orations of Sheridan and Burke."

The Chase trial itself resulted in an acquittal, for enough senators of the Jeffersonian party were convinced by the argument of the defense— "Our property, our liberty, our lives, can only be protected and secured by [independent] judges"—to make the vote for conviction fall short of the constitutional majority. "The significance of the outcome of the Chase trial," says Rehnquist, "cannot be overstated." Had Justice Chase been removed, it would have placed judges, as the closing argument for Chase declared, "at the mercy of the prevailing party." The Chase acquittal, as a matter of history, put an end to the danger of judicial removal on political grounds. Since 1805, although impeachment proceedings have been brought against other federal judges, in none of those cases was the effort to secure removal based on political reasons.

5. *United States v. Aaron Burr*

Aaron Burr is now remembered for two things: his killing of Alexander Hamilton in a duel, and his trial for treason. *United States v. Aaron Burr* (1807) was, without doubt, one of the greatest in our history—as the prosecutor exclaimed, "There never was such a trial from the beginning of the world to this day!"

Despite a mass of trial testimony and archival records, we still are not clear about what Burr intended in his plan for the Mississippi Valley territory. President Jefferson believed that Burr was going to use force to set up a new country in the West and issued a proclamation enjoining officials "to be vigilant . . . in searching out and bringing to condign punishment, all persons engaged or concerned in such enterprise." A presidential message to Congress named Burr as "the prime mover" in an unlawful plan to separate the western lands—his "guilt was placed beyond question." This was a singular pronouncement of guilt before trial. "Surprisingly," Chief Justice Warren E. Burger comments, "for a great libertarian and humanist, Jefferson's campaign against Burr rivals anything undertaken by . . . Senator Joseph McCarthy."

Burr had clearly organized armed men and provisioned them for river travel. But the evidence never showed what his purpose was or how far *he* had gone to carry it out. The trial itself was spectacular, with a galaxy of eminent counsel on both sides. But the principal characters were Burr, who took charge of his own defense; Jefferson, who (though never appearing) directed every stage of the prosecution; and Chief Justice Marshall, sitting on circuit, who presided and made the key rulings that made the case a legal landmark. The Burr trial, Alan M. Dershowitz writes, "could constitute an entire course in criminal [or] constitutional law. . . . The opinions of Chief Justice Marshall in subjects ranging from the definition of treason to the power of the judiciary to subpoena the President are among the formative judicial decisions."

Burr had moved for a subpoena directing Jefferson to produce documents needed by the defense. The prosecutors argued that these were "confidential communications, which the president ought not and could not be compelled to disclose." Marshall issued the subpoena, rejecting the claim that a court had no power to subpoena documents from the President. The president was entitled to "guarded . . . respect" but, unlike the British king, he was not vested with complete immunity. It had been argued that the documents "might contain State secrets, which could not be divulged without endangering the national safety." Marshall, however, found that it was not shown that there was anything "the disclosure of which would endanger the public safety." Executive ipse dixit was not enough; it was for the court to determine whether the claim of privilege from disclosure was properly invoked. Marshall thus established at the outset that the president is not above the law—the principle confirmed in *United States v. Nixon* (1974).

There was, of course, more in the case, with its dramatic testimony and legal arguments, as well as Marshall's opinion on jury impartiality— which has been termed the classic utterance on the subject. But the key issue was whether Burr was guilty of treason.

Most important on that issue was Marshall's rejection of the broad English concept under which it was treason "when a man doth . . . imagine the death of our lord the King." Instead, under the Constitution, the government had to prove by at least two witnesses that there had been an "overt act" of war against the United States and that Burr had participated therein. The government had claimed that, although Burr was in fact absent at the time of the unlawful assemblage at Blennerhassett's Island, he was "yet legally present." While "the doctrine, that in treason all are principals" was settled English law, Marshall ruled that under the

Constitution the traitor must "truly and in fact levy war" and that "fact must be proved by two witnesses."

As it turned out, the trial, in Chief Justice Burger's summary, produced "no solid evidence of any 'army' or any 'ships'—only a few dozen men and some riverboats on Harman Blennerhassett's Island, in the Ohio River near Marietta, Ohio," and Burr himself had never been present at the alleged illegal assemblage. Not surprisingly, the jury found Burr not guilty. His trial remains as another great case exemplifying the principle stated at the end of Marshall's jury charge: "if there be no alternative presented . . . but a dereliction of duty or the opprobrium of those who are denominated the world, he merits the contempt as well as the indignation of his country who can hesitate which to embrace."

6. *State v. John T. Scopes*

The case of *State v. John T. Scopes* (1925)—Clarence Darrow's most famous— was a curious anomaly. "Can it be possible that this trial is taking place in the twentieth century?" asked Darrow during the proceedings. Head-lined as the "Great Monkey Trial," the case pitted Biblical creation against Charles Darwin, and did so in a courtroom atmosphere more resembling a revival meeting than a hall of justice.

Scopes would, however, scarcely be on this list because of its circus-like atmosphere or even because it has become part of our folklore through the play and motion picture *Inherit the Wind* (1960). What makes it great is that the trial helped sever the tie between the law and Christianity that had originally prevailed. In 1844, the Supreme Court declared that "the Christian religion is a part of the common law." As late as 1892, the Court could state, "[T]his is a Christian nation." All this was to change after *Scopes*.

The case arose out of a prosecution for teaching evolution in violation of a Tennessee law that prohibited the teaching of "any theory that denies the story of the divine creation of man as taught in the Bible, and to teach instead that man has descended from a lower order of animals." The trial was a virtual parody of a proper legal proceeding.

In sight of the jury was a large banner, exhorting everyone, "Read your Bible daily." Darrow got it removed by demanding equal space for a banner urging, "Read your Evolution." The trial stars were the lawyers: Darrow, the most famous trial lawyer in American history, represented Scopes and, indirectly, Darwin and evolution. Against him was William Jennings Bryan—the Great Commoner, orator of the famed "Cross of

Gold" speech in 1896, three-time candidate for president—who had volunteered to direct the prosecution. Bryan was the leading fundamentalist of the day. "I am more interested in the Rock of Ages than in the age of rocks," he proclaimed.

The trial high point saw Bryan himself put on the stand. His examination by Darrow, clad in his usual wrinkled shirt and suspenders, has taken its place among legal classics. Darrow questioned Bryan relentlessly, seeking to make his literal acceptance of the Scriptures appear ridiculous.

Darrow began, "Do you claim that everything in the Bible should be literally interpreted?" Bryan replied, "I believe everything in the Bible should be accepted as it is given there." Darrow then asked about different Scripture passages. Did Bryan believe that Jonah was actually swallowed by the whale, that Joshua made the sun stand still, that "the story of the flood [was] a literal interpretation," that "[a]ll the different languages of the earth [date] from the Tower of Babel?"

Bryan answered in the affirmative. Indeed, he said at one point that he would believe Jonah swallowed the whale, "[i]f the Bible said so."

The prosecution secured a paper victory when Scopes was found guilty. But the judge imposed only a $100 fine, and the Tennessee Supreme Court reversed on a technicality: the court, rather than the jury, had set the fine.

The *Scopes* case, wrote the *New York Times*, has attained "mythological status . . . as a successful American shootout between Enlightenment and Ignorance." The reality is not as clear-cut. Bryan was more than the buffoon of Darrow's devastating questioning. Before *Scopes*, Bryan had been a leading advocate of legal and political reform. Indeed, according to Garry Wills, "It is one of the tragic turns of American history that this man who in so many ways extended the Bill of Rights should have been steered by character and accident into a deadly clash with . . . the Bill of Rights."

The tragedy was not, however, limited to the befuddled biblicist. During the first part of American history, religion had inspired many of the most important reforms in law and the society. Bryan himself had been an outstanding example of the fusion of progressive politics and evangelical moralism.

Now, embittered at its caricature by Darrow, the evangelical movement largely retired from the arena of social reform. Liberalism, which has always considered *Scopes* a great victory, was actually skewed by the Monkey Trial. The movement to reform society and law had to proceed on a secular basis, deprived as it was of the religious support that was the mainstay of nineteenth-century progressivism.

The *Scopes* case also had a more direct effect on American law. A quarter-century earlier, the Supreme Court had made its statement about our being a Christian nation without dissent or dispute. To the contrary, Justice Sandra Day O'Connor's endorsement of that view in a 1989 letter led to widespread criticism.

Despite the Protestant presuppositions of our culture, the Bill of Rights provides church–state separation. Only after *Scopes*, however, did this become more than a constitutional ideal. The ridicule cast by Darrow on revealed religion was the starting point for the conversion of American law into the solely secular subject that has dominated recent jurisprudence. The alliance between religion and law that had distinguished earlier periods has increasingly given way to virtual hostility. It was after *Scopes* that the cases began to build a legal wall between church and state. The religious foundation of law that is at the origin of legal systems was replaced by the conquest of religion by the law that has characterized twentieth-century American institutions. Darrow's devastation of Bryan was a prime factor in producing a climate of disrespect for revealed religion in the "educated" part of America. If Darrow designed *Scopes* as a morality play, the ultimate moral was that enlightened opinion had to separate secular activities from religion. It is scarcely surprising that the law was to make the same separation.

7. *Commonwealth v. Nicola Sacco and Bartolomeo Vanzetti*

"So far as the crime is concerned," wrote Justice Felix Frankfurter of *Commonwealth v. Nicola Sacco and Bartolomeo Vanzetti* (1921), "we are dealing with a conventional case of pay-roll robbery resulting in murder." There was nothing about the crime, the victims, or the accused to give the case priority over the many holdups and murders that occur every year. Despite this, a book on famous trials declares, "[t]here has probably never been a criminal trial in this or any other country which aroused more wide-spread interest and protest than the trial of Nicola Sacco and Bartolomeo Vanzetti for murder in the little town of Dedham, Mass., in the summer of 1921."

The crime was committed not far from Boston, when a paymaster and his guard were shot by two robbers, who seized the payroll and escaped in an auto that drove up just after the shooting. The police arrested Sacco and Vanzetti after tracing them through a car used in another holdup. Both made false statements to the police, which, it was urged, showed "consciousness of guilt." The defense claimed that they acted as they did because they were anarchists during the postwar government harassment of alleged subversives. They had lied, they said, because they were afraid of new Red raids and to protect their comrades.

The trial, before Judge Webster Thayer and a jury, took two months. "The only issue," Frankfurter tells us, "was the identity of the murderers. Were Sacco and Vanzetti two of the assailants . . . or were they not?" Every other issue was irrelevant, though the jury may well have been influenced by defendants' radical political views.

The trial saw a mass of conflicting evidence on the central issue. Fifty-nine witnesses testified for the prosecution, ninety-nine, for the defense. Prosecution witnesses identified Sacco as the man who had shot the guard and Vanzetti as one of those in the getaway car. There was also expert ballistic testimony connecting a bullet removed from the guard's body with a gun found on Sacco and a gun found on Vanzetti with one the guard had owned. The defense produced its own eyewitnesses, who testified that defendants were not the men who committed the crime and that they had been elsewhere at the time.

The case thus came down to what is so often the crux of a criminal trial: conflicting testimony. Whom should the jury believe—the witnesses who swore that defendants were guilty or those who gave them an alibi?

This was the prototypical jury case, with the verdict turning on the jurors' credibility determinations. As it turned out, the jury believed the prosecution witnesses and ballistic experts and found both Sacco and Vanzetti guilty. In the vast number of criminal trials with a similar outcome, that would have been the end of it. In *Sacco–Vanzetti*, however, the verdict was far from the end of the case. Instead, as a noted criminal lawyer writes, "[a] student of crime and criminal procedure will seek vainly for a parallel to the succession of amazing events which followed the conviction of Sacco and Vanzetti."

There were widespread protests, both here and abroad, against the verdict. Although the Massachusetts Supreme Judicial Court turned down appeals and Judge Thayer denied motions for new trials, the protests only grew louder—particularly after Alestino Medeiros, a jailhouse acquaintance of Sacco then under sentence of death for another murder, confessed that he and a known criminal gang had committed the murders. The outcry led the governor to appoint a committee, headed by Harvard president Lowell, to review the case. After several weeks of nonpublic hearings, both the committee and the governor issued reports which concluded, in the governor's words, "that these men, Sacco and Vanzetti were guilty, and that they had a fair trial."

The protests, if anything, grew in intensity; even today, so many years after Sacco and Vanzetti were executed, there is still disagreement about the case. As Alan Dershowitz recently wrote, the case "is a murder mystery—with political and ethnic overtones—that has never been solved." Critics urge that defendants were convicted because they were Italian radicals, that when the district attorney concluded, "Gentlemen of the jury, do your duty. Do it like men. Stand together, you men of Norfolk," he was sending them a coded message. In addition, it was charged that Judge Thayer was biased—in Dershowitz's words, "a Brahmin bigot . . . who could scarcely conceal his contempt for the Italian troublemakers."

Such a comment seems unfair. According to a *New York Times* editorial at the time, "The Judge's charge was eminently impartial." And so it seems, at least from reading it. But the prosecution's emphasis on defendants' origins and radicalism may well, as Frankfurter charged, have served to "inflame the jury's passions." Three-quarters of a century later, it is difficult to determine whether this charge was justified. What we do know is that *Sacco–Vanzetti* was a great trial—both for its intrinsic importance and, even more, for the world-wide interest and protests generated.

More recently, a 1962 *American Heritage* article concluded that, based on the author's fresh examination of the preserved ballistic evidence and using scientific methods not available in 1921, the bullets that had killed the guard came from the gun found on Sacco. Despite this, as Dershowitz wrote in 1990, the question of Sacco and Vanzetti's "guilt or innocence is still debated today."

8. *People v. Richard Loeb and Nathan Leopold*

A great lawyer can transform an otherwise ordinary trial into one of the elect. Clarence Darrow's forensic ability elevated *People v. Richard Loeb and Nathan Leopold* (1924) to the trial pantheon. Although the case was a cause célèbre because of the senseless brutality of the crime, it appeared to present little of legal interest, since the defendants' confessions made it an open-and-shut case. Darrow, however, converted the trial into a courtroom platform for his lifelong crusade against the death penalty.

Richard Loeb and Nathan Leopold had committed the senseless "thrill" murder of fourteen-year-old Bobby Franks. Aged eighteen and nineteen, they were the pampered children of wealthy parents. Retained to represent defendants, Darrow knew that a jury would vote a death sentence for so horrible a crime. He entered a guilty plea to have the case tried by the judge alone. Darrow's one purpose was to use the trial to condemn capital punishment, particularly in such a case.

In the trial itself, the state of Illinois meticulously proved every element of the cold-blooded murder. Darrow presented no rebuttal. Instead, he obtained leave to offer evidence in mitigation of punishment. Darrow had no doubt that the two boys were mentally ill. "We intend," he told the court, "to exhibit a condition of mind which does not fall within the definition of legal insanity [but] which should be heard in mitigation." Darrow questioned medical experts (alienists, as psychiatrists were then called), who agreed with his claim that defendants were "mentally diseased." The state presented its own medical testimony in rebuttal.

Then came the Darrow closing argument—the high point that made this more than a sensational murder trial. "The setting," a newspaper reported, "could not have been bettered—the noisy, milling crowd giving point to his argument that the court was the only thing standing between the boys and the bloodthirsty mob."

Darrow spoke for three days—in his trademark shirtsleeves and suspenders, pacing up and down, shoulders hunched forward. Darrow spent a day discussing his clients' mental condition. Their very crime showed that their act was the product of diseased minds. "And yet they tell me this is sanity; they tell me that the brains of these boys are not diseased. You need no experts, you need no X rays; you need no study of the endocrines. Their conduct shows exactly what it was, and shows that this Court has before him two young men who should be examined in a psychopathic hospital."

Darrow stressed the overwhelming public pressure for the death sentence: "Your Honor, our anxiety over this case has not been due to the facts that are connected with this most unfortunate affair, but to the almost unheard-of publicity it has received; to the fact that newspapers all over this country have been giving it space such as they have almost never before given to any case. . . . the public . . . thinks only of one punishment and that is death."

Despite having "placed our fate in the hands of a trained Court," Darrow said, "I have stood here for three months as one might stand at the ocean trying to sweep back the tide." Nevertheless, he was pleading "not merely for the lives of these two unfortunate lads, but for all boys and all girls; for all the young. . . . I am pleading for life, understanding, charity, kindness, and the infinite mercy that considers all. I am pleading that we overcome cruelty with kindness and hatred with love." Above all, Darrow urged, he was pleading for the future when capital punishment would be viewed like the barbarous punishments of a century ago, "where nearly two hundred crimes were punishable by death, and by death in every form; not only hanging—that was too humane—but burning, boiling, cutting into pieces, torturing in all conceivable forms."

Darrow looked the judge straight in the eye: "Your Honor stands between the past and the future. You may hang these boys. . . . But in doing it you will turn your face toward the past. . . . I am pleading for a time when hatred and cruelty will not control the hearts of men, when we can learn by reason and judgment and understanding and faith that all life is worth saving, and that mercy is the highest attribute of man."

By now, late in the last afternoon, Darrow's voice was giving out—at times so faint that he was almost inaudible. Yet every syllable of his peroration could be heard. More important than "saving these boys' lives" was "the progress of the law. . . . If I can succeed, my greatest reward and my greatest hope will be that I have done something for the tens of thousands of other boys, for the countless unfortunates who must tread the same road in blind childhood that these poor boys have trod—that I have done something to help human understanding, to temper justice with mercy, to overcome hate with love."

According to the Chicago *Herald-Examiner*, "There was scarcely any telling where his voice had finished and where silence had begun. Silence lasted a minute, two minutes. His own eyes, dimmed by years of serving the accused, the oppressed, the weak, were not the only ones that held tears."

Most important, Darrow's appeal had its effect on the one person who mattered. Two weeks later, the judge announced his sentence: life imprisonment for both defendants. During his argument, Darrow had stated, "Your Honor alone stands between these boys and . . . the scaffold." In actuality, it was the advocate's forensic skill that forestalled the extreme penalty that all had expected.

9. *Bolling v. Bolling*

If I were asked which American trial I would like to have seen personally, I would choose the case of *Bolling v. Bolling* (1771). The opposing attorneys were two of the great names in the nation's founding: Thomas Jefferson and George Wythe. To have seen them in action in the courtroom would have been a high point for anyone who has devoted his life to the law.

The principal problem in seeing early American law in action is the lack of materials such as transcripts, which tell us what went on in the courtroom. By happenstance, however, there has been preserved the text of the arguments delivered by Wythe for plaintiff and Jefferson for defendant in the *Bolling* case. Wythe was the colonies' leading jurist, and Jefferson had been his law student. Jefferson had been asked by his client "to state it [the case] with written arguments at length in writing." That is why the arguments have been preserved—in a 236-page manuscript, half in the elegant handwriting of Jefferson himself.

The *Bolling* case arose out of a will by Edward Bolling, the brother of Archibald and Robert Bolling, the plaintiff and defendant. The will left Edward's plantation to Robert. Devised to Archibald were "the rest of his estate, negroes, harvest, clothes, and every other part of his estate not already given." The main issue was whether defendant was entitled to the crops growing on the plantation when the testator died, or whether they should instead pass to plaintiff, his residuary legatee, as part of Edward's personal estate.

There were other inheritance-law issues, but the most interesting one was the growing-crops issue, and both Jefferson and Wythe devoted their major attention to it. In addition, resolution of the issue turned on the type of common-law legal reasoning that best showed the early American bar in action.

In law, the growing crops in dispute are termed "emblements." Are emblements to be treated as real or personal property? Jefferson argued for the former; Wythe, the latter.

The *Bolling* trial presents two outstanding legal minds in action. But it is even more important for what it tells us about early law. The quality of the argument confirms the existence of a developed legal system and its central place in the society. The vital role of the law in America, which observers have stressed since Toqueville, was thus apparent before the Revolution.

The *Bolling* argument shows that the American bar was as learned in law as its English counterpart. The Jefferson and Wythe arguments are outstanding examples of the common law in action. Indeed, considering the relative paucity of legal materials available in the colonies at the time, Jefferson and Wythe cite an amazing number of authorities, including cases going back to the origins of English law. American law was already primarily a system of case law.

In addition, both counsel relied on statutes to support their case. Their sophistication in the use of statutes is shown by Jefferson's animadversion on the use of statutory preambles: "Nothing is less to be depended on than the allegations in the preambles of modern statutes. The facts set forth in them, are most commonly mere creatures of the brain of the pen-man, & which never existed but in his brain." The Jefferson censure antic-ipates the recent criticism, notably by Justice Antonin Scalia, against the overreliance on legislative history in present-day statutory interpretation.

Yet if the *Bolling* arguments were primarily common-law arguments, they also had an American cast, which distinguished them from those by their English confreres. Both *Bolling* counsel stressed the social purposes to be served by the view stated by them.

Wythe urged that it would encourage agriculture to have emblements go to the sower's representative, for the same reasons that induce the law to have personal property go to the representative carrying out a testator's will. Jefferson countered that the social interest would be furthered by rec-ognizing a devise as comparable to a conveyance. Jefferson traced the development of the right to alienate property, starting in the twelfth cen-tury. His basic theme was the removal of restrictions on alienation, to encourage agriculture and other productive enterprises. Jefferson based much of his argument on this development: "the purpose of this short account of the progress of alienation is to shew that a devise is but another mode of alienation or conveiance." Hence, "when the testamentary alien-ation becomes perfect by the death of the devisor, the devisee is on the same footing as he would have been if the conveiance had been by deed."

The *Bolling* argument shows that the basic legal techniques used by lawyers today were well known during our law's formative era. Both Jef-ferson and Wythe relied on both the cases and statutes and the social pur-poses to be served by the legal principles they were advocating. Jefferson could deliver encomia on stare decisis and stress the need for fixed legal rules so that, as he put it in his argument, "judges will determine, counsel advise, and even the people themselves proceed, at once with certainty and precision." But emphasis on the social purposes served by law neces-sarily meant that legal rules that no longer served those purposes should be replaced by those that would.

Jefferson the lawyer thus soon gave way to Jefferson the law reviser. The American jurist had to construct a legal system that would answer the needs of what would become a continental community and economy, rather than those of the confined island kingdom in which the common law had developed. Yet it was not only the physical setting that differed so drastically from that on the other side of the Atlantic. American law had to be adapted to the new nation's political and social institutions. As early as the *Bolling* trial, our law had received the instrumentalist cast that was ultimately to predominate in American jurisprudence.

10. *People v. O. J. Simpson*

In 1965, Chief Justice Earl Warren was talking to his law clerk about television in the courtroom. If it is allowed, Warren said, "we can turn back the clock and make everyone in the courtroom an actor before untold millions of people." It "make[s] the determination of guilt or innocence a public spectacle and a source of entertainment for the idle and curious." Warren noted how "[t]he American people were shocked and horrified when Premier Castro tried certain defendants in a stadium." Yet that, he said, was only a step removed from opening trials to television cameras. Televising a trial was comparable to moving it "from the courtroom to the municipal auditorium and from the auditorium to the baseball stadium."

With this view of television in the courtroom, what would Chief Justice Warren have said about *People v. O.J. Simpson* (1995)? Certainly, that trial was, to use a favorite Holmes term, a uniquity. There never has been such a trial and, hopefully, never will be again. In terms of public interest and media coverage, it was the most famous ever held. Throughout the world, people received a concentrated education in trial procedure as they watched the proceeding unfold. Unfortunately, the principal lesson learned was that this was the prime illustration of all that a trial should not be.

Without the media coverage, with the whole world literally the audience, the *Simpson* trial would have been a simple murder trial. The evidence—especially the scientific evidence—of defendant's guilt was overwhelming. The public spotlight, however, converted the proceeding into a television circus, if not a legal nightmare. Instead of the dignified and objective forum for guilt determination, the trial focused increasingly on the sideshows that came to dominate the media coverage.

The country may have been consumed by the trial as it unfolded each day on the TV screen. After all, it had all the elements that are the seismic points of our society: racial conflicts, domestic abuse, horrible murders, operation of criminal justice—all were there. To say that people watched the trial to educate themselves, we would have to believe that people buy *Playboy* for its articles.

Nevertheless, to one who believes that television in the courtroom is an abomination, the *Simpson* trial may well result in the proverbial good coming out of evil. The distortions produced by the television coverage have led other judges to refuse to allow cameras to cover their trials. Is it too much to hope that the ultimate effect of the *Simpson* circus will be to halt what has seemed the inexorable takeover of the courtroom by the television camera?

Legal Morality Plays

"It is not advisable," Catherine Drinker Bowen wrote, "to judge a nation's legal procedure by what happens in big dramatic cases. . . . (Wasn't it Holmes who said, 'Great cases make bad law'?) In such trials, everything is warped." Still, it cannot be denied that great trials make great stories and that the greatest of them reflect not only their legal issues, but the development of the nation itself. That is eminently true of the trials on this list. Not all were held in the courtroom, but all made significant contributions to our law and life.

Some of the trials were important events that made a difference in American history: *Attorney General v. John Peter Zenger*, the first case that turned upon freedom of the press (significantly the first constitutional press guarantee was to be adopted in Pennsylvania, where Zenger's counsel, Andrew Hamilton, practiced); *Rex v. William Wemms*, the culmination of one of the catalysts of the Revolution; the Chase impeachment, which ensured judicial independence; *United States v. Aaron Burr*, which established the limited meaning of treason, saving us from the wholesale conception that had been a blot on English law; and the Johnson impeachment, which confirmed presidential independence and prevented our transformation into a parliamentary system.

Other trials on our list were great because of the performance of counsel. This was notably true of those in which Clarence Darrow participated. His questioning in *State v. John T. Scopes* and argument in *People v. Richard Loeb and Nathan Leopold* are classics of the advocate's art. *Bolling v. Bolling* also ranks because of the attorneys on each side; it adds a largely unknown dimension to Thomas Jefferson and tells us better than almost anything else about the caliber of the bar that was to lead the Revolution and the age of Constitution-making.

Commonwealth v. Nicola Sacco and Bartolomeo Vanzetti would have been an ordinary murder trial except for the public interest and protest aroused by it. The same may be true of *People v. O. J. Simpson*. But that case has also been unique because of its tremendous coverage, which made it a showcase of criminal procedure for the entire world. Again I express the hope that the *Simpson* "circus" will derail what has seemed the inevitable television conquest of the courtroom.

A trial is, of course, a public drama. But drama and histrionics are not synonymous. Most of the trials chosen were not characterized by courtroom theater. Indeed, we can scarcely think of lawyers like John Adams, Thomas Jefferson, Benjamin Curtis, and the others who argued these cases as masters of the wind-blown type of advocacy that people associate with "trials of the century."

Above all, a great trial is more than a forensic contest; it is a morality play, which serves both to educate and to affirm the principles by which the community is ordered. The trials on this list eminently fit within this concept. All were what legal historian Lawrence Friedman terms "representations of morality played out in open forums." All ultimately helped to define the boundaries, norms, and values of our society.

13

TEN
GREATEST
LEGAL MOVIES

A t the outset, I should state that I am not a movie buff. To me, motion
pictures are entertainment, not art. Nevertheless, I recognize that
people have learned more about law from movies than from all the books
ever published. That is why I have included this list of legal movie greats
in this book. All of them are outstanding as films, but they also tell us
important things about the law. They instruct as well as entertain. Most
important, in them the law is not warped by the need to attract a mass
audience. For the law at least, they represent the peaks of Hollywood
productions.

— ★ — ★ — ★ —

— ★ — ★ — ★ —

Ten Greatest Legal Movies

1. *Anatomy of a Murder* (1959)
2. *To Kill a Mockingbird* (1962)
3. *The Magnificent Yankee* (1950)
4. *Twelve Angry Men* (1957)
5. *The Wrong Man* (1956)
6. *Compulsion* (1959)
7. *Inherit the Wind* (1960)
8. *Adam's Rib* (1949)
9. *The Paper Chase* (1973)
10. *The Verdict* (1982)

1. *Anatomy of a Murder*

Anatomy of a Murder (1959) deals with a fictitious case, but it has the ring of authenticity, since it is the screen version of a novel by a Michigan Supreme Court judge who, as he later wrote, "longed to try [his] hand at telling about a criminal trial the way it really was." Both the book and the movie contain the most penetrating account of a case unfolding ever written or filmed.

As in other legal films, the principal protagonist is the defense attorney—here Paul Biegler, a small-town lawyer in the Upper Peninsula of Michigan, played by James Stewart in perhaps his best performance. Biegler is asked to represent Frederick Manion, an army lieutenant accused of having murdered the man who allegedly raped his wife. Manion and his wife tell him that after she came home late, badly bruised, and said that she had been raped by Quill, a tavern owner, Manion went to Quill's bar and shot him three times. Biegler decides to take the case for the fee, even though Manion gives him only a promissory note. The film shows Biegler's difficulty in rounding up witnesses as well as in working up a legal theory on which to base his defense. He finally develops a theory of "irresistible impulse."

Most of the film is devoted to the trial before a new judge from outside the area, played by Joseph N. Welch, the famous counsel in the Senate Army–McCarthy hearing. The prosecutor is the well-known district attorney from Lansing, whose slick arrogant manner provides a contrast to Biegler's laid-back country style. There are realistic scenes involving testimony by different witnesses and the D.A.'s at first successful objections to the wife's rape story. Finally, when the D.A. objects to a police sergeant's telling what Manion had said to him after the shooting (about the rape), Biegler explodes in a stirring scene: "Your Honor, how can the jury accurately estimate the testimony given at this trial unless they first know the reason behind it: why Lt. Manion shot Barney Quill. Now, the prosecution would like to separate the motive from the act. Well, that's like trying to take the core from an apple without breaking the skin. . . . And I beg the court—I beg the court—to let me cut into the apple."

The judge rules in Biegler's favor, and the emphasis shifts to the question of the rape. The key witness is the wife herself, and her cross-examination is the trial's crucial point. It is both realistic and engrossing. Here, best of all, the film conveys its message of ambiguity—when dealing with human beings, it may be impossible to distinguish fact from fiction. Still, the legal process must do the best it can with the evidence presented.

Manion testifies after being prepared by Biegler (many lawyers objected to the implication that lawyers are coached by counsel, but it happens all the time). Manion states that the shots he fired "don't seem to be connected to me . . . they seem distant, far away." The story now is different from what he first told Biegler—obviously the result of an attempt to meet the requirements of his "irresistible impulse" defense.

There are other witnesses, including dramatic testimony. The jury verdict of "not guilty by reason of insanity" is almost anticlimactic; the stress throughout has been on process, not decision. The ending has a sarcastic note: when Biegler goes to collect his fee, he finds a note from Manion, "Sorry but I had to leave town suddenly—I was seized by an irresistible impulse."

Even with the ambiguity of such instances, the picture remains the best portrayal of a lawyer's work in an actual case. The trial scenes are as accurate as any filmed—an anatomy of a trial, not a murder. Despite the clichés—the country lawyer versus the city slicker; the drunken, but wise, sidekick; the last-minute witness; and other forensic surprises—the film works, particularly the lengthy trial (almost two-thirds of the three hour running time). It is still the most realistic depiction of legal procedure in a motion picture.

2. *To Kill a Mockingbird*

A 1992 article, "Atticus Finch, Esq., R.I.P.," criticized the lawyer hero in *To Kill a Mockingbird* as "not an appropriate role model for lawyers." In response, the author was deluged "by Atticans who wrote to equate my rejection of Finch, literally, with attacking God, Moses, Jesus, Gandhi, and Mother Teresa."

To Kill a Mockingbird (1962) is the high point in the idealized movie portrait of the lawyer. Atticus Finch is the lawyer's beau ideal—he has been called "an indelible symbol of the lawyer as the constitution made flesh." A *New York Times* article describes Atticus (like his children we refer to him by his first name) as one "who taught a community and his two young children about justice, decency and tolerance, and who drove a generation . . . to become lawyers themselves." Certainly, Atticus has been a role model for law students and lawyers ever since the now-classic novel by Harper Lee and the film based on it.

The core of the movie is racial injustice seen through the eyes of the Finch children. They learn about the adult world of racial bigotry when their father defends a black man falsely charged with the rape of a white woman—then a capital crime in Alabama. He does so at personal risk and even though he knows that although his client is innocent, he will be fighting a lost cause. Atticus is a Lincolnesque figure as portrayed by Gregory Peck in his Oscar-winning performance. When a mob tries to lynch the defendant before his trial, Atticus, armed only with a book, stops them at the jailhouse door. The trial itself is stacked against the black defendant, but the case is still filmed as the set for a morality play, both for the children and for us.

Atticus presents a picture from which the children learn the difference between right and wrong, justice and injustice, and courage in the face of the world as it is. The unfortunate client's fate demonstrates the law's inability to deal with the injustices to blacks in the courts—manifestations of the all-pervasive racism of the day. What Harper Lee terms "the secret court of men's hearts" makes pretensions of equality before the law a "monumental mockery."

Although he knows it is useless, Atticus fights as hard as he can for his client. His final summation falls on deaf ears, but it is an eloquent summation of the law's ideal: "there is one way in this country in which all men are created equal—there is one human institution that makes a pauper the equal of a Rockefeller, the stupid man the equal of an Einstein, and the ignorant man the equal of any college president. That institution, gentlemen, is a court. It can be the Supreme Court of the United States or the humblest J.P. court in the land, or this honorable court which you serve. Our courts have their faults, as does any human institution, but in this country our courts are the great levelers, and in our courts all men are created equal."

"Character" is the key to Atticus Finch—something most lawyers would still prefer to be most known for, even in a day when the law has become more a business than anything else.

3. *The Magnificent Yankee*

"Let us now praise famous men," say the Scriptures. That is exactly what *The Magnificent Yankee* (1950) does. Oliver Wendell Holmes is one of the most famous men in American law, and the film is a laudatory biography of the Justice. The movie is low-keyed throughout, as was Holmes's personal life (apart from his bloody Civil War service). In fact, to the movie audience, the Justice's life may seem rather dull, devoted as it was to the intellectual life involved in deciding cases. Yet for one to whom Holmes is a legal hero, this screen biography is more engrossing than any film romance.

The film shows better than any other what a life in the law means: dealing with cases year after year—a life devoted to what may seem tedious to the average viewer; yet it was such a life with its constant intellectual effort that enabled the Justice to seem younger and more alive than people his junior by many years. Chief Justice Rehnquist writes that, when he first came to the Supreme Court, "I just felt, literally, like I'd entered a monastery." *The Magnificent Yankee* presents the best movie picture of what it is like to be a part of such an institution.

Best of all, the film has many extracts from some of the best Holmes statements—from his opinions, speeches, and other writings. Happily, these include some of the Holmes aficionado's favorites. There is dramatic license on when the statements were made. Thus Holmes's eightieth birthday speech to his clerks contains some of the most famous aphorisms from other speeches and writings. There are also some minor errors. For example, when Holmes is told he might become Chief Justice, he deprecates the idea, saying that no Associate Justice had ever been so promoted. When the movie Holmes makes this statement, the Chief Justice is Edward D. White, who had been a Justice before being named to head the Court.

Some of the Holmes remarks were made in more dramatic circumstances than the picture indicates. After his last Court session, the film Holmes tells Justice Louis D. Brandeis in the robing room, "I won't be in tomorrow." The statement was actually made from the bench after the Justices had heard oral arguments on January 3, 1932, and Holmes submitted his resignation later in the day. Coincidentally, on that day, Earl Warren, then a California district attorney, had argued his first case before the Court. Warren used to say that his friends accused him of driving Holmes from the bench. They used to tease him, "One look at you and he said, 'I quit.'"

4. *Twelve Angry Men*

What goes on in the jury room is still one of the great mysteries. Many scholars have made studies of the subject, but *Twelve Angry Men* (1957) tells as much about how a jury operates as anything on the subject. Despite the widespread deprecation of the jury, the film illustrates what most experienced lawyers have learned: the give-and-take in the jury room usually leads to the right verdict.

The scene is a steamy Manhattan courtroom. The judge wearily gives his charge. The jury retires to consider what seems an open-and-shut case against a minority slum youth; the peers determining his fate are all white, middle-class men. Lincoln once wrote that a jury frequently has one member who thinks differently. In the film, that juror is played superbly by Henry Fonda. After a brief discussion, he alone expresses doubt and raises his hand for not guilty. The remainder of the film, almost all in the stifling jury room, shows how Fonda gradually persuades the others to share his doubt and ultimately to vote a not-guilty verdict.

The key point made is one that most people forget: that a not-guilty verdict does not require proof beyond a reasonable doubt of a defendant's innocence, but only a reasonable doubt as to his guilt. The emphasis is on the presumption of innocence—what it means in practice and how it is given effect in an actual case. With us, guilt is individual, not collective; but this film shows that that is true as well of jury assessment of guilt. As Lawrence Friedman puts it, "Each juror brings his individual conscience to bear on the collective task of the jury."

No film has shown as much about how a jury functions or how one person can make a difference in the law, as in other areas of life. Critics have pointed out that the movie does not present an accurate picture—that the chance of a single hold-out persuading the others to change their minds is extremely small. In a real jury, it just does not happen that a single star can bring all the others around.

Yet that hardly detracts from the film's impact. It remains the most revealing attempt to show a jury in operation. It makes for exhilarating drama; but it also provides ample food for thought about how a jury reaches its verdict. The emotional tensions among the twelve men underscore the demonstration of how jurors' perceptions of people, evidence, and issues affect the lives of those on trial.

5. *The Wrong Man*

It is hard to imagine a list of movie greats that does not include a film directed by Alfred Hitchcock. *The Wrong Man* (1956) is, however, not the typical Hitchcock product. It is a didactic movie that seeks to instruct, rather than thrill or puzzle. In almost documentary fashion, it makes a point that even those versed in court procedure too often forget: mistaken identification has probably been the single greatest cause of conviction of the innocent.

The film's protagonist, again brilliantly portrayed by Henry Fonda, is a musician who is mistakenly identified as the robber of an insurance office. He has, of course, had nothing whatever to do with the crime, having visited the insurance company only to borrow on his wife's policy.

The robbery victims are, nevertheless, categorical in their identification of him as the perpetrator. The result is a Kafkaesque introduction to the details of criminal procedure, from arrest to a trial that ends in a mistrial. Then the real perpetrator is apprehended and the identification of him is equally positive, so that there is ultimately a happy ending.

To most people, identification evidence is the most reliable, particularly when it is certain. After all, what is more compelling than the eyewitness who is sure of what he has seen? Yet one of the first things law students learn is how frequently witnesses are mistaken about what they have seen, and that is the case no matter how sure they may be. In fact, a common ploy of law professors is to have an unknown person enter the classroom and apparently shoot someone. Students are indelibly impressed by the divergent accounts of what happened and, most of all, by the different descriptions of the gunman.

To be sure, the victim of mistaken identification does not realize this. Nor can he do anything to erase the positive misidentification. Instead, Hitchcock shows graphically how it is almost impossible for his hero to escape from the identification's impact. His life is on its way to ruin—a fate he ultimately escapes only because of the accidental discovery of the real perpetrator. The film helps us to understand the predicament facing the innocent person unjustly accused of a crime. He is virtually helpless when the accusation is based on positive eyewitness identification. Unfortunately, what happens in *The Wrong Man* occurs in real life much more often than most people realize.

6. *Compulsion*

Great trials make great movies, particularly where they are trials in which Clarence Darrow participated. Two of Darrow's most notable trials are on the list of greatest trials and also formed the basis for two of the films on this list. The first is *Compulsion*(1959); the second, *Inherit the Wind*, is next on this list. Both make for gripping theater for anyone interested in law.

Compulsion was originally a novel and play based upon the *Loeb–Leopold* trial. The movie closely follows the facts of the case. To be sure, there are embellishments, notably the attempt by the Leopold prototype to commit a second "thrill crime" at the scene of the original murder. More than half the film is devoted to the background of the two perpetrators, their senseless killing of the fourteen-year-old, and their apprehension through a pair of eyeglasses left at the crime scene. But the high point is the trial, with Orson Welles giving a riveting performance as defense attorney Jonathan Wilk, the Darrow prototype. In the film, too, with guilt established beyond doubt, Wilk enters a guilty plea and makes his impassioned argument against the death penalty. The argument is similar to that in the actual case, though the words are often paraphrases and simplifications of those used by Darrow.

The ultimate climax is Wilk's closing argument. His speech takes fifteen minutes (though perhaps the longest uninterrupted address in a motion picture, that is only a fraction of the three days Darrow took for his summation). The next morning (two weeks later in the actual case), the judge delivered the sentence—life plus ninety-nine years. Wilk, patterned on the renowned agnostic, tells the defendants, "Sometime you might ask yourselves whether it wasn't the hand of God that dropped those glasses. And if He didn't, who did?"

What makes this a great legal film is what made *Loeb–Leopold* a great trial: the performance of defense counsel. Welles was made to look like Darrow himself—hair dyed, body padded, latex bags under his eyes, and in the trademark shirtsleeves and suspenders. As flamboyant as Darrow, Welles displays all the inner conviction that made the great advocate's argument a forensic landmark. The film, like the case, shows how a lawyer can take a seemingly hopeless case and make it a platform for the cause for which he has fought for so many years.

7. *Inherit the Wind*

Without a doubt, motion pictures have influenced the way we view law and lawyers. In the long-running television series *L.A. Law*, two lawyers state their role models: "Gregory Peck in *To Kill a Mockingbird*," says the first, "No," comes back the other. "With me it was Spencer Tracy in *Inherit the Wind*." Both films, of course, are classic legal motion pictures that deserve inclusion in any list of greats of the genre.

Inherit the Wind (1960) is a motion picture version of the *Scopes* trial. The names are changed, but the characters and story are essentially those in the actual proceeding—with Matthew Harrison Brady (William Jennings Bryan in real life) for the prosecution and the Bible and Henry Drummond (Clarence Darrow in the actual case) for the defense and evolution, with the parts superbly played by Fredric March and Spencer Tracy. Defendant Bertram Cates teaches biology (like John T. Scopes) and is prosecuted for teaching evolution in violation of a state law. The film follows the main outlines of the actual trial, even including a cynical reporter modeled on H.L. Mencken, who covered *Scopes*. Of course, there are cinematic embellishments, such as the role given to defendant's film fiancée, torn between her love for defendant and respect for her father, a fundamentalist clergyman. Her dramatic cross-examination by Brady has no counterpart in the actual trial.

The high point of the film, as of the *Scopes* trial, is Drummond's calling of the prosecutor as a witness. Here, too, the discrediting of Brady by close questioning of his extreme fundamentalist interpretation of the Bible is the climax. When Brady declares that only his particular interpretation is correct, Drummond triumphantly declares, "The Gospel according to Brady! God speaks to Brady and Brady tells the world! Brady, Brady, Brady, Almighty!" The spectators, until now Brady's firm supporters, greet his extreme statements with derision. Brady himself recognizes this. Just before the verdict, he sobs to his wife, "They laughed at me, Mother," placing his head in her lap like a forlorn child.

But the moral of the movie is more than the discrediting of extreme fundamentalism that resulted from the *Scopes* trial. In the movie Brady, unable to bear his rejection and overcome by the courtroom's sweltering heat, dies from heart failure a few hours after the verdict (William Jennings Bryan actually died a week after the verdict). In the picture's last scene, the Mencken-type reporter is sarcastic: "how do you write an obituary for a man who's been dead thirty years?" Drummond replies, "Don't you understand the meaning of what went on here today? I tell you Brady had the same right as Cates: the right to be wrong."

In a broader sense, this was the film's basic theme: free thought and expression versus repression of ideas. As Stanley Kramer, the producer and director, stated when it was released, "the real issues of that trial were man's right to teach. These are issues for which the never-ending struggle continues, and they constitute the real theme of *Inherit the Wind*."

8. *Adam's Rib*

In *Anatomy of a Murder*, the husband accused of murder tells his lawyer that he is confident that he will get off because of the "unwritten law" under which, he says, he was justified in shooting a man who had raped his wife. The lawyer replies that "the unwritten law is a myth—it doesn't exist—and anyone who commits a murder on the theory that it does exist has just bought himself room and board in the state penitentiary—probably for life."

Adam's Rib (1949) assumes that the "unwritten law" does still exist, but that it applies only to men, not women. It is one of the best comedies ever

filmed, but underneath the banter is the central idea of the law's continuing unfairness to women. The protagonists are a husband and wife—he
an assistant district attorney, she a practicing lawyer—played at the peak
of their form by Spencer Tracy and Katharine Hepburn. When a woman is
tried for shooting her husband after she had found him in his paramour's
apartment, Tracy is assigned to prosecute and Hepburn arranges to be
retained as defense attorney. The interplay between the husband–wife
attorneys, both professional (particularly during the trial) and personal,
provides most of the action. The mood is light, but that may be the best
way to get across to a mass audience the serious message that, even with
the spread of women's rights, the two sexes may still not be treated
equally by the law in action.

The "unwritten law" defense is, of course, wholly extralegal—one that
should not be considered at all by a jury. But the jury itself is the judge of
its verdict and the considerations behind it. Despite the judge's rulings
and instructions, the jury may decide as it chooses; its not-guilty verdict
stands even if it is contrary to both the law and the facts. As it turns out,
the *Adam's Rib* jury is swayed by the Hepburn argument that the "unwritten law" would have protected a male defendant in similar circumstances, and it is only fair for the same to be true in this case. The jury
votes "not guilty," and the domestic disruption caused by the husband–wife rivalry ends with a reconciliation. Hopefully, the public, too,
has been swayed by the underlying lesson that the law in action is what
counts. The movement toward formal equality before the law has not necessarily meant full equality for the sexes in real life.

9. *The Paper Chase*

Countless law students in the past twenty years have been intimidated by
would-be Professor Kingsfields, who have taken the supercilious Harvard
professor in *The Paper Chase* (1973) as their model. Kingsfield, played to
arrogant perfection by John Houseman, is the dominant character in the
film—far more so than the bland first-year law student who is its nominal
protagonist. Kingsfield transforms the law-school Socratic method into a
modern Inquisition. Yet, torture and all, the Kingsfield class is a crucible
for learning—at least for those able to survive. The neophyte law student
may feel with Dante, at the gates of hell, "All hope abandon, ye who enter
here!" But those able to withstand the Kingsfield treatment also come forth
"to see again the stars." There has been a virtual metamorphosis: the
quondam neophytes are now able to think like lawyers.

The Paper Chase may be virtually devoid of plot; its student protagonist and his colleagues are dim appendages to the standout role of the law professor. Kingsfield's classroom performance shows us the American law school during its golden age, when it furnished precisely the kind of training the potential lawyer needed: training in intellectual independence, individual thinking, digging out principles through penetrating analysis, and reasoning from them in a legal manner. Concepts, principles, and rules of law were studied not as dry abstractions, but as realities arising out of actual cases. Most professors give us rules; Kingsfield gives us the method and the power that can test the reason of rules.

For one who knew the American law school during its Kingsfield day, *The Paper Chase* also presents a poignant picture. In recent years, the case method as practiced in Harvard and its progeny has been attacked as too narrow and too uneconomical a way of learning law—ill adapted for teaching the law's efforts to meet the needs of the changing society. More and more, the case method as taught by a master such as Kingsfield has given way to law-school teaching with a growing hit-or-miss quality. Legal education today too often seems a method in search of a purpose. Instead of the classic Kingsfield approach, law students now are subjected to a smorgasbord of teaching techniques—many of increasingly esoteric character as fad or fancy moves the particular professor.

With all their faults, the Kingsfields in their time made remarkable contributions to legal learning. They did this as professionals offering professional training all but unique in its intensity and discipline. *The Paper Chase* remains a monument to their Herculean devotion (Kingsfield is shown as being at the law school night and day) to training future lawyers.

10. *The Verdict*

"Atticus Doesn't Live Here Anymore" was the title of a 1992 article in a legal periodical. "Atticus Finch," writes the author, "exist[s] in a world far different from our own." The lawyer as hero, crowned with truth and justice, has given way in the antiestablishment post-Vietnam and post-Watergate era, where counsel antics à la O. J. Simpson's circus and lawyer venality are seen as the norm. "You lawyers are all the same," a witness tells Frank Galvin, plaintiff's counsel in *The Verdict* (1982). "You don't care who you hurt as long as you make a buck. You're a bunch of whores."

The golden age of the legal profession in films—with the lawyer and the judge writ larger than life—largely ended with Atticus Finch on his

1962 pedestal. During the next two decades, there were fewer motion pictures with lawyers as protagonists. In the 1980s, however, increasing numbers of movies with legal themes were produced. Now, however, the lawyer was no longer the unsullied icon, but an ordinary mortal, often with feet of clay. This was emphatically true of Frank Galvin, the lawyer protagonist played by Paul Newman in *The Verdict*—the only film in the past twenty years that ranks among the legal film greats.

Galvin is a has-been Boston lawyer—once a promising young attorney with law-school idealism, but now a virtual ambulance chaser, stumbling about his office in a drunken stupor. His mentor shames him into actively pursuing a malpractice suit against a Catholic hospital that Galvin had agreed to take a year and a half earlier, but had done nothing about. Galvin at first is interested only in obtaining a settlement—or, more accurately, in the third he would collect from it. But then he visits the brain-damaged victim and understands the tragic consequences of the doctors' negligence. Now he turns down a $210,000 settlement offer, saying, "If I take the money, I'm lost—I'll just be a rich ambulance chaser."

Galvin's opponent is a mega-sized law firm headed by unscrupulous lawyer Ed Concannon, who employs every trick, ethical or not, to win the case—including using a firm lawyer to obtain information through a romantic involvement with Galvin. A biased judge and difficulties in securing evidence stack the cards against Galvin, particularly when the testimony of his last key witness is ordered stricken from the record. However, he wins a surprise verdict, illustrating the lesson learned as early as the *Zenger* trial that the jury is *the* decider, regardless of the judge's rulings and instructions. As Galvin puts it to them in his closing argument, "*you* are the law, not the lawbooks, not some book, not a marble statue."

The film can be faulted for technical errors, notably in having the case go to the jury after Galvin's case was left without evidentiary support by exclusion of his crucial witness's testimony. In real life, a motion for a directed verdict for the defense would have been made and granted. Despite this, the film is an engrossing presentation of law in action. Most striking is the now-tarnished portrait of the lawyer. The lawyer as hero has given way to unattractive counsel on both sides: the defense is thoroughly corrupt, and Galvin is a pathetic alcoholic, himself not above unethical practices. To have an antihero instead of an Atticus Finch or a Clarence Darrow is, however, only an aspect of the society's pervasive pessimism. *The Verdict* is but a reflection of the growing disenchantment with law and lawyers in recent years.

Today's Legal Mirror

The law, says Holmes, is a magic mirror wherein we see reflected both our lives and the society. This is even more true of the motion picture—today's magic mirror from which most people receive their reflections of life and law. The films discussed are, in my opinion, the ten greatest legal reflections. It should be noted that movies made for television are not included. If they were, *Gideon's Trumpet*—a fine version of the famous case of *Gideon v. Wainwright* (1963)—would be on the list. In addition, these are all films depicting *American* law in operation. If I were not so limited, other films (notably *Witness for the Prosecution* and *Judgment at Nuremberg*) would undoubtedly be included. These are, however, the pictures that, in my opinion, best reflect American law in action.

The movies chosen both instruct and entertain. This is plainly true of *The Wrong Man*—as didactic as any picture ever produced. Yet although it teaches an important legal lesson, it is also a gripping film, holding us in suspense until the end. The other films on this list are not so obviously intended to instruct, but each of them, too, tells us something about the way in which the law operates. *Adam's Rib* may be one of Hollywood's best comedies; but underneath is the serious moral of continuing sex discrimination—if not in the books, in the law in action. *The Magnificent Yankee* tells us how a great judge lived his day-to-day life, its seeming dullness perhaps a necessary accompaniment to his almost monastic devotion to the law. *Compulsion* and *Inherit the Wind* show the master advocate in action. In them, law and the lawyer are at their best; in both films, the courtroom virtuoso uses his skills to advance causes dear to his heart. That is even truer of *To Kill a Mockingbird*; if any lawyer is even more the hero than Clarence Darrow, it is Atticus Finch. *Twelve Angry Men* tells how one person can make a difference in the law and that that person need not be a judge or lawyer; one juror turns around what seemed like a foreordained guilty verdict. The picture also illustrates the crucial role of the jury in our law. That is also the key lesson of *The Verdict* and *Anatomy of a Murder*—both the best depictions of cases in action, from their beginning through trial and verdict. *The Paper Chase* shows what it was like to attend law school during the great days of American legal education; more and more, alas, Professor Kingsfield remains only a relic whose would-be imitators misuse and mangle the method that was once the greatest technique for the training of lawyers.

It is not only legal education that has gone downhill. The reputation of the legal profession—once considered the crown jewel, our true aristocracy according to Tocqueville—has reached its virtual nadir in recent years. Oliver Wendell Holmes, Clarence Darrow, and Atticus Finch now only remind us of the lawyer's former luster. On the screen, Atticus's idealized portrait has given way to the more complex figure of Frank Galvin in *The Verdict*, with blemishes even more prominent than virtues—not to mention Ed Concannon, Galvin's odious opponent, who tries every crooked trick to win his case. The recent article, "Atticus Doesn't Live Here Anymore" deals with the changing face of celluloid lawyers. As in real life, the lawyer as good guy has become almost the exception. On the screen at least, we have not seen his kind since the days of Atticus himself, when the last of my films showing a great lawyer was filmed.

Trivia Questions

Supreme Court

1. Who was the first to wear trousers beneath his Supreme Court robe?
2. Who was the first Justice to hire a law clerk?
3. Who was the only descendant of a Justice to become one?
4. Who was the first Justice who had held no prior public office?
5. Who was the only Justice who served with a relative on the Court?
6. Who was the last Justice to use the spittoon behind the Supreme Court bench?
7. What Justice enjoyed a reputation as a minor poet?
8. What Justices have been known for wearing bow ties?
9. What Justices during this century have worn whiskers?
10. What Justices appeared as supernumeraries in a Washington Opera production, wearing eighteenth-century costumes, including white powdered wigs?
11. What Justice practiced as a frontier lawyer, carrying a pistol and bowie knife?
12. What Justice's major premise was "God damn it!"?
13. About what Justice did another write, "You would no more heed [his] tripe than you would be seen naked at Dupont Circle at high noon tomorrow"?
14. Who is ranked first in every list of great Supreme Court Justices?
15. Who is ranked "great" in every list but one?
16. Who was the youngest Justice appointed?
17. Who was the oldest Justice appointed?
18. Who was the longest-living Justice?
19. Who was the oldest serving Justice?
20. Who was the youngest Justice to die?
21. What Justice was known for playing Trivial Pursuit on the bench?
22. What Justice practiced as a doctor for nine years before giving up medicine for law?
23. What Justice resigned to become a U.S. senator?
24. What Justice originated the legal right of privacy?

25. About what Justice did Theodore Roosevelt complain that he could find more backbone in a banana?
26. What Justice was called by the president who appointed him the "dumbest man . . . I've ever run across"?
27. What Justice was the brother of the builder of the Atlantic Cable?
28. Who was the first Justice to be married while on the Court?
29. Who was the first Justice to be divorced?
30. What Justice had the most wives?
31. What Justice wrote the most opinions while on the Court?
32. What Justice wrote the fewest opinions?
33. Who wrote the most opinions of the Court?
34. What Justice wrote the first dissenting opinion?
35. Why was it the first opinion delivered in the Supreme Court, since dissents normally are delivered after majority and concurring opinions?
36. What Justice delivered the most dissenting opinions?
37. Did the Justice who was known as the Great Dissenter deliver the most dissents?
38. What Justice wrote that he suffered from "dissent-ery"?
39. When President Lincoln visited the front lines and climbed a parapet to see the battle at Fort Stevens, near Washington (with his tall figure an obvious target), what future Supreme Court Justice shouted, "Get down, you damn fool!"?
40. Who was the first Justice to go to law school?
41. Who was the first Justice to graduate from law school?
42. What law school was attended by most Justices?
43. What Justices were Rhodes scholars?
44. What Justices served on the Court with their former law professors?
45. What Justice clerked for the author of a famous sea classic?
46. What Justice signed the Declaration of Independence?
47. What Justices were members of the Constitutional Convention of 1787?
48. What Justice appointed the first female law clerk?
49. What Justice appointed the first African-American law clerk?
50. Who was the biggest member of the Court?
51. Who was the smallest member of the Court?
52. What Justice served as prosecutor during the Nuremburg trials?
53. What Justice served as a bank president?
54. What Justice had his life saved by a United States marshal?
55. What Justices served on the Union side in the Civil War?
56. What Justices served on the Confederate side in the Civil War?

57. What Justices served in World War I?
58. What Justices served in World War II?
59. What Justice had been a general in the Army?
60. Who was the first Confederate veteran appointed to the Court?
61. Who was the first Supreme Court appointee?
62. Who was the first sworn in as a member of the Court?
63. Who was the hundedth Supreme Court Justice?
64. What Justices served without being confirmed?
65. What Justices were confirmed after prior rejections by the Senate?
66. What Court nominee was rejected twice by the Senate?
67. Who turned down appointments to the Court after they had been confirmed by the Senate?
68. What Justices had second Court nominations rejected?
69. When and where did the Court hold its first session?
70. When and where did the Court first sit in Washington?
71. Where did the Court sit after the British burned Washington in 1814?
72. When did the Court get its own building?
73. Who was the only Justice to be impeached?
74. What Justice published the most books?
75. What Justice published the most law books?
76. What was the first case decided by the Supreme Court?
77. What was the first Supreme Court decision to strike down of a state law?
78. What was the first Supreme Court case to review the constitutionality of an act of Congress?
79. What was the first Supreme Court case in which a statute was held unconstitutional?
80. What was the second Supreme Court case holding an act of Congress unconstitutional?
81. What was the salary of the first Justices?
82. What is the salary of Justices today?
83. When did Congress first provide pensions for retired Justices?
84. Who was the first former law clerk to become a Justice?
85. What other former Supreme Court clerks were appointed to the Court?
86. What members of the Court were law-school deans?
87. What Justice was once expelled from the bar?
88. What Justice was an all-American football player?
89. Who was the first Catholic appointed to the Supreme Court?
90. Who was the first Jew appointed to the Court?

91. Who was the first woman appointed to the Court?
92. From what state have more Justices come than from any other?
93. What Justices were foreign-born?
94. What members of the Court were presidents of the American Bar Association?
95. What determines where Justices sit on the bench?
96. In what order do Justices discuss cases at the conference?
97. Who was the only Justice to sit in every chair on the bench, from junior to senior Associate Justice and then Chief Justice?
98. When was the first African-American admitted to the Supreme Court bar?
99. When was the first woman admitted to the Supreme Court bar?
100. Who argued the most cases in the Supreme Court?
101. How many Justices have there been?

Chief Justices

102. How many Chief Justices have there been?
103. What Chief Justice once said that the Supreme Court was his notion of what heaven must be like?
104. What Chief Justice had his picture on U.S. currency?
105. What Chief Justice wrote a famous biography of George Washington?
106. What Chief Justice's brother-in-law wrote "The Star-Spangled Banner"?
107. Who was the oldest Chief Justice appointed?
108. Who was the youngest Chief Justice appointed?
109. Who was the first Chief Justice to go to law school?
110. Who was the first Chief Justice to graduate from law school?
111. What Chief Justice headed the commission investigating the assassination of John F. Kennedy?
112. What Chief Justice had been president?
113. What Chief Justice had resigned from the Court to run for president?
114. What Chief Justice had been a vice-presidential nominee?
115. Who resigned as Chief Justice to become governor of New York?
116. What Chief Justice administered the presidential oath of office the most times?
117. Who administered the oath of office to the most presidents?
118. What Chief Justices were appointed to the Court twice?
119. What Chief Justice had his nomination for Associate Justice rejected by the Senate?

120. What Chief Justice presided over a treason trial?
121. What Chief Justices served as ambassadors while serving on the Court?
122. What Chief Justice presided over an impeachment trial?
123. What Chief Justice originated the handshakes among the Justices before every Court conference?
124. What Chief Justice "called time" on a leader of the bar in the middle of the word "if"?
125. Who served as Chief Justice even though his nomination was rejected by the Senate?
126. What Chief Justice was teased by his friends for driving Justice Holmes from the Court?
127. Who was the first Chief Justice who had been an Associate Justice?
128. Who was the first Associate Justice to be confirmed as Chief Justice?
129. What other Chief Justices were previously Associate Justices?
130. Who served as Chief Justice while he was still secretary of state?
131. What Chief Justice had been U.S. attorney general and secretary of war at the same time?

Presidents and the Court

132. What president made the most appointments to the Court?
133. What presidents made no appointments to the Court?
134. What president chose the most rejected Supreme Court nominees?
135. What president had his power to appoint Justices cut off by Congress?
136. What president appointed a tenth Justice?
137. What president, on appointing a Chief Justice, told his attorney general, "I cannot help but see the irony in the fact that I, who desired that office so much, should now be signing the commission to another man"?
138. What president appointed his predecessor's nephew to the Supreme Court?
139. What president said of a Supreme Court decision that the Chief Justice had "made his decision, now let him enforce it"?
140. What president "packed" the Supreme Court to have a decision overruled?

Greatest Non-Supreme Court Judges

141. What judge on my list designed and made his own false teeth?
142. What judge had the same first name as a city in Montana?

143. What judge used to say that his name had been a handicap in his career?
144. What judge was known as the "American Blackstone"?
145. What judge had Horatio Alger as a tutor?
146. What judge had been a schoolteacher whose pupils included the author of the principal *Dred Scott* dissent?
147. What judge owed his appointment to Earl Warren's veto of the governor's original appointee?
148. What judge was the model for Captain Vere in Herman Melville's *Billy Budd*?
149. What judge was so careless about his attire that he was once taken for a tramp and thrown out of the lobby of a leading Boston hotel?
150. What judge was at first unable to find a publisher for one of the most influential American law treatises ever published?

Trivia Answers

Supreme Court

1. Chief Justice Roger B. Taney. His predecessors had always given judgment in knee breeches.
2. Justice Horace Gray began the practice of employing a young law-school graduate to aid him. At first, he paid the expense of this himself until, in 1886, Congress provided $2000 a year for the purpose.
3. The second Justice John Marshall Harlan, the grandson of the Justice with the same name, who had written the famous dissent in *Plessy v. Ferguson* (1896).
4. Justice Joseph P. Bradley, whose prior career had been entirely at the bar; he had been an eminent attorney in New Jersey before his appointment to the Court.
5. Justice David J. Brewer. When he was appointed in 1889, his uncle, Justice Stephen J. Field, was a member of the Court.
6. Justice Sherman Minton was the last Justice to use the spittoon provided for him behind the bench, which always upset the fastidious Justice Harold H. Burton next to him.
7. Justice Joseph Story. While studying law, he composed a lengthy poem, "The Power of Solitude," referring to it in a letter as "the sweet employment of my leisure hours." Story rewrote the poem, with additions and alterations, and published it with other poems in 1804. One who reads the extracts contained in his son's biography quickly realizes that it was no great loss to literature when Story decided to devote his life to the law. Story himself apparently recognized this, for he later bought up and burned all copies of the work he could find.
8. Justices Tom C. Clark and John Paul Stevens. On January 17, 1986, the Justices were hearing argument on whether Orthodox Jews, with their religious duty to wear yarmulkes, should be exempt from the military dress code's ban on hats indoors. Counsel for the government told the Justices, "It's only human nature to resent being told what to wear, when to wear it, what to eat." "Or whether you can wear a bow tie?" chimed in Justice Stevens.

9. Justices Joseph McKenna, George Sutherland, and Edward T. Sanford and Chief Justice Charles Evans Hughes. More recently, Justice Antonin Scalia grew a beard during the 1996 summer recess and was still wearing it as this book went to press.

10. Justices Ruth Bader Ginsburg and Antonin Scalia in a 1994 performance of Richard Strauss's *Ariadne auf Naxos.*

11. Justice Stephen J. Field, one of the most colorful men ever appointed to the Court. In 1849 he joined the gold rush to California, becoming a frontier lawyer and carrying a pistol and bowie knife. He became involved in a quarrel with a judge, during which he was sent to jail, fined, and embroiled in a duel.

12. A young law clerk once asked Justice Holmes, "What was Justice Peckham like, intellectually?" "Intellectually?" Holmes replied, puzzlement in his voice. "I never thought of him in that connection. His major premise was, 'God damn it!'"

13. "The short of the matter, is that today you would no more heed [Justice Frank] Murphy's tripe than you would be seen naked at Dupont Circle at high noon tomorrow." Justice Felix Frankfurter to Justice Stanley Reed, December 5, 1951.

14. Chief Justice John Marshall.

15. Justice Oliver Wendall Holmes. He is ranked "great" in every list except that in Charles Evans Hughes, *The Supreme Court of the United States* 58 (1928), presumably because Hughes did not list any living Justices.

16. Justice Joseph Story, thirty-two when President Madison appointed him in 1811.

17. Justice Horace H. Lurton, almost sixty-six when President Taft appointed him in 1909.

18. Stanley F. Reed, who lived to be ninety-five years old. He retired in 1957, when he was seventy-two, and died in 1980.

19. Oliver Wendell Holmes, who was ninety when he retired in 1932.

20. Justice James Iredell, who was forty-eight when he died in 1799.

21. Justice William H. Rehnquist. When the Burger Court sat, one of Rehnquist's clerks would every now and then pass notes to the Justice. These were not legal memos but Trivial Pursuit-style questions. Justice Rehnquist would answer them and then hand them to Justice Blackmun for that Justice to try his hand.

22. Justice Samuel F. Miller practiced medicine from 1838 until he was admitted to the bar in 1847.

23. Justice David Davis resigned from the Court in 1877, after the Illinois legislature elected him to the United States Senate.

24. Justice Louis D. Brandeis in an article he wrote in 1890 entitled "The Right to Privacy."
25. Justice Oliver Wendall Holmes. After Holmes wrote an opinion that made Roosevelt furious, "Roosevelt complained that he could carve out of a banana a judge with more backbone than that." Baker, *The Justice from Beacon Hill* 405 (1991).
26. President Harry Truman said this about Justice Tom C. Clark, according to Merle Miller, *Plain Speaking* 225–226 (1974).
27. Justice Steven J. Field was the brother of Cyrus W. Field, who laid the Atlantic Cable.
28. Justice James Wilson, whose wife had died, married Hannah Gray in 1793, when he was serving on the Court.
29. Justice William O. Douglas, who was divorced from his first wife in 1954.
30. Justice William O. Douglas, who was married four times. He received divorces from his first three wives.
31. Justice William O. Douglas authored 1,164 opinions, the most for any Justice.
32. Justice Alfred Moore delivered only one opinion, in *Bas v. Tingy*, 4 Dall. 37 (U.S. 1800), though he served on the Court from 1800 to 1804. Chief Justice John Rutledge also delivered just one opinion, in *Talbot v. Janson*, 3 Dall. 133 (U.S. 1795) but he served only one year as a Justice and briefly during the August Term 1795 as interim Chief Justice. Justice Thomas Johnson, too, delivered only one opinion, in *Georgia v. Brailsford*, 2 Dall. 402 (U.S. 1792); he sat on the Court for less than a year.
33. Justice Oliver Wendell Holmes, who authored 873 opinions of the Court.
34. Justice Thomas Johnson, who delivered the first opinion in *Georgia v. Brailsford*, 2 Dall. 419 (US 1793). This dissent, in the first Supreme Court case in which opinions were delivered, established at the outset the right of Justices to express their disagreement with the result reached by the Court.
35. At that time the Justices followed the English practice of delivering opinions seriatum, one after another. As it turned out, the first opinion was that by Justice Johnson, which disagreed with the Court.
36. Justice William O. Douglas, who wrote 486 dissenting opinions.
37. Justice Oliver Wendell Holmes was known as the Great Dissenter; however, Holmes is in eleventh place on the list of those who have written the greatest number of dissenting opinions. His total was seventy-two.

38. The first Justice John Marshall Harlan. He once wrote to Chief Justice Morrison R. Waite suggesting that he suffered from "dissent-ery".

39. Oliver Wendell Holmes. Lincoln replied, "Captain, I am glad you know how to talk to a civilian."

40. After his graduation from Yale in 1797, Justice Henry Baldwin attended the law school in Litchfield, Connecticut, then the outstanding law school in the country.

41. Justice Benjamin R. Curtis, who graduated from Harvard Law School in 1832.

42. Harvard Law School. Eighteen Supreme Court Justices have studied at the school since its founding in 1817, including fourteen who graduated.

43. The second Justice John Marshall Harlan and Justices David H. Souter and Byron R. White.

44. Benjamin R. Curtis, who had studied with Joseph Story at Harvard Law School; William O. Douglas, who had studied with Harlan F. Stone at Columbia Law School; William J. Brennan, who had studied with Felix Frankfurter at Harvard Law School. At the 1994 Warren Court Conference at the University of Tulsa, Justice Brennan told how Justice Frankfurter had said "at a dinner one night . . . that while he had always encouraged his students to think for themselves, 'Brennan goes too far.' "

45. Justice William H. Moody, who clerked in 1877 and 1878 for Richard Henry Dana, the author of *Two Years Before the Mast*.

46. Justice Samuel Chase.

47. Chief Justices John Rutledge and Oliver Ellsworth and Justices James Wilson, John Blair, and William Paterson.

48. Justice William O. Douglas when he appointed Lucille Lomen in 1944.

49. Justice Felix Frankfurter when he appointed William T. Coleman in 1948.

50. Chief Justice William Howard Taft. He stood 6 feet, 2 inches tall and weighed over 300 pounds. When he was president, he got stuck in the White House bathtub and had to have an outsized model brought in for his use.

51. Justice Alfred Moore. In his book on the Court, Chief Justice Rehnquist writes that Moore was "only four-and-a-half feet tall, and weighing between eighty and ninety pounds."

52. Justice Robert H. Jackson was the chief American prosecutor at the Nuremberg trials.

53. Justice Joseph Story, who was president of the Merchants' Bank of Salem (1818–1830), while he sat on the Court.

54. Justice Stephen J. Field. He was assaulted by former California Chief Justice David Terry, who was shot by a federal marshal assigned to guard the Justice. The incident gave rise to *In Re Neagle*, 135 U.S. 1 (1890), a leading case on executive power.

55. The first Justice John Marshall Harlan and Justices Oliver Wendall Holmes, Stanley Matthews and William B. Woods.

56. Justices Lucius Q. C. Lamar, Horace Lurton, and Chief Justice Edward D. White.

57. Justices Hugo L. Black, Harold H. Burton, Tom C. Clark, William O. Douglas, Sherman Minton, Frank Murphy, Stanley F. Reed, and Chief Justice Earl Warren.

58. Justices William J. Brennan, Arthur J. Goldberg, John Marshall Harlan II, Frank Murphy, Lewis F. Powell, John Paul Stevens, Potter Stewart, Byron R. White, and Chief Justice William H. Rentquist.

59. Justice William B. Woods was a brigadier general in the Union Army (1862–1866). Justice Thomas Johnson also served as a brigadier general in the Maryland Militia during the Revolution.

60. Justice Lucius Quintus Cincinnatus Lamar had served as a lieutenant colonel of the Nineteenth Mississippi Regiment, and his appointment was taken by the country as a welcome symbol of post-Reconstruction reconciliation.

61. Chief Justice John Jay, whose commission of appointment was dated September 26, 1789.

62. Justice James Wilson was sworn in on October 5, 1789, two weeks before Chief Justice Jay.

63. Justice William H. Rehnquist. At the law clerks' annual party on June 27, 1995, Chief Justice Rehnquist fired questions at the clerks in a mock quiz. "One challenge he posed, which had all the clerks stumped, was to identify the 100th Supreme Court justice. After a long silence, Rehnquist reportedly said gleefully, 'It's me!' " *Legal Times*, July 10, 1995.

64. The following received recess appointments and served a period of time without confirmation: Chief Justices John Rutledge (1795) and Earl Warren (1953–1954), and Justices Benjamin R. Curtis (1851), William J. Brennan (1956–1957), and Potter Stewart (1958–1959). Of these all were later confirmed, except Rutledge whom the Senate rejected in December 1795.

65. Justices William Paterson and Stanley Matthews and Chief Justice Roger B. Taney.

66. Edward King, who was nominated twice by President John Tyler in 1844. The Senate refused to confirm either nomination.

67. Robert H. Harrison in 1789, Levi Lincoln and John Quincy Adams in 1811, William Smith in 1837, Edwin Stanton in 1869, and Roscoe Conkling in 1882. In addition, Justice William Cushing and former Chief Justice John Jay declined the post of Chief Justice in 1796 and 1800 after they had been confirmed by the Senate.

68. Justices John Rutledge and Abe Fortas had their nominations for Chief Justice rejected by the Senate.

69. The Court held its first session on February 2, 1790, in the Royal Exchange in New York City.

70. The Court first sat in Washington in the autumn of 1800 in a room in the Capitol basement originally designed as a House committee room.

71. The burning of the Capitol left the Court without its basement chamber. During the next two years the Court held its sessions in the house of Elias Boudinot Caldwell, its clerk, on Capitol Hill.

72. The Court moved into its new building across the plaza from the Capitol in 1935.

73. Justice Samuel Chase was impeached in 1805. His acquittal, writes Chief Justice Rehnquist, "assured the independence of federal judges."

74. Justice William O. Douglas, who published over thirty books, most of them relating to his well-known travels throughout the world.

75. Justice Joseph Story. In 1836, he wrote, "I have now published seven volumes and, in five or six more, I can accomplish all I propose." By the end of his career, he had published nine treatises (in thirteen volumes) on subjects ranging from constitutional to commercial law.

76. *Chisholm v. Georgia*, 2 Dall 419 (U.S. 1793). Although the first session of the Court was in 1790, the Court did not decide its first case until 1793, since the Court had practically no business to transact during its first three years.

77. *Ware v. Hylton*, 3 Dall. 199 (U.S. 1796), in which the Court struck down a 1777 Virginia law that decreed the confiscation of debts owed to British subjects on the ground that it was overridden by the Treaty of Peace with Britain.

78. *Hylton v. United States*, 3 Dall. 171 (U.S. 1796), in which the Court upheld a federal law imposing a tax on carriages used for the conveyance of persons.

79. *Ware v. Hylton*.

80. *Hodgson v. Bowerbank*, 5 Cranch 303 (U.S. 1809), where a section of the Judiciary Act was declared unconstitutional. Overlooking this case,

most commentators list *Dred Scott v. Sandford*, 19 How. 393 (U.S. 1857), as the second decision invalidating an act of Congress.

81. $3,500. The first Chief Justice received $4,000.

82. $164,100. The Chief Justice receives $171,500.

83. The first judicial pension statute was passed in 1869.

84. Justice Byron R. White, who had been a law clerk to Chief Justice Fred M. Vinson in 1946.

85. Justice John P. Stevens who had clerked for Justice Wiley B. Rutledge (1947–1948); Chief Justice William H. Rehnquist, who had clerked for Justice Robert H. Jackson (1952–1953); and Justice Stephen G. Breyer, who had clerked for Justice Arthur J. Goldberg (1964–1965).

86. Chief Justice William H. Taft was Dean of the University of Cincinnati School of Law (1896–1900); Chief Justice Harlan F. Stone was Dean of the Columbia University School of Law (1910–1923); Justice Horace Lurton was Dean of the Vanderbilt University School of Law (1905–1909); Justice Owen J. Roberts was Dean of the University of Pennsylvania School of Law (1948–1951); Justice Wiley B. Rutledge was Dean of the Washington University, St. Louis, School of Law (1930–1935), and University of Iowa College of Law (1935–1939).

87. Justice Stephen J. Field was suspended from the California bar in 1850 as a result of a dispute with a state judge.

88. Justice Byron R. White, popularly known as "Whizzer" White, was an all-star back at the University of Colorado in 1937. He was also later named to the National Football League Hall of Fame.

89. Chief Justice Roger B. Taney, appointed in 1836.

90. Justice Louis D. Brandeis, appointed by President Wilson in 1916.

91. Justice Sandra Day O'Connor, appointed by President Reagan in 1981.

92. New York, from which thirteen Justices have come.

93. James Wilson, born in Scotland in 1742; James Iredell, born in England in 1751; David Brewer, born in Turkey in 1837; George Sutherland, born in England in 1862; and Felix Frankfurter, born in Austria in 1882.

94. William Howard Taft was A.B.A. president in 1913/1914; George Sutherland in 1916/1917; Charles Evans Hughes in 1924/1925; and Lewis F. Powell in 1964/1965.

95. Seniority determines seating on the bench. The Chief Justice sits in the center; the Senior Associate Justice sits to his right. The next senior sits to the Chief Justice's left, the next to his right, and so on.

96. In order of seniority. The Chief Justice begins the conference discussion. The Senior Associate speaks next, and then in descending seniority, with the Junior Justice speaking last.

97. Harlan F. Stone. He moved from the most Junior to the most Senior Associate and was then appointed Chief Justice.
98. 1865, when John S. Rock was admitted.
99. 1879, when Belva A. Lockwood was admitted.
100. Walter Jones, a now-unknown advocate, who argued 317 cases between 1801 and 1850.
101. There have been 108 members of the Court.

Chief Justices

102. There have been sixteen Chief Justices in the Court's history.
103. According to Justice Felix Frankfurter, Chief Justice William Howard Taft once made this remark. This led Justice Frankfurter to write that "he had a very different notion of heaven than any I know anything about."
104. Chief Justice Salmon P. Chase had his photo on the $10,000 bill, which is no longer printed.
105. John Marshall, who published a five-volume biography of Washington while he was Chief Justice.
106. Chief Justice Roger B. Taney married the sister of Francis Scott Key in 1806.
107. Chief Justice Harlan F. Stone, born April 11, 1862, was appointed Chief Justice on February 13, 1930.
108. Chief Justice John Jay, born December 12, 1745, was appointed Chief Justice on September 24, 1789.
109. Chief Justice Melville W. Fuller attended Harvard Law School for six months.
110. Chief Justice William H. Taft, who graduated from Cincinnati Law School in 1880.
111. Chief Justice Earl Warren. The commission he headed is usually called the Warren Commission.
112. Chief Justice William Howard Taft, who was elected president in 1908.
113. Chief Justice Charles Evans Hughes resigned as Associate Justice in 1916 to accept the Republican nomination for the presidency.
114. Chief Justice Earl Warren ran for vice president on the Republican ticket in 1948.
115. Chief Justice John Jay resigned when he was elected governor of New York. A striking indication of the relative importance of the two positions at the time is given in the characterization by a contemporary New York newspaper of Jay's new office as a "promotion."

116. Chief Justice John Marshall, who administered the oath of office nine times to five presidents.
117. Chief Justice Roger B. Taney, who swore in seven presidents.
118. Chief Justices John Rutledge and Charles Evans Hughes. Both had been Associate Justices who had resigned. They were later appointed to head the Court.
119. Chief Justice Roger B. Taney. His nomination as Associate Justice was turned down by the Senate in 1835, ten months before he was nominated to succeed Chief Justice John Marshall.
120. Chief Justice John Marshall, on circuit, presided over the famous treason trial of Aaron Burr.
121. In 1794, Chief Justice John Jay accepted an appointment as special ambassador to England, where he negotiated the treaty that bears his name. Jay's successor, Chief Justice Oliver Ellsworth, served as minister to France, also without resigning as Chief Justice.
122. Chief Justice Salmon P. Chase presided over the Senate impeachment trial of President Andrew Johnson.
123. Chief Justice Melville W. Fuller. "This practice," wrote Fuller's biographer, "tends to prevent rifts from forming."
124. At one time Chief Justice Charles Evans Hughes is said to have "called time on a Leader of the New York Bar in the middle of the work 'if.'" Stern, Gressman, Shapiro, and Geller, *Supreme Court Practice* 587 (7th ed. 1993).
125. Chief Justice John Rutledge presided over the Court during the 1795 term under a recess appointment, before his nomination was rejected by the Senate.
126. On January 3, 1932, after the Justices had heard oral arguments, Justice Holmes casually announced, "I won't be here tomorrow," and he submitted his resignation later that day. On that day coincidentally, Earl Warren, then a California district attorney, had argued his first case before the Court. Warren used to say that his friends accused him of driving Holmes from the bench. They used to tease him — "one look at you and he said, 'I quit.'"
127. Chief Justice John Rutledge, appointed in 1795, had served as an Associate Justice (1789–1791).
128. Edward D. White, who was an Associate Justice when he was appointed Chief Justice in 1910.
129. Chief Justices Harlan F. Stone, and William H. Rehnquist were Associate Justices when they were appointed to head the Court. Chief Justice Charles E. Hughes had been an Associate Justice some years earlier.

130. John Marshall. He served as secretary of state during the last days of John Adams's administration after he had been confirmed as Chief Justice.

131. When Chief Justice Roger B. Taney was first appointed to President Jackson's cabinet, he served as both attorney general and acting secretary of war. During that period, he drew the salaries of both positions. He defended his action in an 1841 letter, declaring, "as I performed the duties of both offices I received the salaries of both. I thought then and still think that it was right."

Presidents and the Court

132. George Washington, who appointed three Chief Justices and eight Associate Justices.

133. William Henry Harrison, Zachary Taylor, Andrew Johnson, and Jimmy Carter. Of these, only President Carter served a full term.

134. President John Tyler. The Senate rejected five of his Supreme Court nominations.

135. Andrew Johnson. To deprive President Johnson of the opportunity of filling expected vacancies, Congress passed a law in 1866 providing that no vacancy on the Court was to be filled until it was reduced to fewer than seven members. After President Grant took office, an 1869 statute raised the number of Justices to nine and authorized the new president to make the necessary appointments.

136. Abraham Lincoln. In 1863, Congress made a provision to increase Union support on the Court by authorizing a tenth seat. Lincoln appointed Stephen J. Field to the additional seat.

137. William Howard Taft, who also told his attorney general at the time that "there is nothing I would have loved more than being Chief Justice of the United States." Taft finally got his wish when he was appointed Chief Justice in 1921.

138. John Adams, who appointed Bushrod Washington, President Washington's nephew, in 1798.

139. Andrew Jackson who is reported to have said, "John Marshall has made his decision, now let him enforce it." The Jackson statement, however, may be only apocryphal.

140. In *Hepburn v. Griswold*, 8 Wall. 603 (U.S. 1870), the Court, then composed of seven Justices, decided that Congress could not issue paper money as legal tender. President Grant then appointed two new Justices (William Strong and Joseph P. Bradley) who were known to

support the constitutionality of the Legal Tender Acts. After they took their seats, the Court overruled *Hepburn v. Griswold*. Legal Tender Cases, 12 Wall. 457 (U.S. 1871). It was claimed by opponents that Grant had "packed" the Court to secure the overruling.

Greatest Non-Supreme Court Judges

141. Chief Justice John Bannister Gibson of Pennsylvania. Like other early-nineteenth-century jurists, Gibson was a man of broad interests. He was a noted student of Shakespeare, read widely in French and Italian literature, and was a gifted violinist. He also displayed talent as an artist; his best likeness is a self-portrait.

142. Learned Hand was christened Billings Learned Hand. He was named after his grandfather, Billings Peck Learned, not the city in Montana.

143. Arthur T. Vanderbilt, who was not a member of the moneyed branch of the Vanderbilts. He often said that his name led people to assume that he was a dilettante who did not have to pursue the law seriously as a means of livelihood.

144. James Kent of New York, whose *Commentaries on American Law* (1826–1830) were the first comprehensive treatise on American law. Justice Story termed it "an American text-book" that would "range on the same shelf with the classical work of Blackstone in all our libraries."

145. Benjamin Nathan Cardozo. During his youth he had a number of tutors, including Horatio Alger, later the famous writer of books in which the hero triumphed over poverty and adversity by courage and hard work.

146. John Appleton. Before he had decided on the legal profession, Appleton taught briefly in a school in Massachusetts. Among his pupils was Benjamin R. Curtis, later the Justice who wrote perhaps the greatest dissenting opinion.

147. Roger J. Traynor. The governor had nominated Max Radin, a leading law professor, to the California Supreme Court. The State Judicial Qualifications Commission, led by Attorney General Warren, turned down the nomination.

148. Chief Justice Lemuel Shaw of Massachusetts. Shaw was Melville's father-in-law and *Billy Budd* was probably written to illustrate the moral dilemma of judges, like Shaw, who had to apply the positive law in slavery cases.

149. Chief Justice Charles Doe of New Hampshire. Doe always refused to conform to accepted standards of judicial dress; he wore the clothes of a country farmer, never shined his shoes, and wore the same Prince Albert coat for over twenty years.

150. Thomas M. Cooley of Michigan. Referring to his *Treatise on the Constitutional Limitations* . . . a commentator states, "No American law book was ever accorded more marked recognition, and none ever had or probably ever will have a more extended influence." Despite this, Cooley had great difficulty in securing a publisher (the senior member of the firm to which it was first submitted later said that he would regret the mistake until his dying day).